Star Crossed
Christine Young

Chapter One

Ireland 1816

    The ring of knuckles hitting flesh thundered through the brilliant spring morning. Casey O'Connell lifted her skirts and raced up the little knoll behind the old white church. She knew her big bro was fighting. They always fought after church on Sunday. For the life of her, she couldn't figure out why.

    "No! Stop it, I say. Patrick O'Connell, you--" Breathing hard Casey barreled through the ring of brawling men.

    "Of course, Casey, anything you say," her brother and his friends laughed as he stepped aside.

    "Get him, Casey! Land a punch for your big brother and St. Patrick," one of the young men called out.

    "The O'Connell's are getting their women folk to fight their battles now?"

"I'll have your head for that, Shaunasey," another joined in.

"Watch your mouth and where you're a starin' or you'll have a black eye so swollen you won't be able to see."

"Woo--eee!" The brawl escalated then seemed to settle around Casey and her off-balance charge through her brother's foes.

Surrounding her she heard raucous cheers, cat calls, and whistles as well as her name. Her arms flailing, she ignored them all and tried desperately to keep her balance.

"Hmph!" She hit hard--a solid rock of muscle--heard the slightest grunt from the object in front of her. Air rushed from her lungs and stars seemed to circle inside her head.

"Oh…" she wailed as the object she hit cradled her with his arms on their way to the dampness of the ground below. Dizziness overwhelmed her. She let her head rest on a muscled chest. *She heard a slow even heartbeat then a low rumble of laughter.*

~ * ~

Moya sat on the softest of flower petals, watching the scene unfold. Oran sat on another petal, cocking his head sideways in scrutiny, his manly features grimacing with disgust. For a quick moment, Moya let her gaze rest on the young men behind the couple, wishing she dared play a trick on them to shoo them away.

"Do you think these two will ever get it right?" Moya asked smiling at her best friend and older brother. A wee spell to send the others on their way wouldn't be such a bad idea.

"I'm not holding my breath," Oran said, brushing a piece of lint from his clothes and looking to the sky as if seeking divine intervention.

"She is lying on top of her true love. What more could she wish for?" Moya sighed, clasping her hands together and enjoying the pure romance as well as the knowledge it was her doing that had brought Casey to the knoll this fine day.

"A little shower of pixie dust? Or maybe a pinch would be enough?" Oran asked a twinkle in his eyes. "I'm thinking they may be needin' more enchantment. They are hell bent on getting this all wrong."

"We have to give them more time. Humans are so..soo..sooo.." Moya let her eyes close, searching for the right word to describe humans. My god, but they were impossible, always ending up in the wrong place at the wrong time.

"Inept?" Oran asked. "Would that be the word you are lookin' for little sis?"

"Foolish with their hearts," Moya told him, trying to give the couple in front of them the benefit of the doubt. Her heart beat hard beneath her breast, her pulse racing in anticipation of Casey finally finding happiness.

"Stupid," Oran shot back with a snort.

"This is the first time they've actually spoken to each other," Moya said, looking wistfully at the two soon-to-be, young lovers. "We knew this wouldn't be easy."

"After all the times we cast spells to put them together, they should be married with children, not rolling around in the grass," Oran said, a note of disgust in his voice. He sighed heavily, casting his gaze again heavenward.

Moya smiled, her dainty hands rested beside her on the lavender flower, her silvery wings moving lazily behind her. "Like it or not, humans rolling around in the grass often times begets children," she told Oran while she laughed at her words and the ancient wisdom.

"You be knowin' what I mean. Don't be twisting my words." Oran hovered over the flower, ready to take flight, his wings beating rapidly, his annoyance obvious.

Moya knew she needed to assuage his feelings and apologize. But she didn't think she had anything to apologize for. "Sit down, Oran. We need to stay put in case they need us. More than likely they will."

"Hmmph." Oran sat back on the flower, crossing his arms in front of him, an elfish glare on his handsome features. "When has a human ever admitted to needin' one of the fae folk?"

"Don't be so fickle, Oran. We both know it's not in their nature to be askin' for advice."

~ * ~

Casey pushed on the green grass, trying to unwind herself from the man beneath her, but fell again. *All right, Casey lass, you're in a heap of trouble right now with no way out. You are seeing the earth whirl and tumble around and you're on top of a brute of a man--a Protestant.*

"All right, lads, we'll meet here next Sunday, same place, same time," her brother's voice filtered through the air as if it floated in the fog that surrounded Casey.

Once again she pushed on the damp grass and didn't seem to make headway, her arms feeling as if they'd changed to soggy twine. *Don't you abandon me, Patrick*

O'Connell. You know I have the Devil's own luck. If you leave me here, I'll never forgive you.

"What about Casey?" one of her brother's friend asked. "She looks a little worse for the encounter."

"Do you think we should leave her here--with Kelly?"

"He's a right stand-up guy. Of course you can leave her here. We'll see her home," a Shaunasey said.

"Well, Kelly is a fine bloke. He won't hurt her. In fact with my feisty lil' sister involved, I fear for him--not her," Patrick said laughing. "She'll do as she pleases. She always does. How can I control her when father cannot? She does not need a second father." He shrugged his shoulders and looked behind him at his little sister as he strolled down the hill.

"She's hurt," another friend called after Patrick. "What kind of brother are you?"

"One who is tired of looking after an accident prone little lass. She has to take responsibility for herself sometime, does she not?"

"She is that," one commented. "You rescue her night and day."

~ * ~

"You should have blessed her with a wee bit o'Irish coordination," Oran said dryly as he flew to a hovering position near the girl.

"And you should remember what our blessed mother told us, 'if you cannot say anythin' nice, don't say anything at all'." Moya rose *above the flower petal, her wings buzzing with her anger toward her brother.*

"I didn't say anything that wasn't the truth." Oran whistled out of tune for a moment. "We could kidnap them."

"And that is your solution to everything?" Moya pointed one finger at him and shook it. "Why, Oran, I believe you may fancy the lass for yourself. I will not have it. Go play your tricks on someone else's charge. She is mine to see to safety and long life. And don't be forgettin' the lad is yours to watch over."

"You best stem your anger, Moya. You're wings have turned golden," Oran said with a hearty chuckle.

~ * ~

"Let Kelly handle her," Casey's brother said with a light chuckle. "He lost and so he must deal with the object of that loss and assume the consequences. It's only fair."

"Hey!" Kelly said, "Don't leave me here with your sister. It will be hell to pay. She's a little girl. What will your father say?"

The others laughed. "Just don't take too long to decide what to do with her. Little girl or not, father will come after you with his pistol."

I just turned eighteen years old--little girl--how dare he…

"Bloody hell, Patrick. What are you thinking?" Kelly cried out.

"I'm thinking the Catholics won this fight. What are you thinking?" Patrick turned his back on the pair and whistled a jaunty tune as he strolled down the hill.

"Revenge will be sweet. Next Sunday..." Kelly shook his fist at the departing back of Casey's brother.

From what seemed like a great distance Casey heard the moan emanating from inside her battered and bruised body. She squished her eyes together, wishing her head didn't pound so fiercely, and the ground spin so wildly. "Who are you?" she whispered next to the man's chest while a soft spring breeze whispered against her heated face.

"Who am I?" the man chuckled. "Lass, you are the one who landed atop me. I should be inquiring into who you are? Only I know." His hands rested around her waist and squeezed as if he were testing--perhaps exploring--entirely inappropriate. Yet for some strange reason, Casey didn't mind the supposed to be unwanted attention. "And I don't think your brother should have left you here with the likes of me. I'm afraid I've landed myself in a dangerous predicament. And I'm thinkin' one that will be very hard to explain."

"Shame on you," Casey said. "You take liberties." The words stole her breath and she had to lean on Kelly once more in order to minimize the pounding of her head and the strange feelings emanating from where his hands were.

"I only want to remove you from--my--ah--person. And if I were taking liberties with you, lass, you'd be near swooning with passion."

"Ah, it seems you are a wee bit arrogant," she opened her eyes and gazed into the bluest eyes she'd ever seen. "The color of a summer sky," she whispered to him, still feeling woozy and not quite sure what he'd just told her--but thinking at the moment something besides the fall caused the earth to spin and the sky to tilt with a crazy, wild abandon.

"What is, lass?"

"Your eyes," she said, struggling against him and finally rolling to the side so she lay sprawled on the grass, staring into the sky she'd referred to a moment earlier and watching a white billowy cloud float past. "I'm not a little girl," she told him. "Don't ever call me that again."

"Then you want me to tell lies?" he asked with a lazy half-smile that stole Casey's heart and left her floundering. "I dinna think I can do that."

"It isn't a lie," she said, trying to sound indignant, yet frustrated beyond anything she'd ever felt before.

~ * ~

"Little girl! What can he be thinking?" Moya's fingers twitched, her wings had changed to a pure gold color. Her body shuddered, her face had turned scarlet.

"Calm yourself, it was just a wee suggestion I be makin' to the lad. If this love thing is too easy, they won't be understandin' each other the way they ought to." Oran grinned from ear to ear as he flew close to his sister. If finding true love and your soul mate is too easy, well…

The taunt didn't go unnoticed by Moya. She turned from him with arms crossed in front of her and calculated the damage she could do to the lad, just enough to get even. She turned back to her brother. "So you be thinkin' this shouldn't be easy are you? What if findin' each other is so hard they give up? Have you been thinkin' of that?"

Oran fluttered back an inch or two. "What mischief have you been dreamin' o'? No more spells or enchantment," he warned.

She smiled, turning her head in a calculating manner but didn't say anything.

"Moya," Oran's voice turned gruff.

"I be thinkin' surprises are infinitely more fun when you know the outcome ahead of time. For now you best be retrievin' Casey's brother. We don't want her compromised before the wedding. Go on Oran; find a way to bring the young man back. Cast a spell or sprinkle some pixie dust on him--remind him he's her brother and he's responsible for her well-bein'."

~ * ~

The heat from the afternoon sun felt wonderful--enchanting--dreamy. When she tried to sit up, the earth whirled around her again. She wanted to feel indignant but she'd brought this on herself. She didn't quite understand why she wanted to convince this arrogant oaf she wasn't a little girl.

"You mind telling me why you tackled me?" he asked.

Casey turned her head to look at the young man. He leaned on one elbow, nonchalantly plucking a blade of grass and sticking it in his mouth. His dark black hair appeared rakishly windblown and his grin was bordered by dimples on both sides. She had the craziest urge to reach up and trace the line of his lips with her finger.

"I don't believe in fighting," she said. "It's absolutely stupid for the bunch of you to come out here on the

Sabbath and fight when the rest of the week you are all bosom buddies."

"Stupid, you say?" he queried. "You dare to call me stupid?" he laughed and extended his hand. "Let me help you up. I don't think I'm ready to meet your dah with pistols on the dueling field. So I think I'd best be seeing you home."

An inferno swept through Casey. She didn't know if she still reeled from the impact or if the dizziness was something else--something magical--something supernatural. When he looked at her, she trembled and her face heated. She touched her hands to her cheeks. They felt cold and clammy. Afraid if he touched her again she might melt, she stared at a puffy cloud floating whimsically overhead.

He bent closer to her. The scent of mint filled the tiny space between them.

"You all right? Did you hear what I said?" he asked, touching a finger to the pulse throbbing at her neck. She tried to bat his hand away even while her heartbeat pounded faster, and she couldn't inhale a decent breath of air.

"Stop it," he said, and paused for a moment in his assessment of her health. "I think you will live."

"Of course I will and I can find my own way home. I'm eighteen. I turned two months ago."

"That old?"

He laughed and she wanted to escape. Yet some little demon inside told her he was the last person she wanted to hide from. She felt as if her body had been taken over by something unearthly, something mysterious or filled with enchantment.

"You're going to have a black eye," she said and touched the bruise forming around his eye. "Does it hurt?"

"Come on, lass," he said still holding out his hand and sidestepping her question.

"You're ignoring me," she told him, getting up without accepting his hand and dusting off hers on her skirt.

"My apologies," he laughed, bowing slightly laugh lines crinkling his brow. "It only hurts when you remind me of it."

"Then I won't be reminding you," she said quickly.

"Casey," her brother said as he rounded the top of the hill. "You coming or do you mean to dawdle here all day?"

She jumped and pressed her fingers along her skirts to smooth them all the while feeling not a wee bit guilty, but a whole lot guilty. *And I have nothing to feel ashamed of.* "What are you doing here? I thought you left me to fend for myself," Casey said feeling a moment of loss at the thought her brother would be walking her home and not Kelly.

"I took pity on Mr. Shaunasey," he said with a low chuckle and a wink cast toward the other young man. "I wanted him to survive the day so we can fight again next week. A few moments in your clutches could be the end of him, if you know what I mean?"

At the sound of Kelly's last name, Casey felt the blood drain from her face. She turned to look at the man who had made her heart pound and her stomach turn over in somersaults. "Shaunasey," she whispered. She no longer had angry words for her brother.

"I don't need anyone's pity--especially the likes of an O'Connell," Kelly said, his voice a low growl and his hands fisting at his sides.

Casey looked to Kelly then back to her brother then back to Kelly as the realization of just who she had been lying on top of in the green grass and having thoughts she just shouldn't have been having. *Shaunasey...*

"Can't be having the likes of a Shaunasey escorting my lil' Casey home," Patrick said, mocking the situation and what might have happened if his friends had not coerced him to return and make sure his sister made it home unscathed.

Casey stepped forward, one finger poking her brother in the chest. "Do you even know what the feud is about, Patrick O'Connell? Do you?"

Patrick shook his head then shrugged his shoulders. "Am I supposed to care? The O'Connell's hate the Shaunaseys. What else is there?"

"A reason," she said with a touch of fury in her voice, her face flushed with heat. She was outraged he would think to carry on a feud such as this one. She turned on Kelly. "Do you know? Do you care that generations of our families have hated each other and no one understands how or why all this started."

He grinned, a devilishly rakish smile. "I think the O'Connell's stole a pot of gold from the Shaunaseys then one of the Shaunaseys kidnapped a young O'Connell lass. Must have been the influence of the fae folk."

Casey clenched her fists. "Both of you--I've had enough of the lot of you. Fighting on the Sabbath, drinking in the taverns on Friday nights and now making up farfetched stories. I can find my own way home, thank you." She lifted her skirts and stomped down the hill, her shoulders squared and her mind shouting to her she must find out the truth.

~ * ~

"If they only knew the entire story," Moya said with a little laugh. "We'd be havin' a wee rebellion on our hands."

"You're not going to be telling them now are you?" Oran trailed along behind Moya who had decided to follow Casey home. She didn't have a problem with a trick or two but she didn't trust Patrick, Casey's brother. Nor did she trust Florence McAffe's mischievous pagan faerie Godfather, Conn. Florence was a suitor of Casey's and she didn't like that one little bit. Nor did she trust Oran. Sometimes, when her brother got carried away with his teasing, he forgot the higher purpose.

~ * ~

"Better go after her," Kelly said to Patrick's back as he raked his fingers through his hair and watched her retreating back.

"Don't be tellin' me what to do," Patrick said as he took the proffered advice and stepped quickly after his sister who was bound to find a pack of trouble on her way home.

Casey heard Patrick's steps thundering behind her, but she kept walking. Tears formed in the back of her throat, and her fists clenched as she grew more determined to leave her meddlesome brother behind her.

Patrick caught Casey, his hand resting on her shoulder to slow her rapid escape from the scene of her most recent humiliation. "Slow down. You're movin' so fast the ground is bound to catch fire."

"Leave me alone. Haven't you done enough?" She didn't want to dwell on her simmering emotions at the moment, and she didn't want to acknowledge her embarrassment.

"Ah, Casey, I don't have a clue what you are talking about." He lifted his hand from her shoulder and paused mid-stride.

"Don't you?" she whirled on her older brother. "I won't ever be able to show my face again." She inhaled a long deep breath wishing she could slow her heart beat and erase the curious feelings coursing through her. Something had happened on that grassy knoll, and it had changed her forever.

Patrick stepped back a moment and looked hard at Casey, his brows furrowing together. He cocked his head a bit sideways then to the other side a slow, arrogant and horrific grin crossed his handsome features. "Why, lil' sis, you've fallen hard--and for a Shaunasey. You fancy yourself in love."

She looked away and tried to start walking but Patrick gripped her arm. "Don't waste your time, Casey.

You know what father would say. He won't allow this--ever!"

She blinked and tried to whisk away the tears without Patrick seeing them. He caught her chin with one finger and forced her to look at him. "I mean it, Casey. He's the wrong kind. You know it and he knows it. It isn't just the feud, he's Protestant. There is no way in h…"

She wrestled her arm away from her brother and raced away, blindly dodging the foot traffic in front of her, tears flowing freely. She bumped off several people before her brother caught up to her again.

"Bloody hell," he muttered. "Are you trying to get yourself killed? That cart nearly ran you over. You should be locked in your room, just to keep you safe."

Casey turned on her brother, stared at him, wondering what she could say. Everything that came to mind had defensive conations. She didn't need or want to defend herself against something that wasn't true.

"Bloody hell, yourself," she whispered to the thinning sunlight. *Bloody hell.*

"Casey," she heard him cry out as she stepped into the street without looking. A horse whizzed by and toppled her to the ground. She sat on the cobblestone, her ego bruised and battered and her heart shattered into a million tiny slivers.

"I'm not in love with anyone," she told her brother as tears streamed down her cheeks. "I am not in love."

He thinks I'm a little girl.

~ * ~

"What a temptation," Kelly muttered, watching Patrick chase after Casey. A chill-premonition swept through him as the sun hid behind a cloud. "The feud was something everyone accepted as a way of life. What had it been all about?" he muttered. "What difference did it make now when no one could remember what it was? Our families hate each other. She is Catholic and I would never convert."

A grumbling behind him brought him abruptly back to reality. "Let's go, Kelly."

"Go ahead. I'll be right there." Kelly waved his friends away, wishing time to think. In those few moments she'd touched him as no other woman ever had. Thinking about Casey O'Connell put a grin on his face, a puzzle in his heart, and a burning need to discover more about her.

Kelly stood with his hands clasped behind his back on top of the grassy hill and gazed into the city. A soft spring breeze changed to a chilling wind and the bright sky changed to a grey overcast. A mist formed high in the sky slowly dropping to the earth as the day slowly changed to dusk.

All the reasons he shouldn't be feeling a burning heat of desire from their brief encounter flashed though his mind. She was a little girl--no, she was eighteen years old. Their families hated each other--had since long before either one of them had been born. She was Catholic. He was Protestant. Despite the dawning of new times, any relationship between the two of them would be frowned upon.

Crazy fool--relationship? They'd just met.

Kelly threw a rock he'd been holding. The missile sailed through the air before landing in a dense growth of bushes. He kicked at a rock, reveling in the pain and wishing he could think of something else, anything beside the feel of Casey O'Connell in his arms. He closed his eyes and let the wind whisper across his face. The gentle caress was unforgiving and unrelenting.

"Little Bro!" His brother must have lost patience. "Kelly," the cry penetrated his mind as the wind was knocked from him for the second time today.

"Ummph!"

The pair tumbled down the hill, rolling, squirming, one getting the better of the other then the roles reversed. On and on the game continued until finally they both lay sprawled on their back staring at the darkening heavens and gasping for air.

Kelly blew a wayward piece of hair from his eyes while he watched the clouds dance across the sky, "What was all that about?"

"Pinin' away like some lovesick fool. I thought I taught you better than that," Liam said with a bit of a chuckle.

"Not lovesick or a fool," Kelly said, but he wondered at the truth of his brother's words. He'd never thought to fall in love--wasn't sure love wasn't just a tale made up by poets and writers.

"Good, I was worried for you," Liam stood and held out his hand to help his brother up, a devilish grin plastered on his mouth.

"Think I'm going to fall for that trick?" Kelly asked as he leapt quickly to his feet, ignoring the proffered hand.

"I'm a better teacher than even I thought," Liam laughed as he strode toward the city, sidestepping the path home.

"Arrogant son of a--"

"I'll buy you a brew at the Black Goat," Liam offered as he turned to look over his shoulder. "You coming?"

"It's Sunday." Kelly's protest was feeble. He knew he would join his brother and would regret it at dawn when he rolled from his bed.

"We have some celebrating to do."

"And what would that be," Kelly asked as he caught up to his brother, matching him stride for stride.

"You conquered your first thoughts of true love-- came out on the winning end--no leg shackle for you."

"You buy then I'll buy." Kelly laughed, knowing his brother meant well but feeling doomed to a headache and a sick stomach come morning.

Inside the smoky room the two brothers chose to sit at the bar. The light was muted, the noise a low rumble, and the scent of stale beer and cigars lingered.

"You aren't planning on seeing the lass," Liam said as he sipped the brew in front of him. "That would not be wise of you."

Kelly's brother's statement hit him in the chest with the force of a Scottish tabor. "Of course not," he said while he mulled over possible ways to do the opposite.

"Why am I thinkin' you're lyin' to me?" Liam swiveled on his chair his eyes narrowing as if he tried to read Kelly's mind.

~ * ~

Conn sat on the bar sipping a glass of the best of the Black Goat's ale when Oran sat down beside him.

"What are you doin' here?" Oran asked, fearing he already knew the answer. Oran was pure pagan and he'd cursed his charge. But that didn't explain anything at the moment.

"Just wantin' to understand the competition."

"What's that supposed to mean," Oran growled, knowing if his fears gave rise to the truth, he and Moya would have an bigger challenge on their hands than just bringing these two humans together.

"And you're thinkin' I'd be wantin' to explain myself to the likes of you?" Conn laughed, and to Oran's ears the sound was pure evil.

~ * ~

"What? Oh, I'm not. I never had any intention of seeing the lass. She's a little girl," he said, flexing his hand around the mug of ale in front of him and remembering the feel of her breasts against his chest and his hands around her waist.

"Her breasts don't look like those of a little girl," Liam said with a low whistle. Liam reached out and stopped Kelly from raising his glass to his lips. For a few more seconds Liam stared hard at Kelly.

"I don't know what you want, Liam. I'm in complete agreement with you. She's a little girl--not interested in little girls." But Kelly's heart raced and he felt the flush of his lie.

"Words won't convince me," Liam said, drinking the last of his ale and waving his hand to order another.

"Ah, you've always been a man of action," Kelly said. When he closed his eyes he saw her, saw her hair flowing around her shoulders, saw her lips, her eyes, and he could feel her as if she was in the room with him.

"You too. Stay away, Kelly," Liam warned.

"Or what?"

The sip of ale Liam was about to swallow stuck in his throat. He choked. "Or I'll stop you."

Chapter Two

"Where is my daughter?" Lady O'Connell asked Casey's long time nurse, Sarah.

"I'm sure she is on her way," Sarah said, wringing her hands in dismay. "She would not be wantin' to displease you."

"Here I am, mother," Casey waltzed into the room, wearing a stunning, blue day dress. "I had to change for dinner. What is it you want?"

"Where were you this afternoon? I went looking for you and couldn't find you. No one knew where you were."

Casey paused mid-stride, her shoulders squaring. She wasn't ready to talk about the brief encounter she'd had with Kelly Shaunasey or the revelation no one in her family or his knew what the feud was about. "I went for a walk."

"Where?" her mother asked with a raised eyebrow as if she already knew. Lady O'Connell continued with her cross-stitch.

Casey smiled. "Around," she said and sat down next to her mother, smoothing her skirts and gazing out the window.

"You should have come home after church. You have your reputation to consider. Young women do not run around town unescorted--without a chaperone. People will talk about you in ways we don't want then you won't be able to find a suitable husband."

"They talk about everyone anyway," Casey said and popped a lemon tart into her mouth, chewing thoughtfully while tearing her gaze from the scene outside to study the expression on her mother's face.

"Really, Casey, have some respect for yourself." Her mother's pursed lips and white knuckles around the frame she held told Casey she'd been a wee bit flippant. Her mother deserved her respect.

"It's not the way it sounds but you know it is true. I walked up the hill south of town and watched the clouds dance across the grassy knoll." At least that part was true.

"Not north?" her mother asked, staring at Casey so hard she choked on the lemon tart and had to grab a cup of tea to wash the crumbs from the back of her throat.

"South," Casey mumbled, feeling the heat climb up her cheeks at her lie. Well, she'd been chastised forever when she couldn't tell north from south. Her mother should believe her. But then her mother questioned her incessantly ever since she turned thirteen, never giving her a moment's peace.

"No scraped knees to show for the walk?" her mother asked with a certain knowing tone that frightened Casey.

Casey looked quickly around the room. Only her nurse Sarah and her mother were there. She lifted the hem of her dress to show her mother. "No scraped knees," she parroted and grinned, feeling relieved she hadn't totally embarrassed herself.

"Thank God," it seemed her mother heaved a quick sigh of what could only be considered as relief. "Your tomboy days should have been over years ago. Climbing trees and swimming in the pond are not acceptable pastimes for young ladies."

"Mother, you know I'm not and never have been a tomboy. You just don't want to acknowledge the fact your only daughter is clumsy and more awkward than anyone you have ever known." Casey nodded, knowing full well God had nothing to do with this. And if her mother saw the grass stains on her Sunday dress, she'd swoon. Well, maybe she wouldn't swoon but she'd ask more questions, questions Casey didn't know how to answer without giving her thoughts about a certain young man named Kelly Shaunasey away.

"She is an embarrassment to her big brother," Patrick said as he sauntered into the room, a devilishly handsome grin plastered on his face. "Always stumbling or causing a scene from which I have to rescue her."

"You're unusually rude," Casey said, immediately regretting her hasty words to her over-arrogant and way too handsome brother. He held her lie in the palm of his hands. If he coughed up the truth of her whereabouts this afternoon, she'd be confined to her upstairs room until her twenty-first birthday or until her mother found someone suitable for her to marry.

"Ah, but you are so cute when you turn that gorgeous shade of crimson," Patrick said, a smug expression on his face. He lounged in a chair, one arm tossed over the back and one leg sprawled out in front of him. Sarah brought him a glass of whiskey from the sideboard. All the while he studied her enough that she squirmed in her seat.

"Stop fidgeting," her mother told her, still working on her stitchery without an upward glance. How on earth did the woman know she was fidgeting when she didn't look at her? "You're a young lady now and you need to act like one. Sit still."

Her brother coughed and wiped the drops of whiskey from his chin with a linen handkerchief he'd been given by someone who was sweet on him, as he'd told her one day. His knowing grin when he directed his attention at Casey sent a shiver of fear up her spine.

Casey smoothed her skirts and glared at her brother, wrinkling up her nose, trying to silently tell him she knew secrets about him far worse than anything he could tell their mother about her.

"Where did you go today, Casey?" Patrick asked a bit of an all-knowing-sneer crossing his face, his expression devilish.

"None of your business, brother dearest," Casey told him, clasping her hands in her lap and staring pointedly at him, willing him to read her dangerous thoughts and the imaginary daggers she sent his way.

"Oh, but I think it is," he said, his voice whiskey smooth, a bland smile on his lips.

"Children, stop quibbling. You're acting as if you are six years old," Lady O'Connell said. "Casey, dear, I've arranged a recital for Tuesday night. You will play and sing and you, Patrick, will attend with a smile on your face," she paused, "and you will be on your absolute best behavior--no pranks."

"Mother," they both cried in unison.

Casey cleared her throat, "I cannot play anything and you know it. I'm horrid. Our friends will run from the room with their hands over their ears in terror they will lose their hearing." Casey's voice was calmer than her rapid heartbeat and racing pulse. "You cannot mean to humiliate me so.

"She's horrid," Patrick agreed. "I for one will not be able to acknowledge she is my sister if you put her through such an embarrassing scene." He rubbed his chin thoughtfully. "I do believe I will find something else to do that evening."

Lady O'Connell shot Patrick a withering heated look that to Casey said, you will not and if you do, I will find a way to make you regret it. But she didn't so much as speak a word.

"I cannot carry a tune nor can I hit the right little ivory keys. Oh, what a nightmare," she felt tears rising in her throat, and she wished she'd catch a cold then perhaps her mother would take pity on her. "I will embarrass all of you and not by choice. I'd rather eat lemons than sing and play."

"Many people like lemons, dear. Florence McAffe will be there. He's asked to court you, and I think this would be a proper way to make an introduction." Lady O'Connell stabbed at her needlework, her brow furrowing in the tiniest of frowns.

"More like a way to scare him off," Patrick said. "But then Casey will have her wish come true. Are you inviting the Shaunaseys?"

"Of course not," Lady O'Connell dropped her stitchery, her face turning pale at the mention of the family who had been their sworn enemies for longer than anyone could remember. "Why would you ask such a thing? You know we never mention that--that name in this household."

Casey rubbed her bare arms, feeling a chill sweep down her spine. She closed her eyes and counted backwards, knowing she might regret the question. "Mother, what was the feud about? Does anyone know?"

Lady O'Connell paused, letting her needlework slip to her lap and looked out the window for a few long seconds. It seemed as if she was gathering her thoughts or recalling some horrific event in her past. She returned her attention to Casey and Patrick. "I suppose the two of you deserve to know. But I have no idea. I married into the feud. As you all well know, I lived in London, my family coming to Ireland on vacations. I met your father and we fell in love. No one spoke of it and since I didn't know the people, I never asked."

"So you have no idea or maybe a guess," Casey felt her hopes die but couldn't resist asking the next question. "Was it love at first sight?"

A whimsical smile crossed Lady O'Connell's face. "I believe it was. Your father was so handsome but as to your other question, no, your father refuses to talk about the feud and so I never pursued the topic."

"Someone should," Casey said, lifting her shoulders in a shrug and ending in a long sigh. Perhaps she would. Where to start?

"Leave it be, Casey," her brother warned, his brows furrowing in a sign of disapproval Casey recognized all too well. "You might uncover something you don't want to know," he warned.

"You do know something."

"Of course not."

"Yes, dear, there is no reason to turn over lose stones that might erupt in more fighting. I believe there was quite a lot of it--violence--back in the day. Some things are better off if left alone," Lady O'Connell said, putting down her needlework. She left the room but not without a backward glance to her two children who were still scowling at each other.

"Patrick O'Connell, what are you thinking?" Casey asked, trying to stare her brother down and wishing she knew what devilry Patrick was scheming. "What do you know that you're not telling? Spit it out."

"I'm thinking you have bitten off more than you can chew, my little sister. Kelly Shaunasey is not the man for you even if there were no feud." This time it seemed to Casey her brother spoke from the heart.

"Why?" she demanded.

"He's dangerous--Protestant--older--a Shaunasey--to name a few things. Casey, he's too much man for you."

"What is that supposed to mean? Too much man? Patrick O'Connell you should be ashamed of yourself."

"Leave it be, Casey. I didn't mean anything by it. He's just too old for you."

"It's the feud," she told herself. She would be stirrin' up a whole passel of trouble if she pursued her interest in this man. And yet she knew deep inside she could not stop herself. If love at first sight were possible, it had bitten her hard. Kelly enchanted her and she couldn't stop thinking about him.

"Casey, it's more than that and you know it. He would never convert."

"But I could."

"That's blasphemy. Never let mother hear you say that. And you know, Casey, you might find an interest in the young man who is coming for your--recital."

"What young man?"

"I forgot his name. Ah, let me think, Florence--yes." Patrick sat up straight, a lopsided grin on his devilishly handsome features.

"He's a fop--a bloody dandy--probably can't be trusted," Casey said, "He makes my insides cringe just thinking about him."

~ * ~

"Well, that much is true," Moya fluttered angry golden wings as she hovered in a corner of the O'Connell home. "And why does her brother think he can threaten her and all I've done just so these two will fall in love," Moya muttered. She tossed her arms in the air and

tiny particles of pixie dust scattered around her. "Hachooo!" she sneezed.

Moya flew around the room, wishing Oran was here. But she knew he was with Kelly. He needed to make sure Liam wasn't able to convince the young man to stay away from Casey.

Moya thought of Conn, Florence's fairy godfather. The suggestion of his presence made her tremble and more pixie dust flew through the air. Conn was pure evil; a black fairy, pagan, and he'd cursed Florence at his birth. There had been no gifts, nothing for the man and Florence was bad, a very bad boy. He was not right for Casey.

~ * ~

Patrick roared with laughter. "And I suppose thoughts of Kelly Shaunasey does something else entirely. You blush every time someone says his name." Patrick put his hands behind his back and rocked on the back of his heels, gazing out at the summer sky.

Casey felt heat rush to her cheeks and immediately clamped her hands there. Patrick laughed harder. "I do not ever think of Mr. Shaunasey. It would not be proper," she declared in a rush of heated emotion.

"Of course not, and you are always the proper little Irish lass." Patrick turned, still laughing but Casey noticed a tender light of concern gracing his handsome features.

"Of course," she said, walking to the window and staring at a velvet sky twinkling with tiny diamonds. She wasn't ready to acknowledge any type of tenderness with the brother who had tormented her forever.

Before she could breathe, her brother stood behind her, one hand resting on her shoulder. "If you are worried about my giving you away, you should be. I won't do anything yet, but don't pursue Shaunasey."

"And if I do?" she asked, ready to do battle even though she acknowledged nothing would come of her feelings for this young man. She knew where the line was drawn, and she would never give up the love of her family or the security they provided.

"I'll have to tell Dah." His voice held a dangerous tone as well as a promise she'd never heard before.

"So I'll be needing saving from a man who dallies with every skirt he sees?" she asked, flaunting his wild side to him as if it would change his mind. He would tell on her if she gave into her feelings.

"If you pursue Shaunasey, you will need saving," Patrick agreed. "And I may be asking a few favors in return for my silence or the savin'."

~ * ~

"Are you out of your mind?" Liam strode toward his brother, his fists clenched at his side and a decidedly grim expression on his face.

Kelly tossed a pebble at an old oak tree standing sentinel, marking the line of the O'Connell property. "Most likely." If his feelings hadn't been so new, intense and strange, Kelly would have laughed at his brother's concern.

Leaning against a street lamp, Kelly watched the light in the parlor window. He'd heard about the recital and for some reason he couldn't stay away. Decidedly bad music had filtered from the window, polite applause followed, and now only party voices floated his way. He'd heard a back door open and close and had wondered about that when no one returned. Impulsively, he'd been tempted to follow but knew how unwise it would be to be caught on O'Connell property in the middle of the night. He laughed inside, amazed at his caution when he felt dangerous and very wild.

"Do I need to drag your sorry butt home?" Liam asked, his stance relaxing somewhat upon hearing his brother's reply.

Kelly tossed another pebble. "Florence McAffe went in there. He's a wolf in sheep's clothing. He'll hurt her and who will pick up the pieces?" *I will. But I don't want her to have her heart broken by the likes of him. I don't want him touching her either.*

Leaves whispered with the breeze, music played from the window, and an old bullfrog croaked from somewhere down the lane. Silence lingered and seeped inside Kelly's soul. Liam didn't have a witty answer to his question and neither did he.

"You're drunk," Liam said.

"Haven't had a drop since last Sunday after I met her," Kelly said too emphatically to convince his brother. He was roaring drunk at the moment and didn't dare push off the lamp pole afraid he'd end up face down on the ground.

"Let's do something to change that," Liam said. "I'm worried about you."

Kelly closed his eyes and let his head rest against the lamp pole. Sounds swirled around him. The scent of spring flowers hovered on the breeze and his imagination played havoc with his body.

"A few of the lads will be there tonight--Black Goat--wanted to know who would join them," Liam said. "You need a night out with the boys. Come on, it'll do you good."

I need a night out with Casey.

"I'm not in the mood for brawling and drunkenness." Before he left this spot he wanted a glimpse of Casey. Perhaps if he saw her, he wouldn't feel the same. Perhaps if she wasn't forbidden, the novelty would die.

"You're a lovesick fool. I'm sure a lusty barmaid will help sway your mind from little Miss O'Connell--a lass you cannot have."

"I'll be there later." Kelly shrugged off his brother's invitation as well as the arm he'd draped across his shoulder. A lusty barmaid held no appeal to him even though a little over a week ago he would have joined his brother with a grin and high expectations for the evening.

"You'll be comin' with me," Liam told him with all the assurance of a big brother who believes whole-heartedly he will always get his own way. "I won't be leavin' you here to make a bigger of fool of yourself than you have already."

"I don't think I can make a bigger fool of myself," Kelly said dryly, wishing he didn't mean his words but knowing the truth. He needed to be with Casey despite her family name. He needed her in ways he didn't understand. Only a week ago he was a carefree and happy man. And now…

Liam looked to the lighted parlor window and back to his brother. "Believe me, you can," he said as if he was the voice of experience. "But you're playing with fire and that, my lil' brother, is entirely different."

"What do you propose?" Kelly asked, cocking his head sideways and knowing what his brother had in mind before he spoke.

"A wild night out with the boys," Liam said again. "Don't think you should be standing here pining away for a lass you cannot have." Liam started to walk away from the O'Connell home. He didn't turn to look back at him, trusting him to follow.

~ * ~

"Florence is meant for the lass," Conn said smugly. "He's Catholic, and he's not involved in the feud," he whispered close to Oran's ear. Conn did a quick little back flip and looked at Oran as he meant to say something else. Instead he fluttered to a nearby bar stool.

Oran felt his temper rise and wished Moya was here to calm him. He wasn't rational at the moment and he felt his anger soar out of control. Sometimes he did things he regretted later. He'd made a pact with his sister and he intended on keeping it.

"You won't win this one," Oran said.

"We'll see," Conn taunted. "Now won't we? You know the bad boy always wins. To humans, there is something primal and intriguing about the bad boy."

"You have a point. But Casey won't fall for him. The only way you'll win is if Casey's parents arrange the marriage. She's already smitten with Kelly."

"A spell here and there will change things," Conn said.

"You mean a curse," Oran said.

"If necessary."

~ * ~

"I just want to talk to her," Kelly said, tossing another pebble. "You think she'd be in her room by now? It's growing late."

Liam stopped. "What? You mean to shimmy up the trellis and sneak into her bedroom?" Liam asked a note of incredulity in his tone. "I thought you were the sane one in this family."

"The thought crossed my mind a couple of times. And I know that would be impossible--stupid. However," he paused, juggling a few pebbles in his hand and looking back to the balcony he was sure led from Casey's bedroom, "perhaps I could get her to come out and talk to me."

"That only works in love stories," Liam said then stopped, horrified at what he'd said. "You, my little brother, Romeo thou are not. Perhaps you have a death wish. This isn't happening," he muttered.

"I don't intend this to be a tragedy and I'm not in love--just curious," Kelly said a bit too quickly to be a convincing argument while he went over ways which he could find to meet Casey without anyone being the wiser.

"Prove it," Liam challenged. "Prove to me you don't care about that girl--that girl you cannot have--that girl who would make our lives and our family's lives a living hell. Come with me to the Black Goat. Have fun tonight and forget about Casey O'Connell."

"Very well, have it your way," Kelly said, darting a look toward the window in hopes of catching at least one glimpse of Casey. When he did, his heart skipped a beat. She stood framed inside the curtains of the parlor, her forehead resting against the window pane. She seemed incredibly sad and lost. He had an urgent need to enfold her in his arms and whisper close to her ear he would solve all her problems and protect her from whatever or whoever had put that sad forlorn look on her face.

Liam grabbed his arm and Kelly had to look at the ground in front of his feet. He stumbled anyway and when he peered backward over his shoulder, she had vanished. The two brothers walked in silence toward the little tavern they liked so well.

Inside it was fairly quiet. The pair sat at a table in the center of the room and ordered ale. "Here's to finding a willing lass to spend the night with," Liam lifted his tankard, searching the smoke-filled room for a diversion for his brother.

Kelly followed suit, not truly agreeing with his brother. A willing lass would not cure his sickness. No one but Casey appealed to him. It seemed she had become a part of him he could not shake loose.

Chapter Three

Casey stared at her reflection in her mirror. She tossed her hair behind her head and grimaced at what she saw. Hair too red, eyes too close together and her little turned up nose made her cringe. She wanted to be beautiful like Meghan O'Cleary or Lizze MacDonald.

"But..." she sighed. "You are no beauty, Casey O'Connell. You cannot play or sing. You trip over miniscule cracks in the floor. If there is an accident waiting to happen, you will be part of it. Why on earth would you think anyone would fall in love with you?" *Especially Kelly Shaunasey--a man who is forbidden.*

Humming off key, Casey wandered to the window overlooking the gardens. She held her lighted candle high, mesmerized by the glow. Flowers were beginning to bloom and the scent of Daphne hung on the air. The night was chilly but not cold. She heard a slight noise and stepped onto her balcony. Another noise peaked her curiosity. Leaning over the railing, she searched through the darkened shadows of the night.

A pebble fell on the balcony floor by her foot. She held the candle light high above her head. "Who is it? Who is out there?" she asked, wondering if anyone would show themselves. Except for the tiny beam of candle light, darkness surrounded her. A tiny shiver of apprehension drizzled down her spine. Her fingers tightened around the top of the railing and the candle holder.

"Show yourself," she whispered, afraid yet strangely not afraid even though a shiver slipped down her spine and the hair on the back of her neck stood on end. If she stopped to let her thundering heart slow, she imagined Kelly Shaunasey out there somewhere, risking life and limb to walk on O'Connell property let alone stand beneath her bedroom window and talk to her.

"Either show yourself or go away," she commanded.

~ * ~

"Give the lad a wee bit of courage, Oran. Do it now before he gives up and leaves Casey alone, wondering what unearthly power was teasing her," Moya whispered in her brother's ear.

Oran stood on the railing to the balcony watching his charge below. Before Oran could cast an enchanting spell on the young man, Conn knocked the pixie dust from his hand. Instead of blessing Kelly with the courage to call out to Casey, Kelly stepped back as if he wondered at his own sanity.

"Conn, you pagan devil," Moya said fluttering her wings so fast they changed from silver to gold in less than a second. "You go on home. Don't you have your own charge to look after?" Moya asked.

"And that is what I'm doin' here," Conn said. *"Florence wants to wed the lass. Even though we all know it will never work out."*

"Go on with you," Oran said, slipping closer to Kelly and blocking Conn from his quest. *"Florence will never marry the lass. I can promise you that,"* Oran growled deep in his throat. Pixie dust shot from his hand. Kelly sneezed and stepped closer, looking toward the balcony.

"I'll give you this one," Conn said and flew away, vanishing into the velvet blackness of the night.

"And good riddance to you," Moya shook her tiny fist at the pagan. *"I pray you find some time machine and leave us forever."*

~ * ~

Casey watched intently as a figure stepped from a shadow hand outstretched. "Who is there?"

"Ah, sweet Casey, cupid has touched my heart. I cannot sleep without thoughts of you and when my eyes close, my dreams are of you. It is I."

Casey giggled then wished she hadn't. "Kelly?"

"Sweet Casey, you mock me and yet I find I am going against the wishes of generations by coming here this evening. The arrow piercing my heart causes pain that will not vanish and a terrifying fear I will never see you again. Come down and walk with me."

"I would never make fun of you. I--" she couldn't profess her undying love. "What are you doing here?" But he'd said he come to her. The part about cupid was touching and so romantic. She closed her eyes, counting to ten and praying this wasn't her imagination working overtime. He wanted her to walk with him. He risked his life for her. Happiness exploded inside sending warm sweet shivers of delight throughout. "Did someone cast a spell on you?"

"What does it look like?" he asked, putting one foot on the trellis and reaching high with one hand as if he might be meaning to climb to the top.

"It appears you are a wee bit tipsy. If not, you are insane," she told him, keeping her voice as low as she could. It would not do for Sarah to hear him out here. While her brother might choose not to tell on her, Sarah would run straight to her mother.

"Perhaps I am tipsy. Perhaps I am under your spell of enchantment. Or I could be crazy--crazy in love. Do you want me to climb up and see how sturdy the trellis is?" His lopsided grin touched her heart.

"Of course not. If the trellis did not fall, you would assuredly be scratched all over from the rose bushes." He was so handsome, so perfect, his eyes so warm. When he looked at her, it seemed as though he saw nothing but her.

"You care..." His whispered words floated on the night wind.

"I would not wish to pick up the pieces if you fell, nor would I want to explain what a Shaunasey is doing at the bottom of an O'Connell balcony with a broken neck." Her heart fluttered with excitement. Thoughts of running out to meet him and walking in the gardens flashed through her head but were quickly put aside. The threat her brother would bring their father into this was very real and potent.

If she had some idea of what the feud was all about, she could fight this and put the anger aside. She had no reason to call this man her enemy when all she wished for was to call him--*my lover*.

"Meet me," he told her. "If you dare," the challenge, undeniable, hovered on the air, real and intoxicating.

"Meet you--where--I cannot." Her pulse raced and her heart thundered so hard against her breast she had to put her hand there in hopes of taming it. She turned from him, wondering why she meant to defy all that was proper to find some way to meet this man. He meant nothing to her. She didn't know him, she reminded herself. But oh, how she wanted to know him--know him in every way.

"You're afraid. I can understand. But I don't want to hurt you or scare you," his voice gentled and she fell deeper in love.

She sneezed suddenly as the air filled with strange tiny golden specks and brushed away a light tickle that floated across her cheek. "My brother…" her words trailed off into the darkness of the night. *Of course I'm afraid*. Who knew what hornets would be stirred up if she met him and they were caught. If she met him once, would that be enough for a lifetime of dreams?

"Mine too. They don't think this is a good idea. They are right. If you are too afraid…" He backed away, one step at a time until she could barely see him in the dim light cast by her solitary candle.

"I am not afraid," she countered. "I understand this is not prudent or wise, but I--something happened last Sunday. I don't know what it was. Maybe it was just the need to understand the feud. Maybe it was something more. I have to find out or I will regret not understanding my feelings for the rest of my life." *Stupid girl, of course it was something more. Your knees turned to jelly, and your insides flamed with the heat from his touch. Stupid girl, your knees are always jelly.*

"Then meet me at two o'clock behind the old church near the town square." He'd moved closer and she saw what was quickly becoming her favorite lopsided grin. "You are my sun and my moon," he said softly. "You are my reason for living."

"I…" she began then stopped to think. He was so romantic. Perhaps he was using her or just seeing if she would be one more conquest. She had always been an impulsive person. But was she also being too forward? She wasn't sure. She'd never had a beau, not a real one. Only the kind who pulled her hair and teased her unmercifully.

"Please," he said extending his hand upward as if asking her to climb down right now and run away with him.

"All right," she told him cautiously. Knowing with her bad luck, someone, probably her brother, would find out about this. Knowing also she had to meet him. If she didn't pursue her feelings for Kelly, she might regret it the rest of her life.

He grinned broadly. "Two o'clock," he told her. "Don't be late. I might not be able to wait for you."

"You don't be late," she told him. Knowing she would wait until dark if she had to in order to get away. And she prayed if it came to that, he would wait for her

"Casey? Casey, where are you? Do I hear voices?" Sarah called from somewhere behind her.

Casey swallowed the lump of fear in her throat.

"I've got to go," she said to the darkness. He had already disappeared into the night.

~ * ~

You're a bloody fool, Kelly Shaunasey--a bloody fool. She's not going to show up here. There's no way. He kicked at a tuft of grass and gazed at the churning waves below him. A storm approached, the sky darkening as he stared at the whitecaps. A whale rose, spouted and dipped below the ocean. The sound carried and Kelly smiled at the sight. Seagulls floated on the air currents and their cries rose from the ocean.

"Kelly," the voice was soft and uncertain. He turned on a heel to gaze at the most beautiful woman he'd ever seen.

"Casey," he pushed her name and the air from his lungs. Surprised and thrilled at the same time at her appearance. "Casey, you came…"

"I told you I would. Did you think I would be leadin' you on?" She walked toward him, her hair flying behind her in a blaze of red. The breeze lifting her skirts around her ankles--the smile on her face angelic.

"I didn't think you would make it here. Did anyone follow you?" he asked looking around her, half expecting to see her brother or her father, pistols in hand. He could not believe his good luck but now that she was here with him, what was he to do?

"Of course not."

~ * ~

Moya chuckled beneath her breath, the laughter sounding like soft tinkling bells to Oran. "Of course, foolish humans, your faerie godmother and godfather followed. We couldn't let you make a mess of this first meeting. And here you are wondering what to do with the girl. You will be needin' some help from the two of us."

"Do you think we are doing too much?" Moya asked. "I wouldn't want things to move too quickly."

Oran snorted. "Too quickly? How on earth? If we weren't here helping them out, things wouldn't move at all. They'd be sixty before they finally found each other. I'm thinking today would be a good day for the first kiss."

"Sixty…you don't really think they are that bad?" Moya fluttered her wings, "Oh, yes, a kiss, a very sweet first kiss.

Oran could do little but shake his head and groan, remembering all the times they'd tried unsuccessfully to help them find each other. He tossed a load of pixie dust in the air. The wind caught the specks. They swirled and danced on the afternoon breeze, settling on the desired target.

"May the fates be with you and may you each take one more, and please make it quick, giant step to falling in love with each other. Never letting anyone, anything or any other fae creature get in your way," Oran said as he thought about Conn and Florence.

~ * ~

The ocean churned and danced below them, waves crashing against the rocks and the sky was lined with pewter grey clouds. Sea gulls hovered on the wind skirting the rocky ledge and the old church's bell tolled three times.

Casey wrapped her arms around herself as she looked out at the sea. Kelly pulled her close, wrapping her in his sheltering embrace, wishing to do more than hold her.

"Let's walk," Kelly said, refusing to let her go. They followed a path down to the ocean. Tiny droplets of rain misted around them and the sun hung in a foggy golden orb dropping slowly to the horizon.

Resting her head against his chest, she wrapped an arm around his waist. "You know I've never been too steady on my feet."

"I gathered that the other day when you steamrolled into me." His hand tightened on her shoulder when she stumbled on a small rock.

"Pick up your feet, Casey," he heard her mumble.

"I won't let anything happen to you," he told her. Kelly felt the most compelling need to make his statement true. He wanted to protect her and keep all harm from her forever.

Casey laughed. "If you mean it, then you have taken on a daunting task. I am the most uncoordinated person on the face of this earth."

"Doesn't matter," he whispered close to her ear. *Roses.* "Hmm---"

"What?" she asked, stopping to look at him. They stood on top of huge boulder. The incoming tide sent waves of crashing mist, rising from the ocean.

"Roses, I smell roses," he said. Ocean mist surrounded them. He backed up a step. "Careful," he said, moving cautiously toward higher ground.

Casey slipped on the wet rocks and seaweed. He held on tight, realizing the waves were crashing all too high and they were far closer than they should have been.

~ * ~

Moya's wings turned gold in the ocean mist, her cheeks flushing to an angry crimson. "Does he think to woo her or kill her?"

"Calm down, Moya. See--he's put her on high ground. They'll be just fine."

"That's a fine start. She's nearly drenched to the bone. He's lucky she didn't slip into a tide pool. Doesn't he know yet she's accident prone?" Moya perched on a slender piece of saw grass, watching the scene unfold.

Oran made large lazy circles around the pair, trying for the power of suggestion, he whispered, "Kiss the girl, kiss the girl, kiss the girl…" Oran grinned, his ploy seemed to be working. "Kiss the girl," he whispered again.

~ * ~

Casey stood in front of Kelly, his arms around her waist the base of his chin resting on the top of her head. He felt as if he heard little voices in his head. Of course he wanted to kiss Casey but there was a right time and a wrong time. She was so young and inexperienced he didn't want to scare her away. But bloody hell, he wanted to kiss her and more.

He swallowed the lump in his throat. His fingers seemed to have a will of their own, making little circles on her arms. He enfolded her hands in his, brought one to his lips and placed a gentle kiss on top of her hand. Slowly he turned it over and kissed her palm. He felt her warm shiver to the depth of his soul.

Sea salt stung his nostrils, roses permeated beyond the smells of the ocean and into every sense he possessed. A soft breeze swirled around them and the sun glowed through the low hanging clouds.

"Kelly?"

"Hmmm, lass," Kelly said, his mind in a fog, his pulse racing and his heart pounding. He was thinkin' surely cupid's arrow had pierced his heart, the potion more powerful than anything.

Casey turned in his arms and gazed at him with her gorgeous eyes. Her skin was flawless, her lips moist, begging for his kiss.

"Do you believe in love at first sight?" she asked a whimsical little smile on her face. Demurely, she lowered her lashes then slowly opened them.

"I do now," he said, his voice husky. He'd never thought to be smitten, never believed in love, let alone love at first sight. Liam would laugh at him. He would call him a fool. But his was a love that was doomed.

She rose, their lips nearly meeting, her gaze upon his, potent and strong. Her fingers played with the hair at the base of his neck. He moved forward, closer so as to brush her lips with his own.

"Kelly! Kelly! Where are you...?"

Chapter Four

"I'm busy," Kelly muttered to Liam. "Go plague someone else." Kelly's fingers tightened around Casey's waist. Wind whistled overhead and it seemed a lightning storm brewed on the horizon. A shriek of wind blasted the couple.

Startled, Casey gasped and stepped away from Kelly. She felt the flush of heat rise to her cheeks. "Liam," she whispered. "What?" but she felt as if she intruded on the conversation about to take place. She saw the angry blaze in Kelly's eyes, and knew he wasn't happy with his brother's intrusion. She wanted the world to know how she felt about Kelly, but it seemed everything was against them.

"Kelly, you've got to hear this. You too, Casey. This foolishness has to stop. The two of you must come to your senses," Liam warned.

"I'm not going to let a hundred year feud keep me from seeing Casey. Perhaps we should delve deeper and find out what has made our families enemies," Kelly said. "It might be something as ridiculous as snatching the last brick of cheese from another's hands."

"No one can tell us what the argument is," Casey turned on Liam, her hands clenched. "No," she said. "No we won't stop seeing each other, and yes, I will uncover the truth." More determined than ever, Casey's fists clenched and her jaw tightened.

"It's not just the feud," Liam said quickly. "It's about religion and politics and…" He shook his head, closing his eyes for a moment as if in thought.

To Casey, Liam sounded frustrated and angry. She knew he wanted what was best for Kelly but he didn't know how they felt, couldn't understand. Maybe she couldn't either. She barely knew Kelly but she loved him. She knew she wanted to spend the rest of her life with him. Everyone would call her daft if she told them how she felt and what she yearned for.

"If that's all you wanted, you can leave now," Kelly said seeming to brush Liam's concern to the back of his mind. "I won't, can't adhere to your wishes." Kelly ran his fingers through his hair, gazing toward the ocean.

Liam's expression was grim as he shook his head at the pair. "There's going to be a fight in town. Florence has issued an ultimatum to your family, Casey."

"What?" Her heart lurched. Patrick would never let a challenge go unmet. He was hot-headed to a fault. "What was it about?"

"No!" Casey felt another surge of heat and fury strike.

Liam turned to Casey, anger written in every line of his face as well as his foot-planted stance. "Patrick has taken the challenge as a personal insult. He says this has gone beyond what is polite," Liam said. "It seems he insulted your character. Had something to do with your seeming infatuation with my brother. So--"

"So it is a challenge against the Shaunasey's too," Kelly said, stepping forward with fists clenched tight. "I will not have Casey demeaned by the likes of Florence McAffe or any other so called gentleman."

Casey stepped forward. "Take me there," she said. "I'm going to put a stop to this." She would not have anyone fighting over her. Her honor? Honor be damned, she could care less. As soon as this gossip blew over, everyone would be fighting over someone or something else. She meant to put a stop to this. She would find a way to put the feud to rest. Loving Kelly for the rest of her life was all she wanted.

"It's no place for a lady," Liam said matter-of-factly. "We'll join ranks with your brother." He winked, "After all it's not Sunday. We can fight a common foe for the good of all."

"You're going home. Liam, see she gets there," Kelly said. "Let me take care of this. I need for you to be safe and in one piece."

"Why Kelly Shaunasey, you've no right to be tellin' me what I can and cannot do. Be off with you. I'm not going home when my brother is about to get in a fight over my honor. And when you seem hell-bent to join in. I can defend my own honor, thank you." Frustration ground away at her temper. She watched them full of themselves and their prowess. Her heart lurched, shivers spiraled down her back and a strange darkness engulfed her soul.

Liam looked a bit sheepish, staring at the ground for a moment before looking back to Casey. All awkwardness vanished in a moment so fast Casey wondered if she wasn't mistaken. "It's not really a fight. I haven't spoken the whole truth." He stared downward at the churning sea, hitting the rocks below.

"What is it then?" she demanded, stepping forward and pointing her finger at Liam. "Tell me the truth--all of it."

"Florence has challenged Patrick to a duel. When he refused, Florence called him a coward. Of course Patrick didn't take to the name calling. I saw the flash in his eyes and they seemed to smolder as if Patrick wanted to fight, as if he there was something eatin' away at his very soul," Liam said.

Casey had thought the same thing the last time she'd spoken with her brother. Something was happening in Patrick's life he didn't want to speak of.

"Duels are not legal," Kelly moved away from his brother and Casey, turning toward the road which would lead him into town. "I can stop this."

"Which makes the situation worse; the survivor will end up in jail," Liam said. "And I doubt if any of us can stop it. They will meet and hopefully no one will die."

"Where are they? Who is to be Patrick's second?" Kelly asked.

"Don't know. They were in the middle of town but I think they will be going to the park," Liam said, his long strides making it hard for Casey to keep up without running.

"Don't they do these things at dawn?" Casey asked, her hands clasped tightly in front of her. The shaking of her legs would not stop and she didn't think they could move any faster. "Duels at dawn," she muttered.

"Don't know," Liam repeated.

Wind whistled through the tree branches overhead. What sun there was an hour ago had vanished to be replaced by dark brooding clouds.

"I'll be his second," Kelly stopped Casey and touched her cheek with a tenderness and longing she'd never felt before.

~ * ~

"Holy smoke, do you think things have gotten a little out of hand?" Moya asked. "Duels, what kind of curse did Conn put on Florence to make him challenge Patrick?" Moya's wings fluttered frantically, wisps of gold grew surrounding her in a golden haze. Everything had been going smoothly, her plans for the couple materializing beautifully. He'd almost kissed Casey, would have if not for his brother interfering. A duel, oh my, what to do? They had to put a stop to this stupidity.

"I think it was the other way around. Florence uttered an ultimatum and Patrick challenged him." Oran was the voice of calm; at least it seemed that was what he tried to be. "It is a mess, that is for sure. A very messy mess indeed."

"He had to be willing. Did anyone force the bumbling fool, Florence, to agree to the duel? This isn't going to turn out well no matter who wins." Oran flew beside Moya who rushed to the park, following behind and in front of the humans.

"We can put suggestions in their heads, but I'm afraid the damage has already been done. What to do? What to do?" She felt moisture well up in her eyes. She didn't want to cry. Crying would make her soggy and she didn't like soggy.

"Don't worry, Moya," Oran said, "Somehow we'll make this all turn out the way it is supposed. You've got to be up for a little challenge now and then."

"We've already been tested, more than I want to be. I didn't expect Conn to be as persistent as he's been. He doesn't even like Florence. So why is he pursuing this?" Moya fluttered beside Casey, watching her and wishing Casey could see her. Casey didn't believe in anything but if she'd become a believer, they could see each other.

"Of course he doesn't like his charge. He's never liked the family. Don't you think that's why he cursed him in the first place? They aren't very nice." Oran seemed resigned to the situation at hand and searched for a solution. He was the antithesis of Moya and very, very good for her ego and her emotions. He kept her in check, kept her from flying off into a ditsy dizzy when things didn't go the way she wanted.

"He didn't have to involve us in his disappointment. He could simply look for a new family. Instead, I think he takes pleasure in the horrible mischief he inspires," Moya pointed out to Oran who she knew already understood what Conn was about.

"You have to put a stop to him, Oran," Moya said, her eyes simmering and her wings flashing golden sparks.

"How am I supposed to do that?" Oran asked exasperated with the situation as well as Moya's insistence he could fix the problem.

"Cast a spell. Put a curse on Florence."

~ * ~

"What light is this I see?" Kelly watched Casey's balcony, his voice weak, his legs shaking. Candle light floated magically from her room. The moon had vanished and only a few stars still twinkled in the growing light of the morning. The duel would be fought today if both participants were stupid enough to pursue the foolishness wrought the day before.

"Kelly? Is that you?" Casey leaned over the balcony, candlelight silhouetting her figure.

"You're there." Kelly's heart lodged in his throat. He prayed she didn't mean to go to the park. He wanted to ask but didn't want to put the seed in her mind. He prayed instead.

"We must end this idiocy. There is no reason for anyone to die and there is no reason for us to be shoved apart. I will give up my name for you."

"I am the enemy. And I would not have you give up all you love and hold dear. I would find a way to change that which we cannot change. There must be a way, for I cannot remain your enemy."

"You will never be the enemy," she said.

"But I am and until we uncover the reason, it will remain so." He climbed the trellis until he was a whisper away from Casey. "I would have the kiss that was denied me yesterday at the rocks," he told her. "Would you be grantin' it? And I would have the kiss before I depart to watch the duel unfold. I have given my word I would be Patrick's second. What a fool I am. The deed will alienate me from my family."

"We can leave. We can go to America or England or..."

"If we left, the feud would grow worse. Right now..."

"I understand," she told him softly.

He caressed her cheek, pushed her hair away from her face and traced her jaw line. With a finger under her chin, he slowly brought her lips to his. So sweet, so very sweet and innocent and he was thinking of ways to take her from her family. He could not do that.

His tongue traced the seam of her lips. Her hands rested on his shoulders then he felt her fingers against his neck. She returned his kiss, opened her lips slightly. He found a way to taste her more deeply, reveling in the sweetness that was Casey.

~ * ~

"A kiss--they kissed," Moya fluttered happily around her young charge, her wings a brilliant silver.

"And did you have doubts? Where our magic is concerned it is a given, don't you think, Moya?" Oran said with an arrogance to his words Moya understood and loved.

"Do you think we should be tellin' them about the feud now that they've taken the next step in their relationship?" Moya watched the pair as he traced the line of her jaw, his eyes alight with passion and love.

"That the feud began because of a piece of white lace?" Oran asked disgustedly. "Belgian lace."

"Well, we both know it was a little more than that."

"Was it? I don't see how. One lady wanted the lace, the other did too then all hell broke loose," Oran said.

"And the hell has lasted more than a hundred years. Don't you think it is time for this to end? I know I do and the young lovers need to be able to--to--love each other," Moya said with a shake of her body that sent faerie dust flying everywhere.

"Look they're kissing again," Oran said, watching Moya. She grinned then turned back to Oran. "You did that to get me off the subject."

"Well how do you plan on letting them know about the feud?" Oran asked her heatedly.

"Sarah, her nurse knows," Moya told him with a little hmmph added for his benefit. She smiled at the young lovers, her heart a flutter with happiness.

"And do you think anyone will believe her?"

"Casey's father knows the truth. Once it is out in the open, no one will question the validity because there are people who know," Moya said, crossing her arms over her chest put emphasis to her words. "They will have to stop fighting."

~ * ~

A sound from behind startled them apart. "I must go," he said. "Someone comes."

She touched his lips with her fingertip, tilting her head slightly to one side. "Take care," she whispered.

Kelly watched her as he stayed to the shadows, slipping through the yard and over the brick wall encircling the house. By the time he climbed over the wall, the shadows were no longer dark. The sun cast a brilliant light on the earth. His pace turned into a lope. He reached the park to find his brother there, and to watch Florence's carriage roll to a lumbering stop. Behind the carriage, Patrick rode on a huge black stallion.

Chapter Five

Casey raced through the streets, her skirts hiked. She dodged the foot traffic, slipping on mud before sliding into the street, her breath puffed from her.

"Get out o' the way," a frenzied driver yelled at her, shaking his fist. "Bloody hell," she heard as the phaeton passed, sending mud and water flying through the air.

"You get out of my way," Casey mumbled under her breath, wiping road dirt from her cheeks, and pulling the ribbon from her hair. She battled the people on the walkways and the carriages on the streets.

To the east the sun stood boldly above the village. She would be late. She would not be there in time to--do what--to stop the foolishness. Men, bah, one would think they didn't have a brain in their wee heads. All brawn and bravado, not a moment of thought marked this duel.

When she stepped into the clearing, the quiet calm surrounded her. The sun warmed the earth while no birds sung in the trees. Patrick's horse whinnied but there were no other sounds. As if in slow motion, men moved through the trees. A hazy morning mist hovered above the green grass.

She closed her eyes, listening; praying somehow she could stop this, knowing no one would listen to her.

When she opened them again, Patrick and Florence stood back to back, pistols pointed skyward. They counted the steps--one, two, three. She cried out, No! But she heard no words. No! No! She raced forward, but tripped on a tree root. Sprawled on the ground she watched. No one paid attention to her. Four--five--the counting went on and she was helpless.

Six--seven--eight--a shot rang out. No! She flew into the clearing. Patrick lay on the ground. Blood. God, blood everywhere.

Liam cursed, men shouted. Florence stood with his pistol pointing to the ground.

"You foul--bloody coward," Kelly roared.

"Everyone will know what you did today," Liam swore again.

"It's just a flesh wound," Patrick said with a grimace as he pushed off the wet grass with one arm and stood. Blood trickled from the wound and pooled on the grass.

"You're lucky the coward is as bad a shot as he is a man," Kelly said.

"And what did all of you prove here today?" Casey said determined to find answers. She turned on Florence, "What did you think? That you could get away with this? If Patrick had died, you'd hang."

Florence shrugged, the smirk on his face telling Casey he had no remorse. "My family would deny wrong doing. And yes, I know what kind of shot your brother is. I thought to save my life. Money speaks louder than words.

In a few days no one will care." He dusted imaginary dirt from his trousers.

Florence walked from the clearing, whistling a tune. Casey heard her brother curse, Kelly too. She knew it took all their restraint from going after Florence. Patrick's temper was well known and Casey admired him.

~ * ~

Moya's wings fluttered and her fists clenched. She flew toward Florence with deadly intent. She hated Conn and what vile thoughts he must have put in the young man's head for him to do such a thing. To top things off, Conn didn't have enough courage to attend the duel he must have had a hand in.

"Hold it," Oran flew in front of Moya, stopping her before she gave herself away.

"Don't stop me! You canna stand between me and my revenge. This is reprehensible." She darted around Oran but found her temper had suddenly subsided a wee bit.

"You must see to your charge. It appears Casey may make a huge mistake. She cannot go with Kelly. Everyone will know about them and it is too soon. Go on, Moya, this will all turn out in the end."

Moya looked back to Casey. Oh yes, Casey had already marched up to Kelly and was about to address him. Moya feared she might say something she shouldn't. Darting that direction she thanked the heaven above. Patrick stepped in front of Casey just as Oran had stopped her before she did something stupid.

Patrick bent low and said something to his sister. The girl flushed then looked at Kelly before she turned around and walked away, Patrick with her.

Moya's heart squeezed tight. Tears welled in her eyes and she brushed them aside with a furious gesture.

"I canna stand to see you cry, Moya. It makes my heart break." Oran flew around Kelly, watching Moya and sprinkling a generous portion of faerie dust on the lad. "Everything will turn out as you wish it," he said. "Go to her tonight."

Moya breathed a dainty sigh of relief as she watched Oran. "Thank you," she whispered softly her hands clasped in front of her. She knew she would have to cast another spell on Casey to make sure this evening's rendezvous turned out the way they planned. Following Oran's lead she sprinkled dust on Casey too. "Go to the landing tonight. Meet your true love and cast your fate with this young man."

~ * ~

"What is this? And this?"

Kelly tossed a third pebble onto Casey's balcony. She stood silhouetted by the light behind her. Using the trellis to climb to the top, Kelly pulled himself over the railing. He couldn't help the grin that spread across his face. He was delighted with this endeavor.

"Get dressed. Meet me at the church--your church."

"What should--the women are crocheting prayer shawls."

"Perfect." Kelly leapt from over the railing and away from the trellis, flashing Casey another smile. He raced to the church, dashing past people strolling through town and even past some who rode horses. Once he reached the church, he paced--first the walkway to the church then around the building, gazing toward the ocean and the eastern horizon.

When he saw her, his breath caught in his throat. Dressed in a lavender day dress, her hair falling free to her waist, she was a vision that would remain in his heart and head forever.

Kelly stepped forward, held her hand in his and gazed awestruck into Casey's eyes. His heart thundered against his chest, his breath raced.

"I hurried," Casey said, breathless.

"You are beautiful."

"I--" Casey stammered, closing her eyes for a second. "You shouldn't say such things."

"For the rest of our lives--I will tell you how beautiful you are." For the rest of his life… Kelly's thoughts hit him in the gut. How? That single notion brought moisture to his eyes. Too many factors stood between them--their religion--the feud.

~ * ~

Moya fluttered around Casey, sighing over and over then sighing once more. She closed her eyes and remembered all the attempts she and Oran had tried in order to get this far.

"Marvelous," her breath whooshed softly from her lips. To see them better Moya opened her eyes, her smile must have reached all the way to her ears. "Don't think I need any magic this evening."

The setting was perfect. A few clouds drifted across the sun. Warm pink and peach colors stretched along the horizon. Evening blues darkened the sky enhancing the contrast between the setting sun hues. Moya's heart fluttered softly, butterflies danced around her, frogs croaked near the little stream wandering its way to the ocean.

"Looks as if all our work is paying off," Oran grinned broadly, giving himself a little pat on his back.

"Dinna slack off," Moya said. "Until they are wed, our work is not finished."

"I wasn't," Oran said, seeming too defensive, his wings rimmed with gold flecks.

"I'm sorry. It is just--well they have too many obstacles in their way," Moya said.

"It's not the feud that bothers me the most. One of them will have to convert. That will set their families against them again."

"Well, you are a doomsayer," Moya said as she watched the young couple stroll hand in hand to the church then disappear inside.

"Should we follow?"

"Are you daft old man? Of course we should go after them. There is no tellin' what mischief Conn will be up to."

"Come on then." Oran flew towards the bell tower.

With a smile touching her lips, Moya watched Oran disappear through the tower. A few seconds later she descended into the church.

"What is he doing here?" Oran shook his fist at Florence who was standing by the altar. A priest stood by him in what seemed to be serious conversation.

"One can only guess," Moya said as she flew to the side room where Casey and Kelly were in deep conversation.

~ * ~

Florence looked toward the side room and scowled, his fury red hot and smoldering. He had plans but with every fork in the road his plans were foiled. The girl was a disaster but he wanted her, needed her fortune, and would move heaven and earth to see the grudge he held against Kelly seen to fruition.

He wanted the glory today. The priest was in agreement. He'd paid the man of God handsomely to help him win Casey's hand in marriage. The lies were circulating and it would not take long for Casey's mother to hear the rumors. Actually most of it was not lies. Casey was seeing Kelly, but he didn't believe Kelly had slept with the girl. But if he didn't move fast…

The moment Kelly noticed him he knew. Sweat beaded on his forehead and his fingers twitched. A spasm swept through him ending with a tick in his jaw. He narrowed his eyes, glaring at Kelly as if he could kill him with that one piercing look.

Casey turned to look over her shoulder, running into an end table, and knocking over a candle. Kelly raced to put out the fire that smoldered on the hem of Casey's dress. Florence grimaced, wondering how the devil he could stand to be around the walking disaster that was Casey. The small flames extinguished, Kelly wound his arm though Casey's, leaning over to whisper something in her ear. The love that emanated from Kelly's eyes hit him in the chest like a sledge hammer. His air rushed from his chest.

"I need that marriage certificate immediately. I plan on going to her parents and having the bans read as soon as humanly possible."

"What makes you think her dah will agree to a marriage?" the priest asked. "I've heard the brother despises you."

"I know things," Florence said, watching the couple disappear into a back room.

The priest coughed, clearing his throat. "I will not do anything I'll regret, Lad."

"You already have," Florence cocked his head sideways, the grin growing on his lips felt evil. He liked the feeling--pure wickedness.

"I'll not be jeopardizing myself anymore." The priest turned, walking away.

Florence set his hand on the man's shoulder, leaning close. "You will do as I say, when I say it."

"Or what?"

"You will regret the day you were born."

Chapter Six

"Wind the yarn in a ball--not too tight." Casey knew she stared at Kelly with stars in her eyes as he held the skein of yarn for her. Love radiated from her entire soul as her heart fluttered with shivers of delight.

"Like this?" Kelly asked, looking up as Casey nodded at him. Casey had seen Florence speaking in hushed tones with the priest. A different type of shiver had swept through her when she saw the man who had just recently asked for her hand in marriage. She would kill herself before she would say yes to Florence's overtures.

She felt a prickle of fear sneak up her spine. Kelly's eyes flashed, his shoulders tensing. Hot rancid breath whispered by her ear.

"I know what the feud is about," Florence whispered, his voice rough and malicious as he taunted Casey.

Casey jerked away from Florence, her knitting needles hitting the wood floor with a dull thud. She stood so quickly all the yarn she held followed the needles, her hands trembling and her stomach churning.

"Don't!" Kelly's words rushed from his mouth as he jumped to his feet, hands clenched at his sides. "Leave her be."

"You can't believe the likes of that young fellow," one of the older ladies told her, pointing one needle at Florence and shaking it. "He's a scoundrel of the worst sort."

"No one knows what the feud was about, least as no one who's willing to talk about it," another interjected. "Wouldn't you like a nice cup of tea, dear?"

"Yes, tea would be nice and maybe a strawberry scone," the first lady said, rising as if to walk to the kitchen to do just that. But she stopped, looking over her shoulder and seeming to wait for more conversation.

"He lies to get his own way," another shook an empty needle his way. "You best be getting home, Mr. Florence, or the devil spirit who haunts you will make you more nasty than you already are. Where are your god faeries when you be needin' them?"

"What about that tea? I'm near starving…" one lady asked.

"Wait!" Casey cried out her voice shaking. "Florence, for God sakes, what is it you know about the feud?"

Florence's lips shifted into a crooked, malicious leer. "It will cost you a pretty penny, my dear. Perhaps a stroll in the moonlight along with a kiss."

"Be off with you. No one wants to hear your lies and mean spirited insinuations," Kelly moved forward his hand clenched tightly at his sides.

Casey rose, stepping in front of Kelly before he made a spectacle right here inside the church.

"Please, Kelly. Let him speak now or forever hold his piece. But he will know I will never take a stroll anywhere with him or kiss the likes of him. Not for any information he might taunt me with."

Florence dusted off the arms of his jacket with milk-white hands. "Don't think I feel like telling anyone just yet. I'll meet you privately, Casey. Then perhaps if I feel--well--feel as if you deserve to know the truth, I might be telling you."

"The hell you will!" Kelly shook off Casey's hand, moving toward Florence once more. "You stay away from Casey."

"Or what?" Florence asked with a sneer. "Another duel in the misty morning? I won't miss next time."

"I'll find out from someone else. I will never be with you as you say, in private," Casey said. "I truly believe there are more people around who do know than who don't." Casey sat down before she fainted. Her legs wobbled and shook as she reached the seat of the chair. She inhaled a few long, deep breaths before she looked around the knitting circle.

"Don't you let that horrible young man hurt you," one lady said. "He may be rich as Midas but he doesn't have a soul."

A collective murmur rattled around the room in a wave of agreement as well as chatter about market places, lace and fairs. Casey strained forward, realizing there might be some knowledge gained here. These women knew and were talking about the feud. But so many voices rang in her ears she couldn't make out the details. Belgian lace…the two words were there over and over again. Florence wasn't the only one who knew. Could this feud that had lasted for more than a century be about Belgian lace? Never, no one was that crazy.

"Belfast? Did you say you met your first beau there?" One lady asked another as if she attempted a diversion.

"Oh, my, but that was a long time ago. I was at church one Sunday and when he looked at me, my heart fluttered and I nearly swooned."

Casey thought she'd had enough of this prattle, but she didn't know how to stop these wonderful church ladies who she knew only had her best interest at heart. "Did you say lace? Belgian lace?" Casey queried, cocking her head sideways, her heart thundering beneath her ribs. She was so close to the answer.

"You best be asking your father, little missy. Mum's the word," one lady said as she cast a baleful glare around the room at the gossipy ladies. "As for the rest of you, all of you, you must have way too much time on your hands. We are all meddlesome old busy bodies. It is long past the time to stop the gossip mill."

"She deserves to know the truth. Star-crossed lovers these two are not meant to be. If her dah won't tell her, I will." With those words said, the older lady stuffed her needles yarn and partial shawl into her knitting bag. She gave all the ladies in the room a nose-in-the-air stare before departing. The room fell silent while Casey mulled over all that had been said.

~ * ~

Moya felt alive with anticipation, her poor little heart fluttering so hard she gasped for air. Casey was about to find out how the feud started. She knew deep down one of these ladies would tell her. She wanted to chant, "Tell the girl, tell the girl." Oran would have a wee little fit if she did. But then it occurred to Moya the discovery would not be the end of the quarrel between the two families. Much had transpired over the 100 or so years and the argument and hatred between the two families had escalated.

"What would you be thinkin', Moya?" Oran asked.

"I be thinkin' these two might indeed be star-crossed. All those ladies can do is gossip. If I could, I'd shout out Belgian lace and tell my poor Casey how this all began. And--I be thinking even if she discovers the truth, there is too much hatred, way too much hatred for the feud to dissolve."

"My head is sore listening to all your thoughts, Moya." Oran rose gracefully from his perch and flew around Kelly, sprinkling some good luck dust on the young man. "I would like to see this resolved too."

A tear slipped down Moya's cheek. She was so afraid their machinations and the faerie dust was not going to be enough to overcome the odds. She and Oran would have to be even more vigilant.

"Come on, Moya, don't be givin' up on the couple yet. It's not like you to lose all hope." Oran flew to Moya's side and hugged her, wiping away the tear drop. He looked at her and smiled. When she smiled back, he chucked her under the chin.

"You say that now, but I remember when Casey's grandda shot Kelly's great uncle. I'm so afraid nothing's going to stop. Either of them could get hurt--s-shot. I couldn't bear it if anything bad happened. They are meant for each other."

"He shot him in the foot, Moya. The act was hardly life threatening."

"I know, but then the uncle retaliated by tearing out the picket fence in front of Casey's grandda's house."

"The years have taken their toll, Moya, but these two will change that. I promise you they will heal all the wounds between these two families. When they have their first baby the parents will be so delighted they will forget everything bad between them. I tell you all will be well."

"Or make it worse. And when were you gifted with the ability to see into the future?"

"Moya, you must have faith."

"I dinna believe you have a wee crystal ball in that shirt pocket of yours? Oran, you cannot be blinded by the facts here. They are star-crossed lovers and I will not believe anything but that until we see them united at the altar with their families standing up for them."

~ * ~

"You're a damned sight better than Florence, but hardly good enough for Casey." Patrick leaned negligently against a tree, tossing an acorn in the air as he spoke. He slanted Kelly a sideways glance before the acorn flew into the air again.

"And who are you to be judging me, Patrick O'Connell?" Kelly skipped a stone across the little stream winding its way behind the church. An owl hooted in the darkness of the night, a lonely sound. *I can be just as cool headed as Patrick O'Connell. I can be cooler, just watch me.*

"Where's Casey?"

Patrick's tone made Kelly jump, his stomach in knots. "Knitting--talking--finding out things I'm afraid to know." Kelly rocked back on his heels, his hands behind his back, feeling helpless. Control was something he wasn't used to losing. This relationship spiraled dizzily out of control. Closing his eyes for a moment, he listened to the sound of whispering trees and the slight mist as it fell to the earth. He smelled the sea and felt the rhythm of the thundering surf as it hit the rocks nearby.

"You ok with Casey alone with the ladies?" Patrick tossed one of the acorns across the creek then another.

"No, but I was about to lose my temper, and I didn't think that would be wise. I had to find some time alone--to think."

"Why would you be losing your temper?" A strange grin spread across Patrick's face as he spoke. "You nervous?"

"Florence."

"Ah, a one word response that makes so much sense," Patrick said.

"He's a threat to both of us." Kelly felt a muscle in his jaw twitch then radiate outward to end up in his stomach. Nerves tensed, every synapse seeming to snap with thoughts of Florence and what he might maliciously accomplish.

"Florence is evil."

"Vile," Kelly said, dusting his hands off as if he could rid himself of Florence with that one simple gesture.

Kelly stood with his hands behind his head, gazing toward the church, ready to storm the knitting circle. Rushing headlong into the gaggle of ladies was not wise and he welcomed the diversion Patrick created.

"I don't understand what he wants. Clearly, he doesn't care for Casey in any way."

"It's about the game--the mischief-- the trouble he creates," Patrick said. "I've known him since we were both in knickers. He hasn't changed."

"The heartache," Kelly said feeling the same churning in his stomach he had earlier. He wanted Casey in his life with an elemental need he didn't understand.

"Go get Casey, walk her home, kiss her."

"I dinna believe my ears, Patrick O'Connell. You givin' me permission to court your little sister? Kiss her?" A kiss--his heart raced at the thought. Casey in his arms--butterflies fluttered in his core--every part of him hardened with need. All he had to do was think about her. The memory of her scent filled him.

"You've fallen hard for my sis. Best you treat her right."

"I have. She's everything to me. In such a short time…"

"There is nothing worse than a lovesick fool," Florence said as he stepped from the shadow of a large oak tree. "And I see one now. You planning on pining away for your lil lass or are you going to show her how a real man would treat her?"

"And you would know this how..." Kelly asked. "You're not a real man, Florence. You're a contemptible creature who thrives on others' pain."

"I'm vile? I'd hardly use that term," Florence said, wiping off his sleeve with a monogrammed hankie. "And I thought you liked me."

A rustle in the night air alerted Kelly, his senses on full alert. This meeting was no coincidence.

"Need any help teaching these two a few lessons?" Two men stepped from the shadows behind Florence, flanking him, fists clenched at their sides.

"Who would be teaching whom a lesson?" Patrick asked, balling his fists. "I would not be so hasty as to jump into this fray without a thought in your wee brain."

"We would be teaching the likes of you two," one of the men said, a crooked leer marking his scarred face.

"I suppose you think the odds are right? Two against three and all, of course Florence doesn't really count as a man. He'll stand behind you two men then claim a victory, if there is one, for himself."

Kelly was pretty sure he and Patrick could beat these two effeminate men even though their biceps were huge. He had a hankerin' for a fight and if that was what these guys wanted, he would be more than willing to oblige. He slanted Patrick a questioning look, saw the nod of the head just before one of Florence's cohorts swung at him. He ducked and punched the aggressor in the gut.

Patrick shouted and with a high kick knocked the other man at shoulder level, decking him with one blow.

The man hit a tree, sliding along the trunk until he sat, legs spread wide on the grassy knoll.

Florence danced flat-footed around the other two men, staying out of reach. Kelly wanted nothing more than to get at the prissy dandy but couldn't find his way past the other man who seemed hell-bent on protecting Florence. It occurred to Kelly the only way Florence could acquire such seeming loyalty would be through blackmail.

"You're a lily-livered little girl," Patrick said. "Fight like a man or call your dogs off, Florence. No one likes a coward or didn't you figure that out at the duel?"

"Or what?" Florence asked. "What will happen to me?" Florence let out a low and long chuckle from behind his protectors--his sneer scalding Kelly's soul.

"Or your reputation will be worse than it has ever been." Kelly danced light-footed around the last body guard. Florence sidestepped behind a tree. "You can cry off now or forever hold your peace."

"Not that I care a fig for my reputation. I have enough coin to pay my way into any circle. If the situation here becomes intolerable and I stop having fun, I can move to London. Can you say the same thing, Kelly?" Once again Florence slid behind the last barrier he had between Kelly's pummeling fists.

"I dinna need to pay my way anywhere. You fit well in London. I hear the depravity in the gaming hells exceeds even your limits. But your limits haven't really been tested have they?" Kelly would love to see the last of Florence. Uneasily though, he knew Florence would never make life easy for him. The hatred ran too deep and had lasted far too long.

"Touché, Mr. Shaunasey. And you will be supportin' Casey on your meager wages--ah, but I could show her off in style, take her to the most fashionable modiste, buy her the newest frippery from Paris. You know her family has more money than I have. She is not used to a life of poverty. Is that what you be wantin' to give the lass?"

"I dinna believe Casey cares for money over love," Kelly said, dodging a feeble punch from the Florence's only protector who was left standing. "We have something few people have, a love that is true and pure. I will make her happy."

"Love cannot feed a family, or put pretty dresses on the wife." Florence's taunt came out in a rush of hot air. He staggered backwards his hand to his face, a look of sudden astonishment in his eyes.

"Take that you whining piece of blubber." Kelly had hit Florence square in the nose and the flamboyant loud mouth went down, bleeding profusely. His friends looked at Florence for a brief moment, shrugged their shoulders in unison and walked away, their backs to their so called friend. They didn't turn around or give Florence a second thought.

"You broke my nose," Florence wailed as he touched it, his hand stained with blood. "You broke it…"

~ * ~

"Oran, hold up," Moya said. "They've finished, quit, done, Florence is going to slink away like the horrible creature he is. The vermin who infests all things good and decent in this world. If there is any justice to be had--that is."

Oran's fists flew in rapid fire staccato, hitting imaginary Florences. A jab here, a jab there, an uppercut then he brought his fist up to protect his face. He let out a karate kick high into the air. "Take that and that," he said as he danced in the air. "I'm going to make you pay for every rotten deed you have ever brought to fruition." His fists pummeled the air--another kick--more punches. A grunt then a groan emanating from Oran.

"Oran, they are quite done. Stop." Moya's wings fluttered fast and furious, her heart a rapid staccato beneath her ribcage.

"Dinna care. I'm having fun here. Don't you stop me from my fun." Punch, jab, kick, punch, jab, kick, "coward, lily-livered rat--take that--and that."

"They will get away and you won't have done anything to help the situation. See, Patrick seems to have takin' a liking to young Kelly. Maybe they will join forces and our young lovers will no longer be star-crossed." Moya brought her clasped hands up to her face and stared lovingly at Kelly. "Ah, Casey darlin', you have found yourself a wonderful lad." The deep sigh emanating from her was long and filled with enchantment.

Oran sucked in a shaky deep breath, gasping for air. Bending over at the waist he continued to inhale then pant as he slowly drew air into his lungs in a normal way. He closed his eyes for a moment, inhaling once more.

"Oran, I dare say you are a wee bit out of shape. You've been imbibing in the ale a little too much of late. Your little ticker is not going to last out your life if you don't see fit to take care of yourself."

Moya never liked it when Oran over did his activity. He wasn't the young man he used to be, and he didn't seem to understand moderation was the key to longevity.

"And you're a model of perfection, Moya?" Oran asked as he finally filled his lungs enough to talk.

"Closer than you."

~ * ~

"I'm going home," Florence said while he scooted backwards on his well-rounded derriere. "I'm…"

"Going to tell your daddy?" Kelly asked a broad smile across his face. "Tell him the truth this time. You can weave a good tale about the fight, three against two."

Patrick slapped Kelly across the back, "Never knew you had it in you, Kelly."

"Who's been kickin' whose butt on our Sunday escapades?"

"I believe the Catholics have won every time," Patrick said, rubbing his chin as if in deep thought over the matter.

Kelly threw a punch then a jab. "You be remembering wrong. Except for one unusual Sunday when a certain little Catholic lass wandered into our fight, the Protestants have won every meeting for the last year."

"Ah--I don't recall anything like that. We've been beating you every time."

Patrick's arm went around Kelly's back, pulling him to the ground. They wrestled, each struggling to overpower the other. Kelly grunted as he threw Patrick onto his back. Minutes later, "Say uncle, Patrick."

"Uncle," he said laughing. Kelly rose, extending a hand helping Patrick to his feet.

"I let you win."

"You did not. I had you from the start," Kelly said feeling a deep giddiness swimming up from his soul. He could be friends with Casey's brother if not for their religious differences. Hell, he didn't care a fig for religion. In his mind religion had started a lot of wars for no other reason than greed and power. True faith was in the way a person treated other people and how they lived their life.

"Shake," Patrick said.

"I love your sister."

"Would you consider converting?" Patrick asked.

Chapter Seven

"Come on, Casey, dance with me."

For a few tense moments, Casey stared at a knothole in the floor, her stomach rolling somersaults and fluttering butterflies. The scene she conjured left images in her head she didn't want to come to fruition. But she didn't want Kelly to beg. Dancing was something girls were supposed to love.

"Case..." Kelly held out his hand, a small gesture but one that went a long way in Casey's mind as to accepting. She hedged, wishing she could run from the room and not cause everyone there to watch her fail miserably. She'd accepted Kelly's invitation, knowing full well she had no business at this Protestant dance.

At the moment she had taken a giant leap, defying her parent's wishes and attending an event that would give them apoplexy if they uncovered the truth. Of course everything she'd been doing and thinking lately would have the same effect on them. She should never be in love with a man her parents did not approve of. Guilt swept through her, yet she stood straight and met Kelly's gaze.

With a shy tentativeness she held out her hand. His fingers closed around hers. Warmth engulfed her and his smile of encouragement filled her soul. Yet she remembered her dance lessons. Her instructor had thrown up his hands in frustration, marching from the room muttering something awful.

"You know I should not be here," she said as he pulled her into his arms. "My parents…" she broke off as he whirled her around in a circle, "Don't approve--the feud--the religion." She stumbled backward.

"Hush love, don't think of things you can no longer change. Watch where your feet are going. I won't let you fall. Just hang on to me."

His muscles flexed beneath her fingertips. His long lean body flowed with the music as they moved faster and faster around the dance floor, her feet barely touching the planked wood beneath her. The music changed, slower now, and Casey relaxed into his arms. Heaven could not be a better place than how she felt. She wanted to spend a lifetime with him. He was her soul mate.

She looked up. His eyes glowed with affection and love. She thought it was love but wasn't sure. She knew she'd never seen that look before. He had said the words, *"I love you."* He'd said the words for the first time last night and once this morning. Would he ever say them again?

"Kelly…" she began, moistening her lips, hoping to say the right words yet not knowing what those words were. Her mouth was dry, her lips parched. If she spoke, she felt sure she might choke and the words would come out like a frog's croak.

"Yes, my love," he bent down and kissed her lightly on the forehead, his hands gently squeezing where they touched.

"Can we--get something to…" Well that wasn't what she wanted to say. "Drink?" She cleared her throat, wishing for courage she didn't have. If she did have something to drink, she would most likely spill it down her front or worse yet spill it on someone else.

He laughed. It was lighthearted. "Of course, follow me. We will have to make sure we get the one that hasn't been spiked." He gave her a devilish wink then sauntered to a table heavily laden with food and drinks of all sorts.

"Of course," she said but she wouldn't be averse to having a little something that might give her a wee bit of daring. She needed to tell him how she felt--that she would spend her life with him if he would always love her. *Now don't jump the gun here, Casey darling. You know he told you how he feels but I'm still afraid to give my heart away. He told you he loves you. But how long have you known him?* And for goodness sakes what had she done?

He ladled punch into a cup, sipped it as if he checked it then gave her the cup. "Want to enter the competition?" He leaned against the table. His long legs mesmerized her, his dark good looks sent her heart racing and his gorgeous blue eyes sent her mind spinning with wicked thoughts. Yet his smile always made her melt. When he grinned lazily at her, she was lost.

"Let's watch," she had to stand her ground on this one. She couldn't let him talk her into dancing in a competition. At best, she would humiliate herself; at worst...well she definitely didn't want to think of the worst that could happen.

"No, come on, Casey. I want to dance. We could win this," he said. "We have nothing to lose and everything to gain." He bent down close to her, "I'm a very good dancer." His whisper sent a lock of hair blowing away from her face.

And I'm a very bad dancer, "It's your life..." she said, knowing she was bound to trip, run into someone, or possibly take a couple out right on the dance floor. "You might be the last one standing if you had a different partner. But you are cursed with bad luck tonight because Casey O'Connell is your dancing partner. Do you see anyone else you could dance with and win?" she asked not wanting to know the answer to that question.

She closed her eyes, picturing the scene. Everyone sprawled on the floor, moaning in pain, Kelly rubbing the back of his neck wondering how on earth he could find himself in such a horrific pickle. Casey saw broken legs and arms, broken pitchers of glassware, food spread all over the planked floor.

Music played. Without her permission, Kelly swept her into his arms and they were dancing. Well, maybe not dancing, more like stumbling without grace. Her nerves seemed to snap while her muscles were a wobbly mess of instability and her mind spun precariously. She closed her eyes and prayed to stay upright.

"Hang in there. We aren't the first..."

"The first what?" she asked breathless and feeling as if she might be getting her sea legs under her or would they be called dancing legs?

"To be eliminated," he bent close and whispered by her ear, sending little chills of delight down her spine.

"Oh!" Casey chose that moment to step on his foot. He pulled her close but not before the stumble was apparent to the judges.

"We're the second. You can stop now and look. Open your eyes, darlin'." He pointed to the dance floor. "Everyone, including you, are still on their feet. You've done no permanent damage to anyone or anything. You can be proud of yourself for trying."

"So we're done." Casey had never been so relieved in her life. She inhaled a deep breath of air. "I don't have to pray to St. Patty now, do I?" She waved a hand in front of her face, hoping to cool her heated cheeks as well as hide her blush.

"Let's go outside. There is a full moon. Besides I don't believe St. Patty is the patron saint of the dance," he said with a wink and a lopsided grin. He brushed a lock of rakish hair away from his gorgeous eyes. She thought she might swoon when he threw her that look.

"The moon will be beautiful for sure." *Maybe he will kiss me.* She caught her lower lip lightly between her teeth and peered at his long well-muscled back as he led the way through the dance floor to the waiting and very romantic scene outside. With her hand in his she trotted behind, bumping into a dance couple on her way out.

Moon glow bathed the porch. A warm spring breeze redolent with the scent of Daphne and roses filled the air. Frogs croaked nearby and a few lazy crickets chirped their own song of pleasure. An owl hooted. Casey sighed inwardly, taking in everything she saw, her hopes and her dreams spinning crazily inside her head.

Kelly pointed to a gazebo surrounded with scented foliage. "Shall we?" he asked his voice a tiny bit hesitant. "We could sit and talk."

"Talk?" she asked. She felt brazen and little bold. She didn't want to talk. "About… about what? The feud…"

"Us, and yes, the feud and the people keeping secrets. About this morning."

Casey hoped he had the same thing in mind as she did. She wanted a kiss tonight, needed to feel his lips on hers and his arms around her. She nodded, her wayward mind having no second thoughts. Her legs did though. They were wobbling so hard she wasn't sure she could walk all the way to the little gazebo.

She stumbled slightly, her hand resting on his back to steady herself. "I could carry you." He didn't wait for a reply. He swept her into his arms, closing the distance to the private sanctuary away from prying eyes.

"Kelly, put me down."

"Never."

"But… I'm too heavy."

"You're as light as a feather." His voice was thick--husky, Casey wondered at the sound and timber. She'd never heard him sound that way before.

In the gazebo Kelly turned her, holding her hands in his, swaying slightly, pulling her body close to his. She swallowed hard, anticipation making her insides quake. She looked up at him and moistened her lips. He was tall, almost a head higher than her, his eyes huge pools of sweetness, promising love and tenderness. As if in slow motion, Kelly leaned forward. His lips met hers in a gentle undemanding kiss--a daytime kiss. He traced the seam of her lips with his tongue.

"Casey, darling, you are so sweet," he said. "I will not take advantage of your innocence and purity." He traced her collarbone with a calloused fingertip, pulling back from her as he spoke softly to her. His jaw tightened as if he fought his emotions, his needs--his love for her. His hold upon her loosened and fell away.

"You are not taking advantage of me, Kelly." She suddenly felt as if she wanted to stamp her foot in a childish tantrum and yell at him--yell, no, tell him how old she was, that she was a mature woman, and she was damn tired of everyone treating her as if she were a toddler just come from her dear mother's womb.

"Ah, but I be thinkin' I am. You are so young and have you ever kissed a boy let alone a man?" he asked, a lopsided grin replacing the serious expression. "I will not have you rue the day you met me or the evening I took you to the gazebo." He laughed softly as if he was enjoying a private joke of some sort. Then his features turned grim once more. "I cannot do this. I've come to admire your brother. While I don't know the rest of your family…" he looked skyward as if seeking divine intervention.

She inhaled sharply, wondering what he was trying to say. Was this just a lark to him, a pastime that meant nothing? Did this morning mean nothing? Were all her feelings for him one-sided? She felt empty and horribly alone at this moment. She stepped back, distancing herself from him and wondering what game he played and if she had misinterpreted his interest in her. Perhaps Patrick was right. Maybe he didn't care for her. She pushed away from him, feeling so many pent up emotions she didn't know what she should say to him. *"I've come to admire your brother." What about me? My brother? Does he want to know the rest of my family? Well that could be disastrous.*

"Why, Kelly Shaunasey, would you be using me? And to what ends?"

~ * ~

Cary flew around the young lovers, an evil smile in her heart, and Conn fluttered up beside her, a devil's smirk on his lips. She enjoyed this, the teasing of innocence. And while Kelly called Casey naive, he was much the same. Trusting, young, inexperienced...

Without guile...

Pure...

"Ha! It's a rare opportunity we can find a moment with these two virtuous creatures without their ever present guardian angels around," Cary said.

Conn had known from the beginning he needed help to carry out his plan. Cary was just the pagan faerie he wanted to assist him with demolishing these star-crossed lovers.

The joy of the star-crossed lovers never finding love made his heart catapult.

"You mean their godfaeries Moya and Oran?" Conn asked, rubbing his hands together in pagan faerie glee. He had never felt so hopeful and he no longer thought he had an uphill battle to wage in order to win the war. Florence had proven himself useless in his bid to win the fair Casey's hand. He was such an arrogant dandy. Conn could barely stand to be around him and he was his god child.

"I wonder what mischief we can do tonight before Oran and Moya find their way here. That little ruse you dreamed up to send them to the wrong place was very clever," Cary said, her evil smile stretching nearly ear-to-ear. "They will be flitting around that empty hall and cursing you until they are blue in the face. But that won't help. They will still have to figure out where to go to find their young charges. I must pat myself on the back--several times. We have already put to a screeching halt their lovers tryst in this very romantic gazebo."

"I be thinkin' the same thing. But common sense will win out. Moya is the logical one. There are not too many places they could be. Their wings will be smoldering hot, but they will get here before the night is done." Conn puffed out his cheeks, flying backwards for a moment then twirling in a tight circle as if he searched the night sky for a sign of the good faeries.

"Is that a gold streak up there?" Cary asked pointing to the north. She blinked twice to make sure she wasn't seeing things she didn't want to see.

"By the grace of God, it is. It must be Moya and Oran. That was faster than I thought. Someone must have tipped them off."

"You little piece of foul..." Moya settled on top the gazebo, cursing Conn and Cary. "Garbage," she yelled, shaking her fist at the two faeries. "You--y-y-you, I have no words to describe the pair of you."

Cary grinned, enjoying Moya's distress. "Garbage? Now, Moya, I'm sure you can come up with something a little more despicable. Something that would fit my personality a bit better. Garbage is just too, too, benign."

Moya's wings fluttered fast and furious, sending a cavalcade of faerie dust swirling in the air. Her little hands were braced on her hips and a scowl darkened her features.

"Now, now, Moya, settle down. We arrived in the nick of time, if I don't mind saying so myself. I be thinkin' the pagans haven't done too much damage yet. At least nothing we can't fix with a little ingenuity and determination."

~ * ~

"I--why Casey O'Connell, how could you be thinking such a thing." He felt as if the love of his life, his soul mate had just kicked him in the gut. He meant to protect her, not take advantage of her. He wanted nothing more than to kiss her again, to make love to her, and more--so much more. "I have only your best interest at heart. Now you are accusing me of--using you of--not considering your feelings to be important."

"Why did you kiss me," Casey asked, "then push me away?" Her expression bordered on furious and hurt. Kelly didn't like that look and was making vows to himself to rectify this as soon as possible and to never see the expression again.

Damn, but she had every right to ask him and to feel hurt. Maybe he was taking advantage. No, he meant to protect and cherish. If he'd kept kissing her, he wouldn't have stopped and he had the strange feeling Casey would not have told him no. *Of course she would not have told him no, she has no idea what kissing will lead to.*

"Casey, darlin', you've got to learn something." He was sweating bullets as he pushed his hair from his eyes then searched for a diplomatic way to talk to her.

She pointed a long slender finger at him, tapping him on the chest, once, twice then three times. "Don't be tellin' me, Kelly Shaunasey, I need to learn how to kiss. That just wouldn't be very nice now, would it? You be knowin' I haven't done a lot of kissing…" She tapped him again and his heart fell to the pit of his stomach. He felt a large lump in his throat. To no avail he coughed to clear his thoughts as well as his throat.

He placed both hands on her shoulders and tried not to draw her close and seek that kiss she was wanting. "You've got to learn how to say no," he told her, feeling a smile radiate upward from his core, understanding the word no was not what he wanted to hear. He needed to hear the soft throaty sounds of pleasure emanating from her when he kissed and touched her.

"No? No! I don't want to tell you no. See, I can say the despicable word. I just don't want to." She placed her hand on his chest. He felt the warmth. An inferno of heat and desire swept through him.

"Therein lies the problem, sweetheart. If you don't say no, I might ravish you right here in this gazebo and that might be a little embarrassing if someone were to discover us--" *Ravish? Where did that thought come from. In the male parts of you she knows nothing about. She has a brother,* he tried arguing with himself.

"Then you want to kiss me." She was all smiles and coquettish looks. She blinked and peered at him from beneath long dark lashes. *God, she has the longest lashes. Well, she has learned to flirt and quite appealingly. Anymore and she might just get her wish fulfilled*--lord, he might have his wish granted. Then the guilt would wash through him. *No, Kelly Shaunasey, if she can't say no, you have to. This is not the right place or time.*

"And so much more," Kelly admitted, knowing he shouldn't. There was so much to settle between them before he could make her his very own. If the century old feud wasn't a formidable road block, the religious issues would make the journey far too difficult to imagine. He knew he had to wait.

"More?" she asked. "Tell me what more means." She quirked a delicate eyebrow upward and flashed him a heart-melting smile. "Please?" she seemed to beg and he was hard-pressed to resist the gorgeous eyes staring into his.

Kelly groaned inwardly. "If I have to tell you, then you really must learn to say no." How does a fella resist this siren's call? She was everything he had ever yearned for in a woman, in a soul mate.

"I want you to kiss me and I think I want the more part too. And I'm really not that innocent or ignorant. I know there is more. I just don't know what more feels like and exactly what more entails. So you will be my teacher. Yes," she paused, "you will teach me all about more and kisses and sinfully decadent things. After all, it is your job." She appeared absolutely happy with herself as if she had solved all their problems.

He wanted nothing more than to teach her everything about love, about making love and anything decadent she wanted to explore. Lord, but he could start right now--this very instant--he would be a well-satisfied man. "Maybe we can keep to the kissing and not find too much trouble." Lord, was he a stupid man. He wanted to make everything right. He needed her in his bed, not in the gazebo.

She looked up and slanted him an all-knowing grin as if she'd just won the first battle. Hell, this wasn't a battle. He wanted this as much as she apparently did. He wanted to surrender to her. The only battle he waged was with his conscience. Hell, his whole body ached to admit defeat. A kiss, what would another kiss be like, and could they both come away unscathed from it? Could he keep said kiss under control, not allowing himself to ravish his lady fair on this very spot. After this morning's events, he knew he would have a lifetime with her.

He pulled her into his arms, holding her tight against him so afraid to carry this further but wanting another kiss from her more than life itself. He knew better. He'd already presented all the arguments against another kiss, but he didn't want to let her go--could not let her go--if he had a choice, would never let her go.

"Kelly..." His name was a breathy whisper in the sultry air inside the gazebo. Did she know what she did to him when she said his name that way? *No, imbecile, of course she doesn't. She is an innocent.*

"What?" He could barely breathe, let alone speak. He asked a question he wanted desperately to know the answer to but was terrified of that answer. What if she had a change of heart? He didn't believe he had ever been as unsure of himself as he was at this moment.

"You're smothering me. Can you just kiss me and teach me everything I want to know? You wouldn't want someone else teaching me, now would you?" She flashed him another coquettish grin as he loosened his hold on her just enough to look down at her and watch her breasts rise and fall with the deep breath she inhaled.

Good God, no.

Smoothing Casey's soft bottom lip with one finger, Kelly stared into the night--into the dance hall. "Patrick," he whispered as a knot formed in his gut. *By all that is holy, what is he doing here?* He felt Casey's jump of surprise and the trembling of her body. This wasn't something he could make right. "As much as I would like to take you up on all of your sweet offers, the timing could never have been worse. I think I see your brother and a few of his friends in the dance hall and if I'm not mistaken, things are heating up in there."

A loud crash and the noise of fists hitting flesh resounded in the air. Casey swirled in Kelly's arms to capture the scene he was looking at. "He's brought his friends. This is not Sunday. You never fight unless it's Sunday."

He felt the shiver of apprehension in Casey, flowing from her into him and sending misgiving spiraling out of control.

"No, we don't," Kelly said.

A young man tumbled from the back door. Another followed in a leap, landing on top of the first. Fists flew furious and fast. Kelly ached to join the ruckus, but knew he needed to stay with Casey. Liam was hit by a punch and landed outside with a few of the other brawlers. Kelly held his breath, pulling Casey into the shelter of his arms. He felt her heart beat and the rapid escalation of her breath.

"What on earth are they all fighting about now?" Casey stepped forward, attempting to push from Kelly's arms, but his hold on her tightened.

"I be thinkin' you know the answer to that," he said, voice calmly resigned. "Your brother and his friends are here for one reason. At that is you."

"Well, tarnation…"

Kelly felt the realization of her statement as she stiffened in his arms. He felt her withdraw from him one vertebra at a time. The knifing sensation in his heart penetrated every dream he just had about Casey. Perseverance had never been so underrated. He would have to hang in there a bit longer. He would win her hand and would convince his family as well as hers they would work out their differences.

She pulled away, shaking her head and turning to him. He saw the tears fill her eyes then slip down her cheeks. "I can't believe he would do this to me. I thought the two of you had just agreed to disagree. What on earth could be wrong with the lot of them?"

Her once smiling face turned serious, shoulders stiffening, he knew he wasn't going to like what he was about to hear. The moments passing between them, the unspoken words, seemed to last an eternity.

"Kelly Shaunasey, I don't believe we can be together until we can figure out how to make our families understand."

~ * ~

"Oh my God. Oh my, oh my," Moya fluttered up and down, her insides churning. "Everything is falling apart. Cary, you are wicked, wicked, wicked, but I'm not going to quit. You haven't won this war yet. You will rue the day you messed with me." Moya shook her delicate little fist at the wicked pagan.

"Calm down," Oran said watching Moya fall apart at the seams. If you go up then down one more time, you're going to make me sea-sick." Oran searched for a way to calm Moya. She would not do anyone any good in this state save the fae pagans, Cary and Conn.

"I know, I know." She wrung her hands and wailed, making a soft keening sound as she calmed a bit. "But Oran, what are we going to do? We cannot stop the fight. There is no amount of dust that will do such a thing. And Casey, how could she have ever said such a thing?"

"You must understand, those two cannot stay apart. Something draws them inexplicably to each other. She is speaking in the moment. You be noticin' Kelly doesn't appear to be agreein' with her." Oran knew he had to think fast. Somehow he had to end the

Catholic versus Protestant war without anyone winning and keep Patrick from haulin' his little sister home never to see her beloved again.

Moya huffed. "It's called faerie dust, you big oaf. And I've plum used up more than half of my month's supply. What about you? Do you have any faerie dust left?" She wrung her hands again; the depression he had seen earlier had seemed to vanish. For a moment Moya looked more like her old self and if that was so, Cary beware of his Moya..

"Tons," but as he looked in the little bag he carried at his waist, Moya must have been able to see he had very little left. Lying to her was out of the question. "Well, I had tons yesterday before you made me sprinkle and sprinkle and sprinkle most of it on Kelly. It seems he wasn't acting up to snuff."

"So we are nearly helpless. We cannot go on..." Suddenly, her keening grew in volume, her distress reaching through to her core. She stiffened then as if she had come to some momentous conclusion.

"Moya, you are never helpless." She needed to boost her ego and find a way to take charge of this quickly turning situation. He had thought she had done just that. Apparently he had been dead wrong.

"Ha, ha, ha!"

The laughter emanating from the top of the gazebo sent a shiver of apprehension down Oran's spine. The chuckle sounded demonic in nature, coming from the pits of hell. He looked to Moya to see how Cary's devilish laughter had affected her.

"You lose something?" Cary's taunt, malicious in nature seemed to give Moya more backbone than she'd had. Oran prayed she would never let Kelly and Casey fall into Cary's conniving hands.

"None of your business, little witch," Moya said, her back stiffening she sped toward Cary in a death defying dive, pulling up just as she reached the pagan.

Moya's fury didn't seem to bother Cary. She held her ground, never flinching. "I can lend you some of mine," Cary daintily placed one perfect nail on her chin. "Hmmm, then you would be on my side. And doesn't that sound intriguing?"

"Pagan," Moya's uttered word was soft but she knew Cary heard it when laughter floated high into the night air.

"Did you know her name is the same as Conn's," she tossed that fact out and it made Moya gasp.

"What lie would you be tellin' now?" Moya asked.

Cary tossed her hair an all-knowing expression on her face. "Let me count the ways. Conn--Son of Connell--Casey O'Connell."

Chapter Eight

Casey marched away from Kelly, a tear in her heart. Desperation drove her to this as well as a burning need to find out why her brother was fighting Kelly's brother. Brothers fighting over…

They can't be fighting over me.

She stumbled but she kept on walking, fisting her hands as she strode toward the mess that had become her life, her back stiffening more with each step. Inside the dance hall the noise reached a deafening crescendo. "Patrick. Patrick O'Connell!"

"Careful, Casey," Kelly said, rushing in a mad dash towards her, his strides long, eating up the distance between the two of them.

Casey made her way to her brother and Liam, her hands outstretched in an attempt to wiggle her way between the two men. "Stop this. Patrick!" A random punch caught Casey in the chin. She flew backwards, landing hard on the grass. For a brief second she lay on the ground, gazing at the heavens above and wondering at the beautiful flecks of gold and silver floating down around her.

"I'm fine," she said. "It's the rest of you who need help. Men…"

"Casey," Kelly bent over her.

"All in a day's life," Casey brushed Kelly's hands aside. "I'm fine," Casey said. "It's the rest of you who need help. Men…" she repeated, mumbling more than was considered polite for a lady.

"Sorry," Liam said a bit sheepishly. "Didn't mean to hit a gal."

More men tumbled from the brightly lit room. Sounds of punches and oooffs resounded through the evening. Kelly lifted Casey, removing her from two men rolling on the ground, fists flying.

"You two have to stop this now," Casey said to her brother, trying to appeal to his good senses and gentlemanly instincts.

"Don't see how?" Patrick grinned at the two.

"Patrick O'Connell!"

"Alright, I'll give it a try, but I'm going to be needin' a little help from the two of you." He pointedly looked at Liam and Kelly.

The two brothers nodded, Liam appearing to be having far too much fun at his brother's expense. But at least Kelly appeared serious. "Go on…"

"Adrian, Clancy, Fallon…hold. The fight is over." In the middle of his friends, Patrick tried to pull them apart. Liam was doing the same, both taking punches while they tried to stop the brawl.

"Keith, Padriac, Rory," Liam called out, his voice rising above the din of the fight. "Do as Patrick says."

Slowly the brawl came to an end. The commotion inside the dance hall died down as well. The night breeze rustling the tree leaves was all that could be heard.

"Why?" Casey asked, her emotions blazing. Her heart raced. She inhaled several long deep breaths in hopes of controlling herself.

"You, my darling sister, do not have permission to be here." Patrick swept his arm out in a broad circle. "I'm taking you home. You will have a bit of explaining to do so think fast. A plausible story would suffice, one with the fewest embellishments."

Emotions blazing, Casey stared at her brother for a moment. She didn't know what to say to the insufferable sibling. But she knew what she wanted to say. Instead she blurted something unbelievable, "You cannot be tellin' me what to do, Patrick O'Connell. Kelly and I are married--as of several hours ago." She suddenly felt sick to her stomach. She touched her once blazing cheeks with the palms of her hands and felt a chill sweep through her.

A chorus of "What!" followed her statement. Pandemonium was on the verge of breaking out once more. She saw fists tighten and shoulders tense.

Oh, my god, I've made everything worse. We weren't going to tell anyone until the time was right.

Casey stiffened, her backbone as straight as a broom handle. Her mind was a muddled mess of crazy thoughts. "Padriac married us." She pointed a finger at Kelly's friend. She watched as Padriac's face paled. He appeared on the brink of denying her statement.

"It isn't legal," Patrick said, looking to Kelly for confirmation. "No reading of the banns, Mother and Father will have the marriage annulled. Any stupidity you accomplished this day can be undone in a blink of an eye."

"Casey," a weak word from Kelly whose face had all but drained of color. "Casey, darlin', you need to stop talking."

"Is this true?" Liam demanded of his brother. Liam seemed to be the only member of the group who was smiling. It was as if he enjoyed this too much.

Kelly's Adam's apple bobbed as he must have swallowed hard. He closed his eyes and for a moment it seemed he would not open them. He began with a stuttered, "I--I--" but couldn't finish. He ruffed both hands through his hair then threw them up as if in disbelief. "Casey--" he began once more.

"I didn't think so," Patrick said a smug look on his too handsome face. "You can't lie worth a darn, Casey. You should never try."

"We've slept together," Casey forged onward. "The marriage cannot be annulled." Her ship was sinking fast. But thank God Kelly wasn't denying anything yet. She didn't understand why she kept blurting out things best left unsaid, things they had both agreed would remain secrets until the time was right.

Liam turned to Padriac. "You've just recently been ordained. Is this some kind of sick joke? So which is it? Married or not married?" Liam stepped up to his friend. Casey couldn't tell what emotions were flitting through his head.

"I'm not sure," Padriac said as he looked heavenward as if seeking some kind of divine intervention.

"Of all the…" Liam said. While his brother's face was ashen, she saw color flood his cheeks. He was angry, no doubt about it.

"It's true, all of it," Kelly rubbed the back of his neck. "We wed this morning, said our vows with Padriac blessing our union. True, we didn't do this all proper but the marriage is legal. The certificate is at home in my bible."

"Have you slept together?" Patrick asked. He appeared ready to renew the fighting. For some strange reason he held back.

"That is none of your business," Kelly said. Casey moved closer to Kelly's side. Protectively, he circled his arm around her.

"Who was the witness?" Patrick asked, seeming to search for a way to annul this marriage. "I will have this undone. I promise."

"Fallon."

"Congratulations then," Liam stepped forward to give Kelly a pat on the back.

~ * ~

"Oh my, oh my," Moya fluttered above the group dropping faerie dust as if it were water. "How did we miss a wedding? How could that happen? I've barely left her side, haven't slept in weeks and eating--that hasn't happened. I'm wasting away." She turned to Oran. "What about you? I thought we had our schedules mapped out."

"How indeed?" Oran said, sounding puzzled but not overly surprised. "I went with some friend to the pub this afternoon. They weren't even together. I don't have a clue but we can't be anything but pleased."

"Did you know?" Moya demanded an answer. "Did you know and is that why you left? We would have had to alert someone. They shouldn't have done it this way." She would never have missed the wedding day. She's had great hopes of attending the huge event Casey's parents would have insisted having.

"Well, I don't like the way this is playing out," Cary said with a disgusted sigh. "I guess our job is done before it even began." She rose above the crowd, staring down at them and fluttered her wings. "I'm leaving." But she hovered in the air as if she still didn't want to miss any new developments.

"No way," Conn said. "These two will never be happy. If this is true, they've gone against their families." He joined Cary, hovering in the heavens and watching as the scene still unfolded. "There still might be a fight. I'm ready for a jolly good one. Bloody eyes, but they stopped too soon for my liking."

"We will find a way to make it right," Moya said, flying up to Conn and shaking her little fist in his face. "They will have a proper wedding and the blessing of their families. You just wait and see."

Cary let go a devilish laugh, "Time will tell." She did a little back flip in the air, followed by a cartwheel, laughing all the while.

"I wish you away from here," Moya said vehemently. "You are the devil's spawn and I cannot abide your evil treachery."

"Never," Cary stopped her antics and grinned at Moya. "Never, not until all this is finished and the happy couple is no longer so jubilant."

~ * ~

"Congratulations… Bloody hell!" Patrick swung at Liam, his fist hitting the man squarely in the jaw.

"Bloody…" Liam tackled Patrick around the waist. They went down, tumbling on the grass, grappling to get the upper hand and grunting with the exertion needed to accomplish just that.

The friends joined in the ruckus. Fists flew, groans resounded in the night air. An owl swooped from the trees and gave a loud "hoot" in approval or disapproval before flying into the darkened night.

"Kelly, stop them," Casey said, clutching his arm, her fingers biting into him. "They can't fight, not on our wedding day."

"Leave them be, they are letting off steam. It's good for them and us. Let's go." He slipped her hand into his and gently tugged. "Come on, they'll get the frustration from their systems and meet us at the pub for a pint of ale. At least we will see Liam there. He always ends a fight with a few drinks."

Kelly gave one last look at the ruckus in front of him, swept Casey into his arms, and trotted toward the pub. The joy he felt spiraled soul deep. He looked at his wife of a couple of hours and grinned. Anticipation swept through him.

"Put me down."

"Not on your life." He always wanted to hold her close to his heart. A heart that raced while his blood pounded within.

"You'll drop me."

"There is more of a chance if I put you down, you will trip over one or the other foot." He groaned at his words. He never wanted to reinforce her notion of clumsiness.

"That was not nice."

"But..." About to say true, he stopped himself mid-thought. No, she didn't need anyone's protection. She was an incredibly strong woman and he liked her that way. She had a penchant for accidents but that was because she challenged her physical limitations and didn't always emerge the winner.

Casey sighed, not seeming to have anything else to say and rested her head against his chest. He inwardly smiled as his heart beat hard and fast in eagerness to consummate their marriage. He wasn't sure how this would all play out, but he meant to have her in his arms and his bed before the night ended. They were married and he needed to make sure there was no way her parents could annul the marriage.

A warm glow from the pub beckoned the lovers. Laughter and talk flowed from the Black Goat, a place that was known for the best ale in these parts. The scent of sizzling meat floated on the spring breeze.

Kelly set Casey down inside the pub. His mother stood behind the bar waving cheerily. She bent over and placed a quick kiss on Kelly's cheek. "Now who is this?" she asked, a motherly twinkle in her eyes.

"Casey O'Connell." The hesitancy in Kelly's voice sent a chill down his spine, stopping his heart for a brief moment. He cleared his throat, his gaze on Casey. "My wife." His mother backed away, a strange expression on her face.

She cocked her head sideways as if assessing her son's betrothed. "Hmm… You be jokin' now…"

"No," Kelly sighed inwardly, running his hands through his hair while he searched for the right words. "We were wed this afternoon. Padriac--did the ceremony--gave his blessing." Wholeheartedly he wanted his mother's approval as well as his father's.

"Why, Kelly Shaunasey," his mother's hands rested on her hips, her lips thinned. "What was the hurry? Why couldn't you wait and have family attend? And my gosh, is this Casey O'Connell one of the…"

"O'Connell's who we are feuding with? Yes, the very same. Now would you be carin' to share the tale as to what this disagreement is all about? We don't believe the feud should stand in our way of happiness." He held onto Casey's hand, giving it a small squeeze to reassure. Although he needed the reassurance as much or more than he thought Casey did.

"I don't know why we hate each other." Kelly's mother poured two pints. She paused. "Never really thought about the feud--never had a reason."

"At this moment, I don't hate any O'Connell and with all my heart I love Casey." Kelly's words and voice dared anyone to refute him.

"You two are talking around me. It's as if I don't exist." Casey punched Kelly on the arm. "We love each other and didn't expect our families to bless our union. Yet…" She looked at him, her eyes shining with what he thought was love.

"Enough," Dorinda said. "I am glad you are now a Shaunasey." She set a pint of ale in front of her and gave Kelly one too. "Are you wantin' a wee bit of privacy tonight? I have an open room upstairs the two of you can enjoy, this being your wedding night and all." She wiped down the counter and put the rag in the sink.

Kelly nodded, watching the blush stain Casey's cheeks. She sipped the ale, looking into her glass. His heart expanded with such joy he'd never known before. "What do you say, Casey? Do you want to take Mother up on the room?" Lord, but he prayed she would say, yes. This was, after all, their wedding night. He tucked a loose strand of hair behind her ear, smelling roses as he did so.

She sipped again. "I suppose." Her voice squeaked yet she said, yes, sort of. He wondered at the lack of eagerness or was it fear?

"That doesn't sound very enthusiastic," he said, trying to understand her innocence. Compassion filled him. He felt sure she was apprehensive. She'd had no one to speak with her about lovemaking. The wedding had been so spontaneous. Usually the mother would tell the daughters what to expect. She'd had no one.

She swallowed a large portion of the ale. "I," she moistened her lips, "feel a wee bit fuzzy." She smoothed her skirts.

Kelly laughed. "It's the ale speaking. I'm not too sure you should drink any more. Have you ever…"

"No," she said with a crooked smile. "I like it though." She finished the glass, setting it on the counter and looking to Kelly's mother as if for another pint.

Dorinda set another in front of her. "It will ease the wedding night jitters," she said. "If you have any questions…"

"I think I'd like her awake, though." Kelly tossed back the rest of his pint, knowing his mother was giving him a bad time.

Dorinda laughed, the wink that followed surprised Kelly. What was she thinking? His mother seemed eager to get the two of them in bed. Were mothers supposed to think that way? Well, she couldn't be as eager as he was to hold her in his arms, kiss her, make love. Lord, he closed his eyes trying desperately to stifle the groan that threatened to rumble from deep within. His imagination overpowering his constraint.

"I'm awake." Her words slurred together in a charming way. Kelly knew he'd never forget this picture.

"Room?" Kelly asked his mother.

"Upstairs, the one at the end of the hallway."

"Come on." Kelly scooped Casey into his arms and with high hopes he walked up the stairs to his fantasy suite. Casey melted into his arms, kissing him lightly on the neck and snuggling deeper into his embrace. Ah, lord, she was his and he was about to make love to her. He'd dreamt of this night since that Sunday on the knoll when she'd tried to stop the weekly fight.

He set her on the bed and turned to disrobe. Hesitant, because he wasn't sure how fast or how slow he would need to proceed. He shucked from his shirt and set it on a chair near the bed, his heart racing.

She lay on the bed, her hair in glorious disarray around her, her breasts rising slowly with each breath. He laughed softly. Her cheeks, rosy from the ale, made her peaches and cream complexion irresistible. Sitting beside her he stroked her cheek, traced her jaw line then farther to run his finger across the visible flesh above the bodice of her gown. Her lips parted, beckoning his attention.

"Casey."

She opened her eyes for a brief moment. One hand rested on his forearm. "I'm so sleepy."

Kelly stretched out beside her, kissing her softly on the lips. Startled, he backed away, frustration mounting.

"Casey?"

~ * ~

Oran tugged on Moya's arm. "Darn bless it, female, we have to leave. Right now."

Moya brushed Oran's hands away. "I know. But we have to make sure everything goes right. And we have to make sure Conn and Cary don't show up to make trouble."

A malicious laughed echoed in Moya ears. "Too late, too late you are. I dinna believe they will consummate the marriage tonight." *Cary continued to chant.*

"Get out!" *Moya was beside herself with anger. Her wings fluttered to gold and faerie dust flew.* "What have you done?"

"Prolonged the inevitable," *Oran said. He flew circles around Conn as if he tried to push him out the window.*

"Hey," *Conn said as he found himself flat against cold night air.* "I'll go. Don't want to see adults cry, you know."

Moya watched then decided to try the same tactic on Cary. She swirled and somersaulted, dodging Moya's futile attempt, laughing as her antics kept her within the room.

"Go on, leave with your evil friend, Cary. No one be wantin' you here."

"You going to stay and watch the pair sleep?" *Cary taunted.*

"I'll stay as long as they are asleep, but you won't be here," *Moya said.*

"We haven't seen the last of those two," *Oran said.*

Chapter Nine

Warm sunshine filtered through the lace curtains. For a moment Casey wasn't sure where she was, but yesterday's adventures crashed in on her sending her mind swirling. She smiled, reveling in the moment. She was married and at this moment, she felt Kelly's warm body next to hers, his arms wrapped protectively around her. She snuggled against him, knowing she would remember this feeling for the rest of her life.

"Casey," his voice ruffled the hair on the back of her neck, sending goose bumps down her arms and warmth into her heart.

"Hmm…" she said, feeling dreamy and not wanting to move one muscle.

His hands roamed the length or her back, settling on her hips as he turned her then brushed the hair from her eyes. Their bodies brushed against each other. *Oh my…* Her heart raced, knowing what she could expect.

His kiss was soft, long, slow, and passionate. At first he was gentle, running his tongue along her lips almost as if asking her to open for him. When she inhaled slightly, his tongue strayed inside. She settled her hands behind his head, threading her fingers in his hair and moving enticingly against him.

"Tell me if I do anything you don't like," he spoke softly in that raspy voice she heard when he kissed her.

"I--" She really couldn't talk. Her heart pounded against her chest and the heat sweeping through her raised an inferno within. She loved everything, even some of the more startling and new feelings. His hand cupped her breast, pushing aside fabric until he touched her nipple. "Oh, my..." *Oh my...*

He rose above her and watched her. "Oh my, indeed."

Suddenly his mouth was on one nipple, his fingers teasing the other. She moaned and arched as if she could make him take more of her into his mouth. Her fingers tightened on his shoulders, her nails, she was sure would leave marks.

He kissed her belly then lower, spreading her legs, touching her there, everywhere. She clung to his hair, running her hands through it. She smoothed her hands across the broad expanse of his back.

"Kelly, I--I've never felt this way..."

"Good," he said smiling at her.

"Do you think you should do that?" she asked, knowing how stupid a question that was. She wanted this more than anything. She just didn't quite understand.

"Easy now," he whispered close to her ear.

She cried out at the pain then there was nothing but pleasure as time spun and he brought her to a place she had never known existed.

"Casey?"

"I--"

"Tongue tied?" he asked, laughing. "Are you all right?" Kelly pulled her close. Once again she delighted in the feelings, his protectiveness, and the safety. Everything in her world was right and nothing could change that.

She reveled in the moment, closing her eyes and resting her head on his chest. "I'm fine." For a brief moment the earth stood still and nothing but Kelly mattered.

"Casey! Casey! You better not be in there!"

The door crashed in. Kelly pulled her close as he drew the covers over her.

"Father…"

"Let her go. Casey, you are coming with me," her father said.

"No." Kelly's one word echoed in the crowded room as he pushed Casey behind him.

"Father, we are married. You cannot be here, I--" she said peeking around Kelly's broad shoulders at her father.

"I will have the marriage annulled."

"This marriage is valid and consummated. It cannot be annulled. Now, my wife and I demand you leave."

Dorinda arrived and jumped in to help the newlyweds by escorting Casey's father and mother from the room. "Let the children dress. They will join us downstairs as soon as they can." She looked to her son.

"Thank you," he said and nodded.

Casey was thankful too. She was sure if Dorinda had not intervened, both her parents would still be arguing, mindless of their state of dishabille. When the door closed, Casey sat back against the headboard and closed her eyes.

"Did we do the right thing?" she asked.

Kelly kissed her lightly on a cheek. "Yes, they would have never allowed a marriage. This way they will learn to accept it. My mother has."

"Your mother, yes, she seems to have accepted. Do you think it is easier with a son than a daughter?"

"I don't know. Come on, let's dress less we be invaded again." His laughter echoed around the room.

"My heart was beating so hard, I thought I'd just run a race."

Kelly stood, tossing the covers back. Casey watched, mesmerized by his strength, his muscles, the power emanating from him as he walked gracefully to his clothes. Casey still had the covers pulled high. My goodness, but there was no room for modesty. Only this morning he'd touched every inch of her.

"I will meet you downstairs," he winked at her and left after quickly pulling on his pants and shirt.

Casey scrambled to her clothes, dressing and washing quickly. Looking in the mirror, she touched up her hair and pinched her cheeks.

"All right, I guess it's time to face the music."

By the time Casey reached the tap room, only Dorinda and Kelly were there.

"Your parents left. They told me to tell you congratulations."

"They were furious."

"Livid," Dorinda said. "But like all parents they will come around."

"They will disown me."

Dorinda set a plate of strawberry scones in front of Casey. "I'm not saying any of this will be easy. But in the end, they will want what is best for you--what will make you the happiest. Parents have a way of learning their children have grown up and have minds, thoughts, hopes and dreams as well."

~ * ~

Moya's clasped her hands in front of her chin and heaved a sigh of relief. It appeared as if all was right, well almost right, with the couple. They were truly wed. And perhaps the parents of the bride would grant them a grand reception. Perhaps, too, they would reveal the reason for the feud.

"You look the proud God-faerie today, Oran."

"I am, just look at the two of them. He cannot keep his eyes off her. He is so very in love."

"As is she," Moya said. "They are no longer star-crossed lovers."

"We will have to concentrate our efforts on the parents. A little faerie dust might loosen up their hearts."

"Ah, but look there," Moya said pointing to the door. "The forgiving part did not take as long as we thought it might."

"And how do you be knowin' they have forgiven?"

"Their smiles tell me all I need to know." Moya swirled in the air showering all in the tavern with golden dust.

"Stop that," Oran said. "Not to throw a damper on all of this, but I'm sure Cary and Conn will be showin' up soon. We are going to have to come up with a master plan--a strategy that cannot be bettered."

"I don't think so," Moya said. "On my way here I saw a strange object out on the cliffs and a little tiny dog running circles around it and barking his head off. Cary and Conn were flittin' about and I think they will be engaged there for a bit."

"Really, what did it--this strange object--be lookin' like?"

"I cannot be sayin'. It was strange and huge, a circle of sorts. Florence was there too. He was walking around it, trying to stay away from the dog."

"Hmmm…"

"My thoughts too. We will have to check it out. Go see what is happening."

"As soon as we are positive about the forgiveness here."

"Look, Casey's mom just gave her a peck on the cheek." Moya fluttered to the ceiling then back down, sighing.

"Do you think we can check out that--that thing you saw?

"Oh, yes."

~ * ~

Florence walked around a huge cylindrical shaped object. Rubbing his chin he looked it up and down. "Oh, my and what would this be?" He ran his hand over the surface, curiosity overcoming rational thought.

Just then the thing opened, a doorway of sorts, and a small dog darted through the dark portal. Running around him, nipping at his heels the dog barked incessantly. "Mangy mutt."

The dog lifted his leg and peed on him. Florence kicked at the dog but missed. "Damn," he shook his foot trying to dislodge some of the liquid. The dog darted and pranced then sprinted after a butterfly toward town. "Good riddance, you mangy mutt."

Frustration over Casey's marriage had led him to seek solace. Watching the waves rise and fall then crash against the cliffs had always had a mesmerizing effect on him. Today he had come across this gigantic red thing. He had no other name for it--had never seen anything like it before.

He should know better but the thing drew him and the dark opening beckoned to him. He needed to see what was inside. There had to be a way to turn a profit here. Perhaps he could use it against Kelly--or Patrick--or both of them. He'd love to watch the men squirm.

He stepped inside. Sweat beaded on his forehead, sliding down his cheek and neck to soak into his perfectly white, silk shirt.

"Oh, my, oh my." Gadgets whirled and hummed. Lights flashed, blinking non-stop. He felt slightly nauseous. He put his hand on his ears to deafen the noises thrumming around him.

I should get out--leave now. But some unknown force kept his feet firmly planted on the floor of the thing. He closed his eyes, murmuring a prayer for himself then feeling satisfied nothing could hurt him, he opened his eyes.

The machine went quiet. The silence terrified more than the noise. He squinted and saw one blinking light. The light called to him. "Florence, Florence--Florence come see. Come here and find out what I am. I have been made just for you. I will make you rich, rich, rich--as Midas."

Good God, had he gone daft? He was talking to machines and listening to the same machine talk to him. Granted, they seemed to be talking to him. But...his thoughts trailed into oblivion. A blue light began to flicker. Captivating, enthralling, spellbinding his every sense. *Back off, Florence,* a little voice in his head faintly spoke. *Back off or you might regret this strange inquisitiveness.*

He could not leave. Nothing within him would allow retreat. He had to find out what this was, how it worked. The tales he could spin if he could figure this out. At first he had frozen, his body numb, but now he felt more relaxed, more in control.

Cautiously he walked to the panel of lights and buttons. Pushing one he discovered a little cigar shaped object pop out. His thoughts centered around the yappy little dog who had exited this machine a few minutes ago. *Interesting.* Bending down he picked up the object and ran it under his nose. *Hmm...smells of meat or,* he wasn't quite sure. He put it in his mouth as if to smoke and tried to light the end. Nothing. Tasted alright though he didn't think he would like to eat it. It was a bit hard.

He tried a pink button which said, FOOD. The cigar shaped object must not be food. A bar shot out from the slot. It was a, as the label said, a fiber bar. What the bloody hell was a fiber bar? He opened it and gingerly bit into the bar. *Hmm…good.* Chewing slowly he finished the bar then found another button.

Drinks… He pushed. A cup burst out then ice to be followed by a dark liquid. He watched in awe. Shaking his head in disbelief, he picked up the cup and tentatively sipped. *Good too*, he drank a large gulp of the fizzy stuff then belched.

"My oh my," he said again. *What have I found?* He lost his original caution and began pushing buttons to see what they would do.

START. *Alright what will this start?* He pushed. Suddenly the machine kicked into action. Buzzing and humming, whirling and blinking the big red thing seemed to rumble loudly to life.

Excitement roared to full throttle inside Florence. The thrill nearly had him jumping out of his magnificently shined Hessians. His heart pounded. A fierce need to know what was happening to him took hold. *Could this move?* Roars echoed inside his head. Two chairs materialized beneath him. As if human a machine-like person escorted him to a chair and strapped him in to it.

"Good Lord, I'm going to die!"

"Taking off," a calm male voice spoke from above. "Fasten your seatbelt and enjoy the ride--an adventure of a lifetime--I always say."

"Ride? What kind of ride? I don't want to take a ride--maybe I do. I'll be able to patent this and make a fortune." *If you survive*, a voice inside his head reverberated.

"The weather is sunny and warm here in Oregon. Prepare for a rare spring day of sunshine."

"Oregon--where the hell is Oregon?" Florence clenched the chair, his fingertips digging into the soft fabric. The machine sputtered and rocked then suddenly it stopped.

"You have reached your destination," the male voice told him.

~ * ~

"By all that's holy!" Conn said.

When Florence pushed the start button and the machine roared to life the momentum sent Cary flying into Conn's chest.

"I'm not likin' the feel of this," Cary said shakily as she regained her composure and fluttered nervously around the big red machine.

"Me neither. What do you suppose is happening?"

Gold dust flitted around the small space as if it were dust highlighted by sunlight. "That little scamp of a dog sure was eager to get out. And where the devil is this Oregon? Never heard of it before."

Cary's heart beat so hard she could feel it when she put her hand to her breast. "Oh, lordy," she moaned softly. She flew to a counter in the machine and sat there afraid she would faint. Her head spun crazily and her stomach churned.

Conn flew from side to side as if he paced the floor. When the machine stopped abruptly, Cary fell from the counter to land sprawled on the floor and Conn found himself rammed against one side of the machine, buttons imbedded in his flesh.

"Oh…" Cary's wail of fear brought Conn to her side.

"We have to leave this place now!"

"Do you know how?"

"Looks as if Florence has the same idea. He has pushed the button which opens the door. See--" Conn pointed one finger as the countryside slowly came into view. He grabbed Cary's hand and they were out the door, Florence a step behind them.

Epilogue

"Here's to the happy couple." Casey's father stood on a chair, saluting them with good wishes and a mug of ale in one hand.

Casey's heart swelled with pride as she sipped the brew handed to her by Dorinda. She leaned into Kelly, reveling in the warmth and good cheer between the families. Somehow they all had managed to put their quarrels aside. She wondered if she dared ask about the feud and if it would bring up bad memories. Best she left her questions unanswered.

"Sarah." Casey stood her arms open for her nurse.

Sarah ran to Casey, enclosing her in her arms and whispering to her. "I will tell you of the feud later. Don't ask anyone. We don't want to be puttin' a damper on your big day, now do we, lass?"

The warning went straight to Casey's heart, echoing her feelings. Realizing the knowledge would soon be hers, she nodded her acceptance then turned and smiled brightly at the people in the room.

"Here is to my little sister and the man she loves, may he always catch her when she stumbles," Patrick said laughing good naturedly.

Casey blushed, oh how much truer could he be. He teased her and many there did not know how very clumsy she was.

"Patrick," her mother said, sounding astounded at what her brother dared to say. "Play nice, this is an important day."

Patrick held out his arms, shrugging his shoulders with a wide wicked grin pointed to his sister then Kelly.

Casey felt the tears rising to her eyes. She waved her hand in front of her face just as Kelly wrapped her in his arms and swung her from her seat. For several long seconds he whirled her around the room, "I love you. Don't you ever forget that and don't let what your older brother said make you unhappy."

She nodded, sniffing.

"Promise me," he said looking seriously at her almost as if he demanded her happiness.

"I promise. I love you too." She let her head rest on his shoulder, closing her eyes for a brief second before lifting her head and smiling broadly.

"Good, let us finish with the celebration then." Kelly kissed her on the cheek to the roars of the others in the room accompanied with a few ribald jests.

An Irish jig kicked in then young and old danced.

"It seems that at least on the surface our families are accepting of the marriage," Casey said, gazing around the room and smiling.

"It does and for that I am thankful. It doesn't mean we will not have the rocky roads ahead of us," Kelly said.

"But we will have each other."

"And what would you be meanin' by that?" he asked, kissing her once more.

"We have not been together all that long. There is much we haven't discussed or come to a decision on."

"What are you talking about?" He held her back slightly, a curious look on his face.

Casey felt heat rush to her face and the blush surfacing. "Children," she spoke softly. "We haven't talked about where we will live, or…"

"Hush, there is plenty of time for all that. I'm sure we will find compromise in everything we do. As for children--unless you want more than ten or less than one--I am fine."

Casey's heart fluttered so fast her head spun. She had truly found her prince charming, her knight in shining armor. What more could she ask for? She leaned close and whispered to him once more. "I love you, Kelly."

"And I love you, too, my sweet, sweet Casey.

Meadows of Gold
C.L. Kraemer

Chapter One

A gentle breeze sighed, undulating the meadow grass lazily and whispering past the forlorn figure slumped on the tree trunk, hands clasped tightly in his lap. Thomas, a forest leprechaun, released a long melancholy breath between his cracked, dry lips. A single plump tear meandered down his stubbled cheek.

The sun sent bright shafts of light through the pine boughs and around the wooden pedestal upon which the morose figure resided. Ignoring the dancing beams, the leprechaun pulled a shuddered breath into his lungs and stared at a spot in front of the stump where a crumpled daisy chain necklace lay withering in the warmth of the afternoon. Another plump tear snaked down his unshaven face.

In the distance, a lone figure scuffed up the lane, which crossed in front of the tree stump. Thomas paid no heed to the approaching form, pulling a thin silver flask from inside his rumpled vest. He blindly opened the lid, placed the opened top to his lips and pulled a deep draught from the container. Refitting the cap to the top, he slipped the silver spirit holder back into his vest. His next shuddered breath was interrupted with a hiccup.

The figure on the road drew closer. Thomas raised his head and squinted his eyes. Was she coming back? He hiccupped and straightened up. Maybe she had been teasing him when she ran away and now she realized how much he cared for her. His eyes brightened and a smile began to touch his lips.

The figure came around the bend and toward him. The last he'd seen her, she was wearing a diaphanous, thin dress. Had she changed? The form nearing him was clad in leather breeches, a braided leather tunic, and knee-high, soft leather boots. A sword blade strapped to the figure's back flashed in the sunlight. Was Cary so angry she meant to cut him in little pieces? His heart began to pound in his chest and inside his mouth his tongue stuck to the roof.

The figure stopped two lengths from him and raised a hand to shade its eyes from the brightness of the day.

Thomas realized he was shaking. This was it…his life was over. He hung his head.

"Thomas?

The voice was familiar but it didn't sound like Cary. If it wasn't her…

~ * ~

"Thomas! What are you doing?" Tiamoon, a warrior gnome of the valley clan, stood with her feet planted shoulder width apart in her full leather armor on the roadway to her home. She'd just reconnoitered the meadow area for evidence of the marauding night elves. The local hill clan had been raiding the gnome settlements and wreaking havoc on the inhabitants. The gnome community was rallying together to protect their families against further damage.

Thomas narrowed his eyes and looked through his veil of tears.

"Oh, Tia (hic) moon, itsch you."

Tia rolled her eyes heavenward and leaned toward the wobbling leprechaun, wrinkling her nose in disgust at the sour smell of alcohol surrounding the disheveled lump occupying the tree stump.

"Thomas? How long have you been sitting here?"

"Dunno. What day is it?"

"Tuesday."

"Really?" Thomas lifted rheumy eyes to meet Tiamoon's clear blue ones.

"Yes, really. So how long have you been here, Thomas?"

"Uhm, (hic) since Saturday."

"Saturday!"

Tiamoon stepped to the stump, in the process crushing the daisy chain necklace. She reached out to grab the leprechaun as he dissolved in tears.

"You (hic)... you stepped on (hic) the necklace. (hic) Just like she (hic) stepped on my heart."

"Good heavens, Thomas, pull yourself together. She who?"

She wrestled the drunken leprechaun to his unsteady feet. His weight surprised her. He was sturdy and muscular beneath the rumpled clothing.

"Cary, the love of my life."

"Heavens be cursed. Thomas..."

"Wha-a-a?" He turned red-rimmed, green orbs her direction.

"You fall in love with every female who crosses your path."

"Do *not*!"

"Really? Okay let me guess...she flirted with you and teased you until she got you out here at the edge of the meadow where you promised to tell her where your secret stash of gold was hidden if she'd kiss you and be your mate."

His eyes ricocheted in the sockets, making Tiamoon's head hurt.

"You were (hic) sshpying on ussh."

Tia got her shoulder under his armpit and hoisted him up. She wrinkled her nose at the stale body odor emanating from his clothing.

"No, Thomas. It's a pattern everyone in the woods knows. Come on. You need a bath, some food and sleep."

"But what if (hic) she comesh back?"

"Thomas? I can guarantee that won't happen today. Come on."

She dragged him along the road. His head was slumped on his chest and his leather shoes were dragging, toes down, in the soft dirt of the two-lane thoroughfare. After a mile of struggling with the leprechaun, she turned down a single file path winding through the trees. Thomas had hiccupped in Tia's ear through the entire journey, his head lolling from side to side.

She'd reached the end of the path as well as the end of her patience. When the path stopped abruptly at the river's edge, so did Tia. She allowed the momentum of her pace to transfer to the inert leprechaun.

The moment the figure hit the icy water, he screamed.

"You're killing me! Gods in Heaven! You're trying to kill me!"

"For crying out loud, Thomas. Just dunk your head under the water and quit yelling. Maybe if you bathed more often, you wouldn't chase away the ladies."

The figure floundered in the icy stream.

"I can't swim! Tia! I'm drowning!"

"Thomas?"

"Help! I'm drowning!"

"THOMAS!"

The roar echoed through the woods.

"Put your feet down!"

Blustering until his face was crimson, the drunken man splashed furiously. His head went beneath the water and he rose up sputtering, unconsciously standing on the stream's bottom. He quit flailing his arms.

"Oh."

"Yeah, oh." Tia drew her sword and pointed it his direction. "Now get yourself and your clothing sopping wet.

If you even think of getting on the bank without attempting to wash off some of that stench, I'll split you from gullet to gizzard."

He glared at the gnome warrior.

"Fine."

She stood pointing her sharpened blade at him until he and his clothing were sufficiently soaked.

"Now, let's go. My mom will have some stew to put into your stomach."

"But I don't wa..."

Thomas stopped his whine at the glare he was receiving from Tia.

"Lead the way."

Chapter Two

Cary stretched her arms above her head as she yawned. Her moss bed lay in a sunspot inside her temporary oak tree home and she took every opportunity available to steal a nap. Today was no exception. She'd had a run-in with the leprechaun Thomas. He'd gotten sloppy drunk and proposed a union between the two and had the nerve to act surprised when she'd turned him down.

Had he been so drunk as to think his offer of gold could sway her?

"Fool. I have something worth more than his pitiful pot of gold."

She splashed water on her face from the acorn bowl nitched in the cradle of the root of her tree. She wiped her face and hands with an oak leaf. Staring out a gap that served as a window, she noted the rippling heat waves rising to the cloudless sky from the swaying meadow grass. The wind blew hot across her face and she turned from the opening to nibble on some bread. It had been a strange fortnight. Cary still wasn't sure *exactly* what had occurred. She and Conn had been scheming, no, make that planning to undo the wedding of Casey and Kelly and were in right good position to see that happen when, whoosh! they were spirited away along with that pompous human, Florence, wherever here was.

The rustlings across the room set aside Cary's concentration and alerted her to the fact Conn was beginning to move about from his nap.

"Have we food?"

Cary looked at her rumpled roommate. "Always thinking with your stomach, aren't you? If the bread I secured is not enough for your fine palette, then get out and find suitable food."

"Why do I have to be the one to supply the meals?"

Cary fisted her tiny hands to her hips and cast a deadly glare at Conn.

"Because of all the talents in this world, you're gifted at putting food on the table."

He slogged his way to the sink and splashed water on his face. He sucked in a surprised breath.

"That's cold!"

"Might be because the water flows directly from the stream?"

Conn wiped his face and hands and headed for the makeshift door.

"I'm out to find food and trace the whereabouts of Florence. As we have lived in this... place for a fortnight, my senses tell me he might be in need of my services. Left alone to his own devices, he fares poorly.

"I'll return then we can sit down and make plans to locate Casey and Kelly. They've been having enough time to learn to dislike each other by now. Our plans will be easy enough to initiate. This time next week, all will be as it should."

"Are you daft?" Cary fluttered to land lightly on her feet in front of Conn.

"Beg pardon?" A scowl covered his face.

"We're not in the green isles, you fool. We're of a different time and different place. I know not exactly and will be out myself to see if I can steal the knowledge from one of the locals. When I have this information, we'll talk about what plans to make. Not before. You go and hunt for Florence, but don't return reeking of wine and foolishness." Cary stamped her foot and turned her back to Conn.

His face reddened and he yanked open the piece of wood they'd been using as a door. He let the bark drop on the ground and flew from the tree.

He buzzed close to the earth, taking in the smells of this new place. There was much greenery here and the trees grew tall and lush. He had to admit to himself Cary was right. This was not the Ireland he knew. What he could smell of the earth was dark, fertile ground. His ears caught the sound of a very angry, very large horde of bees. He shifted his direction and came upon a scene foreign to his eyes. Strangely dressed humans held shiny steel weapons. They seemed to be attacking the forest with a tree-eating monster that buzzed very loudly while eating its way through the wooded area.

Conn was frightened and shot away from the scene. Though certain he could not be seen, he wished not to take any chances. He heard a loud rattling sound and the grinding of metal-to-metal coming very close to him. Darting to hide behind a large evergreen, he peeked at the aberration that nearly crushed him.

It was very large and black. The wheels upon the black wagon had a foreign substance all around them. This padding substance was why the large cart approached him in relative silence. There did not seem to be any horses at the front pulling but the metallic cart moved forward with a deafening high pitched grinding of metal. The wagon stirred up the dust and dirt on the trail. Conn felt a tickle in his nose and, before he could think, he sneezed loudly.

"Ach! I can't be giving away my location. Who knows what monsters lie in wait in this forest? I need to find Florence. I have seen more abominations today than I care to ponder. The explanations must surely be simple."

Conn lifted his wings and tentatively flew toward the direction where the sun slid behind the hills. He sensed Florence. With each wing beat, his sensation of his ward grew stronger. He would find his charge and answers would be forthcoming. Until that time, he was charged with being vigilant and wary. Despite Cary's warning, Conn knew he was going to need some mead to settle his nerves.

"She can threaten all she wants, but until she's been as close to the mouth of this monster as I, she can't know the terror. Only mead can soothe this kind of fear."

Having justified his visit to the pub, Conn let a smile touch his lips. Finding Florence was important but not as important as Conn settling his nerves. He couldn't be expected to pump information from his charge and find food without a bit of the mead, could he?

Of course not. He began to whistle a lively reel as he flew toward town. This would turn out to be a positive day after all.

~ * ~

Cary was irritated at Conn. It really was his fault they were in this mess. If he'd been watching Kelly as he was supposed to instead of dashing about the fight egging the boys on, they'd still be back home in familiar surroundings instead of this place. She had no name for this land. All she knew was everything recognizable had disappeared. She needed to find a place where she could get the information without giving away her ignorance. Cary hovered just above the grass line. She sensed other beings close by and headed their direction. As the human voices grew louder, she slowed her flying, finally touching down near a whitewashed building sporting a porch out front. Silently, she climbed up the boxes on the front to look into the window. Her eyes beheld a business selling assorted items. She could hear a bell ring and decided to investigate.

She skittered inside the opened door and sidled up to the wooden counter. Peeking around the side, she noted items in jars on shelves behind the front counter. A human with a white apron stood behind the divider and helped other humans by retrieving merchandise from the containers on the shelves. He would then go to a large metal box, pushed some metal things jutting out from the box and stand back while a portion on the bottom of the box jumped out at him. It was the box which made the bell sound. Cary had flown up to the counter to investigate the box when her skin dimpled in chill bumps. *Someone is watching me!*

She raised her eyes to look directly into the cool, blue orbs of a female night elf. Cary panicked. Night elves! She had not encountered a night elf in years. Now, in this place where she knew nothing, she was going to have to keep her guard up against night elves?

Before Cary could react, Gitty Saun casually leaned over and snatched the faery from her hiding place and placed the tiny being in her leather carryall.

"Curses on your father!" the little fae screamed to the darkened leather prison walls.

Well, now she'd done it. She was no smarter for her travel and her current state of freedom was in question. Cary dropped her chin to her hand as she sat on something metallic and uncomfortable. The jouncing of the bag as this creature walked was making her nauseous. If she had been but a moment quicker…

She twittered then chuckled and finally allowed herself the luxury of laughing out loud. She had to give credit to this giant--were she able she would have made the same move. She could only hope the appetizer for tonight's dinner was not being carried in this leather prison.

Chapter Three

Florence sat in his room squinting out the window. He had indeed indulged himself a bit too much last evening. The light in his eyes pierced through his head causing the muscles of his neck to spasm in pain. If he were just to have a bit of the powder the witch woman in his village kept on hand, he might survive this day.

A tap upon his door sent him to moaning.

"What would you ask of me now?" Florence pushed the heels of his palms against his eyes.

"Mr. Florence? It's Dorinda. May I come in?"

His head ached and he tried his best to recall a Dorinda. When the door opened a crack and the smell of fresh soap assailed his nose, his brain kicked into gear.

Ah, yes; the slender serving wench from the tavern.

"Please, my lady. Do enter my chamber."

The door hinges complained with a high-pitched squeal, setting his ears to twitching and his head to pounding.

"Ah, lass. Could you be but a wee bit quieter?"

"So sorry, Mr. Florence. I thought you might be...hungover a bit from last night. I brought some aspirin to help relieve the pain. If you swallow them with this glass of water, it should help take away some of the pain in about twenty minutes."

Dorinda placed two aspirin on the table next to the glass of water she'd brought.

Florence lifted bloodshot eyes to the night table then to his guest.

"What's this poison you place before me? A draft to kill?"

Dorinda's face drained of color, her eyes widening in horror.

"Oh, no, Mr. Florence! This is medicine to relieve the pain. If you don't want to take it, I'll take the pills away."

Florence looked at the tiny white spots on the table stained with brown rings and burn spots.

"This not be poison?"

Dorinda vigorously shook her head.

"Medicine to take this evil from my head in less than the peal of one bell?"

She hesitantly nodded.

"Then I shall ingest this...medicine and wait to see if you skirt the truth. But know this, woman, should I expire from your ministrations I shall curse you and all the kinsmen of your clan."

He put the pill into his mouth and started to chew.

"NO!"

Florence squinted his eyes and hunched his shoulders against the reverberation of the shout in his head.

"Swallow the pills whole and wash them down with the water."

Bitterness exploded in his mouth, and he sensed he was close to losing the contents of his stomach. He lifted the glass and washed down the remainder of the pills. A hint of sweetness remained on his tongue as he swallowed to quell the bile rising up his throat.

Dorinda took the glass from his hand.

"When your headache is gone, come to the kitchen and I'll make you breakfast."

A slight nod of his head sent her out of the room. Florence lay back on the soft bed and closed his eyes. His head spun from the events of the last fortnight. The strange clothing on his body had appeared after he had first stumbled into the inn and had been subjected to the jeering of the patrons. The slender serving wench had taken pity on him and steered him to this room he occupied. Somewhere she had secured the local dress of the area so he would not appear out of place. But he *was* out of place and it was up to him to determine his whereabouts so he could return to his life in the emerald land of his birth.

He was respected in his home village. People knew his father was a wealthy man and they catered to his wishes. Somehow the knowledge had not traveled to this village. He would have to right the situation.

Florence's eyes drooped then closed as the aspirin began to work. Within fifteen minutes, he was snoring, the headache temporarily forgotten.

~ * ~

Cary was close to losing the battle with her stomach when the swaying stopped and her leather prison was unceremoniously thumped on to a solid, unmoving surface. As she stood up and tried to get her legs under her, the top of the bag was wrenched open, blasting a glaring light directly on the little fae causing her to throw her hand over her eyes.

"Well, well, well. What do we have here?"

A large, porcelain colored extremity snatched the wee folk by her waist and pulled her into the light of the room.

Cary blinked furiously, trying to adjust her eyes to the surroundings. The abode was as large as any castle she'd seen but not hewn together with any stone she recognized.

A magnificent fireplace stood guard at an end wall but no logs crackled a warm welcome. The furnishings scattered about the room were bulky, imposing and cold, making the little fae shiver.

The large fingers wrapped around the fae exuded warmth. Cary tried to wiggle herself free to no avail.

"I don't think even you have the strength to escape my grip, but you're welcome to try."

Cary turned and cast a wary look in the direction of the speaker.

"How is it you can see me?" She tilted her head to one side considering the tall, pale blonde with fair complexion.

"Because, wee one, I'm not a human."

Cary raised a brow, the hint of a smile touching her mouth. "No?"

Gitty pulled up one side of her lip and snarled. "No! I'd rather have my heart ripped out and fed to me than be part of the human race." She held her chin high. "*I* am a night elf. We are far more clever, smarter, better looking and live considerably longer than those human curs. *And* we are able to see magical creatures of the forest."

Cary pursed her lips together. She crossed her arms and considered this creature that had hold of her.

"So you can see the fae?"

"Yes, and because I can see the fae of the woods, I know you're a newcomer to this area. Who are you and where did you come from?"

Cary stared into the icy blue eyes of this night elf. No warmth radiated from their depths. In fact, she could see nothing resembling compassion in the elf's eyes no matter how hard she looked. She pulled up as straight as she could, unfolding her arms and adjusting her skirt.

"I am Cary of Innisboffin and I have absolutely no idea where *here* is. Maybe you could be so kind as to tell me where I am?"

Gitty chuckled. "Why so you can enchant me and leave? I don't think so. I think, for the time being, you'll be a guest in my home. When I feel I can trust you, I'll let you go, but not until then. So, wee one...back in the bag."

"NO!" Cary squirmed and pushed at the extremity clutching her body so tightly. "I hate the dark and that leather thing makes me sick. Please don't!" She sobbed and struggled, using all her strength. But alas, she was dumped unceremoniously into the pouch and the top was tightened closed.

"Now, what?"

Hiccupping and sobbing, Cary covered her face. Because of that darn Florence and his curiosity, she and Conn were who knows where. The clothing, language and homes she'd seen so far indicated this was not her beautiful Ireland. But if this was not Ireland, then where in all the world could she have landed?

It was a question whose answer would have to wait. Cary's eyelids traveled to her cheeks and before long the gentle snoring of a tiny faerie emanated from the leather pouch.

~ * ~

Florence woke to the sun streaming in his room. He reached up and touched his head, noting there was no pain remaining. Gingerly, he swung his legs to the floor and sat on the edge of the bed.

"The little white dots the wench gave me worked. My pain has passed and I'm starved. Think I'll find my way to the kitchen for a meal."

After a brief stop at the facilities, Florence entered the kitchen, his nose taking in the pungent smells.

"Ah, lass. what do you have for me this beautiful morn?"

Dorinda turned and graced him with a shy smile. "Morning, again, Mr. Florence. How does pork, potatoes and scrambled eggs sound to you?"

"Like a bit of heaven." *And home.*

"Looks as though the aspirin worked for you."

"Indeed it did, lass. I feel ready to take on the world." Florence noted the sudden sadness in the innkeeper's eyes. "What is it? Has something I said offended you?"

"No, sir. Just your comment about taking on the world leaves me no choice but to let you know of the consequences of your actions last night. You might want to take a seat."

Florence swallowed and pulled out the chair at the kitchen table. He plopped down.

Dorinda fussed around the stove shoveling eggs, bacon and fried potatoes on the platter. She placed the food in front of her boarder who grabbed his fork and dug into the meal. She added a plate of toast on the table within arm's reach.

She poured two cups of coffee, placing one in front of Florence. He grabbed the cup and started to gulp the contents.

"I wouldn't..."

"Owww! That's hot!"

Sitting at the chair opposite, Dorinda cradled her own cup between her hands. "As I was about to tell you, it's very hot. You might want to let it cool for a bit."

Florence touched his fingers to his burnt lip. "Right. Now what were you going to tell me about last night?"

Dorinda gazed into the dark contents inside her mug. She took a small sip then blew out a shuddered breath.

Florence grabbed a piece of toast and mopped up the remaining bits of food from the plate. When he finished the toast, he brushed his hands over the plate, shoved the soiled platter to the center of the table and leaned back to enjoy his coffee.

"Well?"

"Well, Mr. Florence, you insulted one of the new landowners in the valley who you challenged to a duel."

Florence's mouth dropped open. "I what?"

Dorinda squirmed in the chair. "You challenged him to a duel."

Pulling up, he placed the mug of coffee on the table and cleared his throat.

"How...how did that happen?"

"Best as I can tell, you called his girlfriend a saucy trollop and he took offense."

Florence lowered his head to his hands. "I take it he feels the need to defend her honor?"

"Yep. And as drunk as you were, you challenged him to a duel with swords."

Florence groaned. "I'm much better with a pistol."

"Too late. The duel is set for this evening at the edge of the meadow. If you don't show, he'll hunt you down and 'dispatch you'."

I've done it now. Not only do I have no idea where I might be but I've riled up the villagers. Florence huffed out a breath. "Tis done now. Have you a blade with which I might practice?"

Dorinda lifted a brow. She rose from the table and reached beside the icebox, retrieving a worn sweeper, its bristles splayed and bent.

"No, Mr. Florence. But I do have a broom. Best I can do on such short notice."

Florence took the proffered weapon, glancing up and down the shaft.

"Will have to do. Thank you, Miss Dorinda. Should anyone seek me, I'll be in the yard... practicing. Please call me in time to clean up before I leave for the inn."

Dorinda hid a smirk. "As you wish, Mr. Florence." *He's gonna get himself killed.*

~ * ~

Conn slipped past a farmer in bib overalls as he opened the door to the inn. The fae winged his way to a corner of the pub and watched the assorted villagers enter and leave. His thirst was increasing with the passing of each human. This place didn't have a designated corner as they did back in his land where the humans understood fae still existed in the land. How was he to slake his thirst if no one offered him mead? His mood darkened until a movement from the corner of his eye caught his attention.

Sitting with his back to the wall, a tall, elegant man ordered himself a glass of mead with a second smaller container set to the side. He carefully moved his long, blonde locks behind his shoulder and looked directly at Conn.

The fae held his breath and froze in his position.

"I can see you, little brother. Come sit with me. Surely, you thirst?"

Conn's heart thundered in his chest. He was certain the man had been speaking to another.

"Come. I *can* see you, wee one. I know you must have a great thirst. Join me and quench the fire in your mouth." The hint of a smile touched the blue-eyed man's lips.

Conn was sorely tempted. This stranger had a familiarity about him that made Conn cautious. The long blond hair, blue eyes and ability to see the fae? He shuddered. A night elf; what were night elves doing in this faraway place?

I'm so thirsty but if this elf captures me...oh, what the heck. What more do I have to lose except my thirst? Conn winged his way to the table and landed just out of reach of the elf.

"Greetings, kind sir."

The elf slid the small glass toward the fae.

"And to you, sir."

"Call me Morgan."

"And I'm Conn." The little fae eyed the elf warily. "Can you be trusted, Morgan?"

The corners of Morgan's lips curled in delight.

"I sincerely hope not."

Conn blinked his eyes, furrowing his brow then threw his head back and laughed.

"Ah, good. A man after my own heart. I think we shall get along."

Morgan dipped his head and grabbed his glass.

"You speak the truth, Conn. To a new...partnership."

Conn pushed his glass toward the elf, furiously using his wings to move the large container.

"To a new partnership." He then stuck his head in the glass and pulled a deep draught from the amber liquid.

"Ptah! This is milk for children!"

"You speak the truth but it is the best these villagers can produce. It's better than water."

"Well spoken."

The unlikely twosome drank quietly. When the liquid dropped so far down the glass the fae was unable to get to it, Morgan signaled to the barmaid to bring a straw.

"What brings you to this inn, Conn?"

Conn was certain Florence had frequented this place but was still a bit leery of the night elf.

"I felt a need to drown my thirst and observe the humans of this village. Has there been any excitement lately?"

Morgan downed his drink and signaled for another. "Yes, there has. Some blighter showed up a fortnight ago and started horning in on my territory, if you know what I mean?"

Conn took a pull from his straw, eliminating the need to answer.

"Anyway, he comes prancing through the door last night like some nancy-boy and sidles up to my companion for the evening. After several glasses of whiskey, he made a rude comment about her character when she rebuffed his advances."

Good heavens, Florence. Not in town for a moon and you've poisoned the water. Maybe you don't need my help.

"What happened?" Conn balanced himself on the rim of the glass.

"I demanded he apologize to the lady and myself. He laughed, issued more inappropriate suggestions regarding my lady friend then challenged me to a duel."

Conn slipped from the rim and saved himself from falling in the mead by quickly winging his way to the tabletop.

"Does your sheriff *allow* dueling? In my village, the sheriff would lock everyone up should he have knowledge of such a happening."

"I'm above these quaint humans laws. I live by my own rules."

The elfkind's wrinkled nose and down turned lips showed his disgust for the local constabulary.

Conn gulped. He had to ask the question burning in his brain.

"Wha-what weapon did he choose?"

Morgan allowed a big smile to lighten his face.

"Fool chose blades."

Conn started coughing.

"Are you alright, friend?"

The fae held up one hand while the other clutched his stomach. He nodded then lowered his head to his knees in an attempt to catch his breath. Once he had his composure back, he pulled upright and continued.

"Can I assume you're talented with the blade?"

Morgan's smile widened. "If I say so myself, I'm very adept with steel."

Oh, you've done it now, Florence.

Conn moved to his perch on the glass' edge.

"So, what would this nancy-boy's name be, Morgan?" He pulled in a mouthful of beer and quickly swallowed.

"I've no idea. What does it matter?"

"The name will be important for placing on the headstone."

"Ah, my little friend, you do have a point. Let me see..." Morgan tapped his finger on his chin. "I believe it was Terrance. No, more along the lines of Lawrence to the best of my recollection. I wasn't really interested in his name; just his apology to my lady friend."

"As well you should have been. If interlopers are allowed to insult your companions, they'll have no compunction about insulting you. You can't have that in your village."

"Thank you, Conn. It's good to see someone who understands my position. I'm afraid my sister isn't as comprehending of a gentleman's duties."

Conn looked at the elf lounging elegantly in the opposite chair. He'd just mentioned a sister so that meant there were at least two of these night elves in the vicinity. He wondered how many were in their clan.

"Tell me, Morgan. When is this duel to occur?"

"This afternoon at the set of the sun."

"Shouldn't you be practicing?"

"His defeat can be accomplished with one hand held behind my back."

"Maybe I'll stick around and observe."

Morgan signaled the barmaid. "I'm feeling a mite peckish. Would you care for dinner?"

"Love some."

Conn smiled. His day had morphed from dismal to delightful in the span of one glass of beer. He and Cary may have been stranded here because of Florence but Conn was going to make the very best of it. If Florence had to be sacrificed in the process, well, such were the consequences.

The barmaid brought soup in a bowl for Morgan and, at Morgan's request, a small cupful for *the wee ones* he'd told the barmaid with a wink.

She shook her head and rolled her eyes but complied with his request, as he was known to be a big tipper.

Conn tucked into the soup. *I could get used to this. Wonder where Cary is?*

The thought flitted in and out of his mind. He was too busy eating and drinking to give it any real consideration. Things would turn out as they were destined. They always did.

Chapter Four

Tiamoon had settled Thomas at the family table after coaxing him to change into dry clothing she'd located in her brother's room.

"Don't even think of moving." She narrowed her eyes at the weaving leprechaun.

Thomas picked at the sleeve of the shirt. "This isn't mine. Where's my clothing?"

Tia unbelted her sword and placed it inside a small closet beneath the stairs of the cottage.

"Your clothes are out on the line drying. Maybe some fresh air will help rid them of the stench."

She went in search of her mother. In the back of the small building, divided into equally marked plots, lay the pride and joy of Tiamoon's mother, Skye--her garden. From the cool, damp days of spring through summer's heat, Skye charmed the earth into producing bushels of food. It was in this haven Tiamoon located her.

"Hello, mum."

"Hello, Tia. Can you hand me the trowel near your feet?"

Tia picked up the small spade and carried it to her mother.

"I've brought home Thomas, the leprechaun from the meadow clan. I was hoping you might have some of your potato soup left."

"There's some on the stove. Why did you bring him here?"

"He's a mess. He's been drinking for who knows how long and was visible to any that chose to look. He'd have given us away to the humans."

Skye rose from her knees to face her youngest child. "Daughter, you have to stop bringing home strays." Patting Tia on the shoulder as she passed, she moved in the direction of the cottage. "I'll warm the stew but you have to make the toast."

Tia surveyed the bounty of fresh food growing in the plot. Every year she watched her mom create life from the earth and it still amazed her. She hadn't the patience. Clashing swords was more her style.

Skye had stoked the fire and was stirring the warming soup when Tia strode into the room. On the small table next to the drain board sat the wire toaster and a couple slices of bread. Tia popped a slice into the wire and with a dishtowel opened the heated handle of the cast iron wood stove. Mere minutes provided the needed heat to brown the bread. Smearing the toast with fresh churned butter, she placed it on a small plate and, with a full bowl of heated soup in her other hand, carried the food to the dining table and the sleeping leprechaun.

Tia placed the food far enough away from Thomas as to be safe, then walked to his chair and shook him awake.

"Get up, you fool. My mother has worked hard to provide food for your mangy self. Least you can do is eat it."

Wiping away the drool from his lips, he leaned back and inhaled deeply.

"Smells to be a good potato soup--and toast. I, uh, I think I might actually be hungry." His eyes opened wide and he grabbed for the dishes.

Tia slapped a hand on the table next to his watching him jump in reaction.

"Now that I've got your attention, listen up. You'll eat politely and not make a mess. You'll finish everything on these plates then you'll excuse yourself and wash up. After that, I'm putting you in my brother's room for the night. Tomorrow, you'll go home and stay away from the spirits until next week. Do I make myself clear?"

Thomas nodded, his attention riveted on the steaming bowl of soup.

Tia slid the bowl to him and retrieved a spoon from the sideboard.

She handed him the implement. "Politely."

Watching him devour the contents of the bowl, Tia wondered how he ever managed to take care of himself. Seemed someone in the meadow was always looking after him. *Might be how he planned it.* Tia looked hard at the leprechaun. *Nah, not clever enough.*

She walked to the front of the small cottage and stared out the window to the meadow. The name Thomas had uttered in his drunken stupor was new. She was familiar with most of the meadow, forest and mountain fae in this area and none bore this assignation of Cary. It rang of the old country. She would have to investigate this new visitor.

The loud buzz of snoring interrupted her thought and Tia turned to find Thomas asleep at the table. She bundled him from the chair and dragged him back to her brother's room. Securing him in the bed, she closed the door and went to sit in front of the cottage where she gazed at the scenery.

She couldn't quite put her finger on the uneasiness roiling about her. Her nerves tingled on the top of her skin and she jumped with the slightest provocation. A change was about to happen to her valley, Tia was sure. Just what that change was--she wouldn't even hazard a guess.

~ * ~

Cary moaned and rolled to her back. This was absurd. Why was she tiptoeing around this night elf? The wee folk had taught many of them the magic they used! She had more ability in her tiny finger than the cold hearted, stony-eyed giantess who held her captive had in her entire body. Mustering her courage, Cary stood and began to chant a spell her mother had taught her. Again and again, she chanted the lines, feeling the dormant power surge through her veins. Radiance began to glow around her and the leather container opened. Cary zipped through the mouth of the bag, coming face to face with the night elf.

"I wondered how long it would take before you employed your power." Gitty smirked and reached to grab the tiny fae.

Cary loop-de-looped away, winging herself a safe distance from the elf. "You'll not be holding me prisoner any longer."

Gitty swiped at the floating fae and missed again. A frown marred the porcelain face. "And what makes you think I can't?"

Cary flew straight at the elf and stopped directly in front of her.

"Because the width and breath of my magic surpasses anything you can imagine. I'll have no hesitation to use it to bring you to my size and pummel the life from you!"

Sparks flew from the wee one's fingertips as she pointed at Gitty.

The two stood staring at each other; Cary hovering in front of the elf and the night elf standing feet planted shoulder width apart, hands on hips, glaring.

The air crackled and popped. Wind whipped hair wildly around their heads. The clock on the fire's mantle ticked loudly, echoing in the silence of the room.

Then Cary giggled. Gitty raised her eyebrows and a smile hovered over her lips. The tiny fae clutched her sides as she broke into laughter, her shoulders shaking.

Gitty snickered and soon was laughing as well.

The wee one drifted to the shoulder of the night elf.

"I must say, Madam Night Elf, you seem to be a soul after my own heart. What say we join forces? I can use a partner in this new place who has knowledge and position."

Gitty chuckled. "You've proven yourself bold, Cary. I believe you have the flint of a steel blade backed by the powers of a great mage. Your convenient size would help me in my pursuits, too. We have the makings of a perfect partnership.

"Shall we call it done?"

The wee fae flit off Gitty's shoulder and pirouetted in front of her.

"Done!"

Chapter Five

Florence pulled the handkerchief from his back pocket and swiped at his forehead. He couldn't remember the last time he'd sweat this much. Tucking the soaked cloth in his pocket, he picked up his broom and began the parry-lunge-withdraw routine his father had taught him as a boy.

My only hope is the lessons father tried to impart to me will come back automatically.

"Mr. Florence? Mr. Florence?"

Dorinda carried a glass of sparkling water to the red-faced warrior. She handed the cooling liquid to him and watched as he gulped the contents.

"I think you should come inside and have dinner."

"I'm not really hungry."

"It will help to bolster your strength and spirit. You might also consider a shower before you leave. I've washed your clothing and shined your boots. You'll look very dashing in your outfit."

Florence stopped and turned to look at Dorinda. Her blue eyes gave no hint of guile.

"Sounds a good idea to me. I'll shower before dinner, if you don't mind."

"Not at all." *Whew. I'm glad he suggested it first.*

She led the way to the kitchen.

Florence continued to the bathing room and found his clothing carefully laid out. He admired the high gloss of his riding boots and noted his shirt had never been so spotless. It appeared nearly new. He held the trousers to his nose and pulled in the scent of fresh air. His hand lightly caressed the sharp crease, which had been ironed into the fabric. He'd wash himself especially well using some of the sweet smelling soap in the bathing room then smooth his hair with the slicker Dorinda had shown him how to use.

He strolled into the dining room, his nose seduced by the delicious smells coming from the kitchen.

"Have a seat at the table."

Florence sat in the chair before which a plate and silverware had been placed.

Dorinda brought in a plate of crisp, golden fried chicken. She set it on the towel and slapped at Florence's extended hand.

"Not until all the food has been brought out."

He licked his lips. His stomach complained loudly but he knew not to push his luck.

Dorinda finished placing mashed potatoes, homemade gravy, baked biscuits, home grown corn and fresh butter and honey on the table.

"Now we say grace."

The two bowed their heads and Dorinda offered the blessing.

"Lord, please bless this food and those who eat it. Watch over Mr. Florence tonight so he returns safely to our house. Amen."

"Amen."

Florence looked at Dorinda and raised his eyebrows.

She smiled shyly. "Yes, Mr. Florence, you may start." *Eat hearty, man. This may be your last meal.*

~ * ~

The buzz around the meadow increased all through the day.

Tiamoon snagged Cheney, head of the wood clan of gnomes, as he headed toward his forest home and asked about all the excitement.

"Haven't you heard?"

"Would I have asked if I had heard, Cheney?" Tia frowned and crossed her arms.

"Uh, right. We've had visitors arrive in the last two weeks who seem discontent with the peace of our valley."

"What are you talking about?"

"A human arrived and was accompanied by a couple of fae I've not seen before." Cheney nodded his head at the fact.

"You wouldn't happen to have the name of the fae, would you?" Tia dropped her arms to her sides.

He furrowed his brow and narrowed his eyes. "To the best of my recollection, the she-fae is called Mary. No, that's not it. Derry, no, humph." His eyes rolled to the sky as he thought. "Cary! That's it. She's Cary and he's Conn.

The human they accompanied has some fancy girly name like Flossie, or Francis. Something like that."

So this was the name of the fae Thomas the Leprechaun muttered in his drunken stupor.

"What has all the valley folk wagging their tongues so furiously?"

"The human male challenged Morgan to a duel...with swords." Cheney's grin covered his face.

"Is the man out of his mind?!" Tia began to pace. "He'll be skewered. We can't have these humans and night elves dueling in our valley. If the human is killed, the human authorities will come out here and trample our homes in their zeal to find the culprit."

"Hmm. Hadn't thought of that."

"Apparently nobody has. When and where is this to happen?"

"Tonight at the meadow's edge. All the valley-kind will be there. Listen, I want to go home and eat before the duel. I'll see you there, Tia."

With a quick wave of his hand, Cheney disappeared into the greenery of the forest.

It was bad enough the night elves were raiding the homes of the faerie and gnome clans. With teamwork and dedication, the gnomes, faeries, wood nymphs and other small folk of the valley might be able to protect their homes and hold back the scourge of the elves. If humans got involved in the mix, the valley folk would surely lose.

Tia shuddered at the thought. With someone else responsible for patrolling the meadows and forests tonight, she'd planned a quiet evening at home. Taking care of

Thomas had drained her energy. However, her quiet evening would have to wait.

Anytime the night elves were involved in a fracas, nothing good happened from the outcome. Tiamoon needed to witness this event and plan accordingly.

~ * ~

Morgan pulled the brush through his white hair one last time, settling the locks behind his shoulders.

"Looking magnificent." He smiled at the reflection in the mirror.

"My lord, brother. You're worse than any human woman I've met. I take it you have a heated rendezvous tonight?"

Morgan slowly turned to face his sister. "I have a meeting but not with one of the local women." A smile touched one corner of his mouth accenting the dimple in his cheek.

"I've been challenged to a duel."

Gitty had sprawled across the white divan. Her eyes grew in astonishment.

"You? Dueling? Please. Whatever brought this on?"

"There's a cretin of a human being who showed up a couple weeks ago and tried to sweet talk his way into my territory. Last evening was the final straw. He insulted my lady friend and I demanded an apology.

"He's the one who challenged me to a duel. He just made the mistake of choosing swords."

Gitty sat up and considered her brother. "Well, if nothing else, I can give you the edge on swords. Next to me, you're the best swordsman in the clan."

Morgan rolled his eyes. "I can outfight you any day, sister. Once I've finished this interloper, we can set a time and date to meet and prove who's best."

Gitty propped her feet on the table in front of the divan.

"No thanks, little brother. I've better things to do with my time than beat you soundly at a sword fight."

Morgan huffed out an impatient breath. "I haven't time for this. I'll be at the meadow's edge at twilight should you wish to witness my victory."

He flipped his cape over one shoulder and pulled open the heavy wooden door, allowing it to close behind him.

Gitty turned to the small figure seated quietly on the back of the divan.

"Well, Cary, fancy a night on the town?"

The little fae's eyes lit up. "Yes!" She flew up and turned a somersault before landing on the night elf's shoulder.

"Lead the way, partner."

Chapter Six

Rays of rose-colored light extended warm fingers from the setting sun to the golden meadow in the valley. Surrounding mountain sentinels glowed a deep burgundy and purple, hiding their forests in indigo shadows.

Standing head and shoulders above the gathering crowd, a lone white-haired figure towered, replete with flowing cape and polished black boots. Securely tucked at the figure's side in a hand-tooled leather scabbard shone a finely honed sword engraved with the bearer's name and family crest. At his feet, a plain practice weapon reclined.

Morgan unconsciously brushed his hair behind his shoulders as he unbuttoned his cloak. With a flourish worthy of a film star, he whipped the cape from his shoulders and folded the plush material in one smooth motion. Sunlight flashed off the hardened steel blade and he placed his bundle on the cleanest log he could find.

Conn winged to the cape and took a seat. He winked at Morgan and wiggled his brows. There was nothing quite as exciting as a good fight. Rubbing his hands together, he giggled. If Morgan quickly dispatched his opponent, maybe they could go to the pub and have more mead before he went back to face Cary.

With carefully staged movements, Morgan drew his weapon from the scabbard, the quiet hissing of the blade against the leather lost in the growing murmur of the multitude.

Morgan was a patient man, but the cowardice of his opponent was becoming evident by the lack of his presence. Should the interloper fail to appear, he would win by default and not have to break a sweat. He felt confident this stranger was more bluff than action. More to his advantage. He would appear as the wounded party and fall back in the good graces of the ladies.

Just as Morgan decided to resheath his weapon, a ruckus at the back of the growing mob caught his attention. People parted and a lone figure in riding breeches, white billowing shirt and shining boots marched toward him.

Pulling a monogrammed handkerchief from his sleeve, the outsider whipped it across Morgan's cheek.

"I formally challenge you to a duel."

The corners of the night elf's lips curled in amusement. He pulled himself tall, staring directly at the man and replied.

"I accept your challenge." Turning to the crowd, he searched but was unable to see his sister. *Where is she?*

"Is there someone here who will act as the referee?"

"Didn't you pick one before now?" A raspy male voice from the gathered mob hollered.

Morgan drew himself to his full height. "There was no time."

"I'll referee." From the midst of people, a parting of the crowd showed a small being swathed in leather from head to toe and carrying a blade upon her back.

Morgan raised a brow and looked down his aquiline nose. "And who might you be?"

Tiamoon looked around at the gathering. She would need to be... cautious with her response.

"I'm Tia from the far side of the meadow. I have knowledge of dueling and can be an impartial referee."

Morgan let his eyes rove over the small creature standing before him. Should it decide against him, two swift swings of his blade could end this creature's existence and no one would be the wiser. *Why not?*

"I've no objection." He turned to his opponent. "And you?"

Florence blinked his eyes to be sure he was seeing the sight standing before him. His knowledge of the wee ones imparted to him in bedtime tales covered gnomes and as sure as he was standing here getting ready for a sword duel, this being was a gnome.

"I've no problem."

Morgan swung his blade with his wrist, twirling the shining metal past his shoulders.

"Shall we begin? I've provided you a weapon over there." He indicated with a jerk of his head toward the practice sword on the grass.

Tia strolled to the weapon and lifted the metal spear. She drew her thumb down the blade and turned to glare at the night elf.

"The blade is dull. You will give him a stone and allow him ten minutes to sharpen this weapon."

Morgan rummaged in his pocket and tossed a whetstone to his opponent.

"There. Ten minutes, no more."

Tia looked toward the crowd. "Is there someone with a watch?"

A hand went up.

"Please let us know when ten minutes has passed."

Shirring sounds of stone against metal and shuffling feet filled the air. The spectators soon began to mumble and fidget.

"Time!"

Florence looked up, a shadow of fear passing over his face. He regained his composure and walked to the blonde giant. He handed the stone to its owner.

"Thank you."

Morgan smirked. "You're welcome."

"Please make a large circle so the challengers have plenty of room to spare."

The crowd shuffled back, raising a dust cloud silhouetted in the twilight. When sufficient space had been acquired, Tia turned and looked at both men.

"Stand with your backs to each other."

When the two competitors were back to back, it was clear Morgan had the advantage of height and arm length.

In the crowd, Dorinda watched in horror and wrung her hands.

Leaning against a tree behind the majority of the gawkers, Gitty propped one leg up against the trunk. Her line of vision was unimpaired by the shorter townsfolk.

Cary settled on her shoulder, her eyes popping at the sight of the opponent. What the devil had Florence done now?

"Are they really going to fight with swords?"

"Looks like it."

Good heavens! Fool was going to get himself killed! He was better with a firearm than a blade. Unfortunately, all she could do was sit back and observe.

"Who do you think will win this?"

"Oh, Morgan will make quick work of this. You watch."

Cary fretted for a moment then settled to study the duel. Florence had been given his chances. After all, wasn't the fault his they were stuck here?

The referee continued.

"Please take five paces. One...two...three...four...five. Now turn and face each other."

Morgan whisked around and looked into concerned brown eyes. He could sense fear from the intruder. *As well he should be.* He pulled his weapon to the front and grasped the hilt with both hands. Quickly he covered the ground between himself and his opponent just as the man had put up the blade in front of himself.

Morgan swung down with crushing force pushing the blade to the ground, the clanging of steel on steel echoing between the darkening mountains.

Florence sucked air into his lungs. The fierce attack of this blonde giant had taken him by surprise. He shoved upward, catching the steel of the other man's sword and flinging it up toward the giant's shoulder.

The blonde warrior turned into the surprise move and jammed Florence's weapon up and over, catching the blade and flipping it from his hands. Morgan then pirouetted and ran the interloper through from front to back.

Shrieks and cries were all the gathered observers could do. On the ground, red staining the white shirt, lay the stranger.

Morgan walked to the edge of the meadow and wiped the blood from his steel. He'd do a careful cleaning when he returned home.

Dorinda burst through the throng and ran to her houseguest. She fell to her knees, gently cradling Florence's head in her lap.

He looked into her eyes and smiled weakly. Mouthing the words, thank you, he expelled his final breath.

She hovered her hand over his forehead and sensed the spirit had left his body. Lowering her head, she allowed tears to course down her cheeks.

Cary watched curiously from Gitty's shoulder then flew closer to observe the reaction of this other human. The female human was crying real tears over Florence. *How strange.* She, Cary, was supposed to be his guardian and, yet, she couldn't bring herself to feel sadness.

Winging her way back to the night elf, she realized she'd changed her alliances. This was the fate of her new life. Nothing ever stayed the same.

Gitty stood and straightened her leather jacket.

"I might as well congratulate Morgan. He'll be impossible if I don't."

The pair wended their way through the meandering crowd. As they neared the edge of the meadow, Cary narrowed her eyes. *If I didn't know better...*

"Well, brother, you did well. Congratulations."

Morgan turned to face his sibling. "Where were you? I couldn't see you in the crowd. Did you catch the whole thing?"

"Yes, I saw the whole thing. I thought duels were supposed to be between equally matched opponents."

Morgan shrugged his shoulders as he leaned to pick up his blade.

"I can't help it if he chose the weapons. Point is I won. Thought I might head to the pub and have a beer or two. Care to buy me one?"

Cary dropped from Gitty's shoulder to the log holding the cape.

"Conn! You devil! Where have you been? Why weren't you searching for Florence? Explain yourself!"

The male fae jumped from his perch at the bark of his name. He twisted around and winged backward.

"Cary! I, uh, I was looking for Florence." He pointed to the form lying recumbent on the ground. "See? I found him."

Cary punched him in the chest. "You idiot! How are we supposed to get home now?"

Conn winged his way above Morgan's shoulder. "I'm not sure I want to go home. What's there for us? More work? No thanks. I like where we are right now."

Gitty and Morgan looked at the two fae arguing.

"New friend, sister?"

Gitty bristled at Morgan's tone. "Yes. Just like yours. Useful and very devious. I see a way to get what we want without putting ourselves in danger."

Morgan slipped his blade into the scabbard and grabbed the cloak from the log.

"Tell me over a brew. I've worked up a thirst and I believe my small friend is in need also."

The siblings moved in the direction of the tavern while the wee folk continued their argument as they winged behind the night elves.

From behind a tree a small figure emerged.

I need to find out what they are up to before everything I know is destroyed.

Tiamoon pushed out a breath between her lips. She was going to have to go into the lion's den. If it meant saving her people, then so be it. The lion's den it was.

She set off toward town. This time tomorrow she would have the knowledge she needed to formulate a defense plan or die trying.

Chapter Seven

Darkening shadows stretched long across the valley. Tiamoon, lounging against her favorite oak casually swinging her blade, surveyed the meadow. Chills inched down her back, setting her nerves to tingling. Seeking solitude from the crush of the humans in the pub, she'd returned to observe the mortician's ministrations to the outsider. His body would reside in a pauper's grave. Tia could only hope his soul would find better accommodations.

Rocks crunching beneath boots alerted her to the approach of unwanted visitors. Two night elves deep in conversation strode her direction. She squinted her eyes and caught the flickering of wings from tiny fae surrounding the elves.

Tia felt her chest tighten. Faeries and night elves didn't normally mingle. *This doesn't bode well for the rest of us.* She leaned over and pulled her blade toward her as she slowly rose and slipped around the tree in sync with the night elves movement.

"What are you rambling on about, Morgan?" Gitty slowed her pace. "You're going to collect your practice sword, aren't you?"

Strolling to the red-stained metal shaft, he bent down to retrieve the implement. "Of course. We'll need every blade in the coming days. Weren't you listening at the last clan gathering?"

Cary and Conn, sensing a squabble brewing, flew themselves out of danger's range and hovered above the siblings.

Cary leaned toward Conn. "You smell of mead and tobacco. I thought you'd gone to search for Florence?"

Conn snapped his head her direction. "I was tracking him down. I can't help it if the journey took me to the pub, can I?"

Staring at the blood soaked ground; Cary wrinkled her forehead in consternation.

"Well, you did a slap-up poor job of finding him, now didn't ya?"

Conn noted her brogue deepening. If he didn't defend himself now, she'd start a railing that wouldn't stop until his ears bled.

"I located Morgan who let me know where Florence was to be. It's not my fault the fool went and issued a challenge he couldn't win. Besides, I was hungry and thirsty. What was I to do? Morgan was kind enough to offer me food and drink. Saying no would've been impolite."

Cary flew to inches in front of Conn's face. Gritting her teeth, she lowered her voice to just above a whisper.

"You're his faerie godfather, Conn. Your responsibility was to guide him and watch over him. What about that?"

The fae straightened his back and reverse winged until he could look Cary in the eyes. "I guided him through his childhood. His decision to disregard my advice as a man had nothing to do with my efforts. I couldn't force him to use his common sense. Don't place the blame on me for his boastful nature. Florence developed that without my help and against my guidance."

Cary's wings slumped and she heaved a sigh. "Tis the truth. We can but lead them. We can't force them to use their knowledge. I'll give you that, Conn, but if I find you're only purpose in going to the pub was to quench your own thirst..."

He held up a hand. "On my honor as a fae godfather."

She eyed him suspiciously. *I've naught but to believe him.*

Their attention was drawn back to the night elf siblings sniping at each other.

Gitty pulled her sword from the scabbard and twirled the blade, switching the fine steel claymore from hand to hand.

"Why should I listen? Most of the talk is you boys blowing your own horns about your conquests. I can live without knowing how many notches each of you has on your belts."

Tiamoon hunkered at the foot of the oak, her dark brown leather blending with the tree's bark coat. She keened her ears, held her breath and concentrated with all her being.

Morgan whipped around, covering the distance between himself and his sister with purposeful strides. His arm shot out and grabbed the twirling blade, yanking the weighty steel from her grasp. Standing toe to toe with his older sibling, he narrowed ice blue eyes at her.

"You arrogant ass. The council voted to interrupt the raids on the valley folk. Someone has gotten to them. They're talking about setting down a peace treaty with the locals. Do you really want to live on your little piece of land?

"We started this because we're far more intelligent than the local villagers and ruling is in our blood. Wasn't it your plan to own your own mountain and valley? Have you discarded that idea?"

Gitty placed her hand in the middle of his chest and shoved him.

"Don't ever get in my face like that again. I'll cut out your heart and feed it to you."

She snatched the saber dangling in Morgan's hand. Flipping it up and sheathing the metal, she walked toward the road then turned.

"I'll have my kingdom and you won't be allowed inside the borders." She tromped toward home, rising dust with each stamped footstep.

Morgan watched her ramrod straight back march away from him.

Cary sped up to catch Gitty.

Conn winged lazily to Morgan's side. "Is she going to be mad forever?"

Morgan jumped. "You startled me. No, she won't be mad forever, but being on Gitty's bad side is not good. I'd never tell her to her face but my sister is a formidable opponent. It's best when she's *got* my back, not trying to attack it. By the time she gets home, she'll come around to see things my way."

Morgan wiped the bloodied cutlass on the dew-laden grass until the blade appeared clean.

"What *are* you planning to do, if I may ask?" Conn cocked his head ever so slightly, frown wrinkles creasing his brow.

Morgan looked about the area.

Tiamoon held her breath and concentrated on trying to hear the night elf's plan.

Morgan meandered to the edge of the clearing and gazed at the meadow surrounded by forested mountains.

"This land is the richest I've ever seen. The local villagers are ignorant farmers and laborers with no knowledge of the wealth beneath their feet. So far, our clan has been able to flash a few gold coins in their eyes and buy up the property. The humans aren't the problem. This Depression they complain about has made them easy targets.

"No, it's the forest folk; the fae, gnomes, leprechauns, nymphs and sprites that are causing us the biggest concern. We need to run them out of the area. If they can't pay taxes, they can't live on the land. But the little blighters have dug in and won't be chased away."

Morgan turned to Conn. "Your people are very tenacious, little partner. Maybe you can offer me insight into a way to get them to leave?"

"Uh, I, uh, will have to put my mind to the task. Let me think it over and I'll get back to you."

Morgan leaned over and picked up his practice cutlass. "Don't take too long. We're planning a raid in the next few days and I want to be certain I'll have success. Before the next moon, I will own all my eyes can see."

He set a fast stride down the same path Gitty had taken, the little fae winging frenetically to keep pace.

Tiamoon counted to twenty then emerged from her hiding spot. Things were far worse than she'd imagined. She needed to rally her clans and pull in as many of the fae and others as she could.

She slid her blade in its casing on her back and trotted down the road toward her home. As she neared the cottage, she smelled the sweet wood her mother burned in the fireplace. Tia vaulted over the gate and burst through the front door.

"Mum, mum!"

Stirring a vessel on the potbellied wood stove, Skye started at the noisy intrusion.

"Why in the world are you yelling? Slow down, Labhoise, and take off your boots. You're tracking in mud all over my clean floor."

Sitting at the table looking a sight better than Tia had seen him in two days was Thomas who quirked an eyebrow and one corner of his mouth her direction.

"Labhoise?"

Before the last syllable had left his lips, a blade with razor-honed steel was at his throat. He gulped, feeling the cold steel prick his skin.

"Yes. It is my name but will never be uttered by the likes of you. If I find you have spoken this to anyone in this forest, you won't be able to tell anyone of your stash of gold.

"Are we clear?"

Thomas slowly moved his head up and down.

Tia removed the blade from his throat and propped it in the corner. She sat on a three-legged wooden stool by the fire's side and removed her boots, wiggling her toes to bring warmth to them. She gazed at the crackling flames, sagging on the small settee. Her simple life was getting too complicated and all of the problems pointed to the interlopers in the valley: the night elves.

Skye, her warring leathers traded for the comfort of a house smock, stirred the vegetable stew. Glancing at her daughter, she sensed unease in the young woman.

"What bothers you, daughter? What creates such deep longing and confusion?"

Tia stood and turned her back to the fire's warmth. She clasped her hands behind her and rocked lightly on the balls of her feet.

Nodding in Thomas' direction, she questioned. "Has he had any of the spirit today?"

Skye narrowed her eyes at the leprechaun.

"Not as far as I can tell. I upturned his flask in the sink and have kept a close eye on him while he was here."

Thomas shot a thunderous glare at Tiamoon. "I'm as bloody sober as I ever want to be, thanks to you. Can't say much for the condition."

"Good." She walked to the table and sat opposite Thomas, indicating her mother should sit.

"What I have is news...not good at best, disastrous at worst."

The frown melted from Thomas' face and Skye leaned toward her daughter.

"Wha-what news?" Thomas' voice shook and his lip began to quiver.

"Quit thinking of yourself, Leprechaun. This news will affect all the inhabitants of the valley."

Skye held up a hand. "If this is serious, I need to have my pipe to think. Thomas, would you care to indulge?"

"Yes, ma'am."

Tia huffed out an impatient breath. She tolerated her mother's smoking but wasn't an indulger herself, never having developed the taste for it.

After Skye and Thomas had packed and lit the long ebony carved pipes, Tia began to relate the information she'd gleaned from the night's reconnaissance as the other two settled in to listen.

Wispy tendrils of fragrant smoke curled above their heads. Skye and Thomas kept the pipes clenched tightly between their teeth and refrained from commenting.

"What I'm about to tell you came directly from a night elf known as Morgan. He and his sister reside in the abode on the top of the hill that overlooks the valley. To this point, they've caused little problems...or so we thought.

"I've just learned they are buying up as much of the land from the humans as they can. Somehow, they have gold when others do not. They aren't worried about the humans. They are worried about the valley folk.

"Morgan mentioned the other clans have become tired of warring and are happy to settle with what they've received from the humans. He, on the other hand, wants as much land as he can get and domination over the entire valley: magic *and* nonmagic folk.

"He's making plans to raid in the next few days. He wants us gone before the set of the next moon."

Skye pulled deeply on her pipe. She appeared to be concentrating on a spot across the room. Slowly, smoke trickled from her mouth, lazily clinging to her burnished red hair.

"I've been part of the talks with the night elves."

Tia raised her eyebrows.

Skye pulled the pipe from her mouth and pointed it at her daughter.

"It's not necessary for me to tell you everywhere I go. You were busy patrolling the valley.

"At the last meeting, we'd come to an agreement to sign a treaty. If the young bucks have taken it in their minds to start raiding, I think it's time to call in the head of their clan. The elder night elves are tired of the warring and wish to settle on the lands they have now. There's enough for all of us to live without encroaching on the other's territory.

"I must think on this, daughter. It's time for dinner."

"Food?" Thomas put his pipe on the table and rubbed his hands together. "Sounds good to me!"

"Bah! All you think about is your stomach." Tia got up and grabbed the bowls and spoons. Maybe her brain would work better if her stomach were full.

It couldn't work any worse.

Chapter Eight

Shuffling sounds filled the room as participants from the clans settled at the table. One side of the long wooden slab seated heads from the night elves; facing them were the gnome, faerie, leprechaun and wood nymph clan leaders.

Skye stood and cleared her throat.

"I want to thank everyone for attending tonight. We have much to discuss. I'll get directly to the point. Are all the clans represented?"

She watched a familiar figure rise across the table from her, his white hair flowing around his muscular shoulders.

"All the representatives of the night elf clans are here." The smooth baritone of the speaker reverberated in the room.

Skye swallowed hard. *I have to keep my mind on the proceedings.* She pulled in a calming breath.

"Thank you, Aethel. I think we can achieve our goals quickly so we can all go to our homes before the sun rises this time." A shy smile covered her face.

Ahhh! That man makes my knees go wobbly.

Aethel stepped around his chair, moving to the head of the table.

"What is so urgent we need to meet three days prior to our scheduled time?"

Skye moved so she was opposite the clan leader. Her palms had begun to sweat and she knew if he got too close he'd be able to see her heart pounding wildly in her chest.

Pulling to her full four foot eleven inch height, Skye plunged ahead.

"Are you aware within the last rising and setting of the sun a human was killed by a night elf?"

Stunned expressions and crushing silence was her answer.

Skye avoided looking directly at Aethel. Her eyes connected with the other clan leaders as she continued. "A young night elf known to frequent the meeting places of the humans engaged in an altercation with a newcomer to the valley. Their verbal sparring peaked in a duel challenge."

Whispers morphed to murmurs and the participants at the table sent furtive glances toward Aethel, whose flushed face belied the straight line of his lips and determined set of his jaw.

"The humans gathered last evening in the meadow next to their drinking place. When the challenge had been dealt and accepted, two figures stood in a circle of witnesses.

"It's my understanding the actual duel was brief; the night elf dispatching his opponent painlessly and quickly."

Aethel pulled out the chair at the head of the table and dropped onto the wooden seat. A vein on the side of his neck visibly throbbed.

"When the duel ended, the humans went to their pub and continued as though nothing had occurred. Their keeper of the dead came out and took away the remains. What happened next is of concern to each and every council member here."

Skye paced the floor, biting the side of her lip and contemplating how to cautiously phrase her next thought.

"A conversation was heard between the victor of the duel and a female night elf."

Aethel's shoulders flinched.

"The young night elf boasted of a raid to be staged in the next few days. The tone of his comments indicated we have young ones not willing to listen to the judgment of their elders. He spoke of power, possession and domination of all creatures of the valley.

"If this is indeed the climate of feeling among the young warriors, we could be facing dire consequences."

Skye looked around the room and noted each clan member deep in thought. It wasn't a comforting sight.

"I'm asking for your solutions to stop this bloodshed before it happens."

"You're wrong."

She looked up to face the voice of dissention.

"What makes you say that, Glade?"

The night elf of the woods clan stood and peered down his straight nose at the gnome leader.

"I have spoken to my clansmen, young and old, and they tire of the constant threat of war. Many of the young men are seeking to settle and raise families. Who is your source for this outrageous story?"

Skye gritted her teeth. Glade was known to be argumentative. Sometimes, she thought, just for the sake of arguing.

"I don't wish to speak the name."

"There you have it." Glade slapped his hand on the wooden tabletop. "If you won't reveal your source, how are we to know what has been spoken is the truth? Maybe you're making this up to catch us off guard and attack us." He shrugged his shoulders. "Who knows? Unless you can provide a witness to this conversation, we only have the word of a...gnome."

The curl of Glade's lip left no doubt about his feelings.

The door to the meeting hall slammed shut.

All heads turned toward the sound.

"You dare to call the head of my clan a liar?" A young male gnome planted his feet shoulder width apart, sword drawn and at the ready.

Skye turned to the figure. "Terran, please. The man is entitled to his opinion."

The gnome Terran strode to Skye's side. "Aye, he is, but not when he fouls the clan's honor."

The night elf Glade yanked his sword from the casing and, in two swift steps, stood next to the gnomes, weapon in hand, towering dangerously over the two.

Aethel rose, his chair scraping across the floor. He threw out his arm, toppling the cutlass from Glade's hand.

Whipping quickly around, right hand fisted and swinging, Glade's dark green eyes sparked as Aethel caught the thrown punch mid-air.

"Glade." Aethel's low warning held menacing undertones.

The night elf of the woods clan wrenched his hand to his side.

"This is not over, Aethel. You may head this council, but I don't recognize your authority and won't be bound by the decisions made here."

He leaned in and dropped his voice. "Prepare yourself and your little friends. I believe Morgan has the right idea and I may consider joining his campaign."

Stepping away, he gave a quick jerk of his head. Chairs dropped to the floor of the meeting hall as several clan leaders jumped up, clomping their boots and banging the doors on their way out.

Skye pivoted on her heel and headed for the door. Hesitating at the exit, she twisted to face the rest of the clan members shuffling to leave the table.

"I think we'll need to regroup and meet at another time. I'll send messages via the mouse network. Everyone take care when traveling homeward. Tonight has shown we've come no further than we were a year ago. Terran, we head for our home. Aethel...good to see you again."

Skye acknowledged the night elf with a quick head bob. She left the meeting hall and slipped the dagger from her belt, hiding it up the sleeve of her shirt. Terran trotted behind, his hand on the hilt of his blade, surveying the landscape in all directions. In a complete reversal of previous congresses, tonight's meeting put the council back to where each clan had stood at the very first get together, and Skye no longer felt safe in her land.

She feared a bloodbath was about to ensue, regardless of the careful negotiations accomplished to this point. There really was nothing as headstrong as a young man trying to prove himself to the world.

Skye tread lightly, scanning the surrounding meadow and woods as she moved toward home on soft leather boots.

Terran, straining to hear beyond the hushed footfalls of Skye, brought up the rear; walking in the same spots.

Skye was deep in contemplation. She'd fallen for persistent attention lavished on her when she'd been but a young warrior. A tall, elegant white-haired night elf had stolen her heart and sweet-talked her into ignoring the common sense whispering in her ears. Furtive meetings in dense forest locations had produced many memorable nights...and a daughter. The night elf had disappeared out of Skye's life as quickly as he'd appeared.

It wasn't until many years later she'd learned of his arranged marriage to the daughter of a chieftain, putting an end to generations of warring between the clans. The woman quickly gave birth to two children: a daughter and a son, expiring while giving the son life.

She felt blessed her daughter resembled her and not the father, making explanations unnecessary.

Skye and Terran reached the cottage. Smoke spiraled from the chimney and a candle glowed in the window.

"We're welcomed," Skye whispered.

"Good, I'd hate to have to fight my way back in my own home."

Skye could tell her son was smiling. Joy bubbled through his voice.

A quick entrance and the two warriors stood inside the living room. Thomas, the leprechaun, was snoring in the armchair facing the fire, his feet stretched in front of him, pipe smoldering in the abalone shell on the side table. Tiamoon sat on the three-legged stool, gazing into the fire.

"Hello, daughter."

She swiveled on her seat to acknowledge her mother when she caught sight of another figure skulking in the shadows of the room.

"Who's there?" She sprung from the stool clamping her hand on the fireplace poker and wielding the implement as a weapon.

The figure chuckled then burst into laughter.

"Do you know how silly you look, sister?"

Tia glared at the figure until his words connected with her brain.

"Terran?" Tia set the poker against the flagstone hearth. "Is it really you?"

The young gnome stepped into the glowing ring of light cast by the fire.

"Yes, sister. It's me."

Tia quickly covered the floor space and smothered her brother in a hug.

"When did you arrive? What have you found out? How many bought swords are we facing?"

Terran wiggled free from her grasp and held up his hand. "Whoa, big sis. Let me unstrap my weapon and sit in front of the fire. My body is tired from the journey. I wish a warm cup of mother's broth and to remove my boots."

"I'll get you the broth and some bread but you're on your own for taking off your boots." Tia wrinkled her nose, much to Terran's delight.

"It's good to see little has changed since my leaving." Setting in the other armchair facing the fire, he ripped the bread into pieces and dipped a piece in the broth, bringing both to his mouth. Eyes closed in delight; he swallowed and released a long sigh.

"I have missed this."

Skye slipped to her room. The children could update her with the latest news in the morning. The council meeting had tried her patience and worn her out. There was also the matter of seeing Aethel again. It had been many a year, but her heart still skipped a beat and her stomach hurt every time she spotted the night elf. A good night's rest would put things back into perspective.

~ * ~

Tia watched as her brother gorged himself on the broth. When he had finished and removed his boots, she drew the stool next to his chair.

"What have you found, brother?"

Terran stared at the flames dancing in the hearth.

"The threat we've suspected is real-very real. There is a faction of night elves determined to rule this valley. They have enlisted the help of mercenaries from afar and make plans in the dark of the night. The elder clansmen have no knowledge of the plans or the mercenaries. I think we're on our own."

Tia used the poker to shove the logs in the grate around then added a new one on the dying stack. Flames flared up, expelling heat and light.

"What are we to do, Terran?"

Brother and sister stared into the fire.

"Nothing tonight. I'm exhausted and can't think clearly. After a good night's sleep, I'll tackle this problem again."

Tia rose and strolled to her room. Terran was right. The evening had dragged and Thomas' constant whining about not having any liquor to drink had worn on her. She was no good to anyone at this moment. Sleep, indeed, appeared to be the best idea.

Chapter Nine

Wan flaxen rays of sunlight reached across diaphanous pillows of fog covering the dew-laden meadow. Gitty stood holding her coffee cup, staring at the light playing off the mist. Steam curled around her nose, wafting the pungent smell of freshly ground coffee beans to her olfactory senses.

Before her lay the fertile meadow gently sloping up to the velvet green mountains covered in usable forests. A smile touched her lips. *My meadow, my forests.*

Oh, yeah. Morgan might have illusions of power, but Gitty would guarantee the reality of ruling. From what she had ascertained about the meeting last night in the few mumbled words her father had spoken as he had stomped past her to his bedroom, the peace committee had been disrupted and temporarily put on hold. It was her duty to make sure the treaty was never signed.

Morgan stumbled into the living room and through to the kitchen. Several minutes later, Gitty heard him plop himself on the settee.

"Tough night, little brother?" Gitty turned to face him.

Squinting up at her, he grunted.

"Aren't you just the picture of polite conversation today?"

Morgan gulped a large mouthful of coffee. "Better things to do than make small talk with you. I've an important meeting to attend. I'll be out all day."

Gitty raised a brow. "Really. Since when do you leave the house before 4 pm?"

Morgan rose from the couch, grabbed his cup and tromped toward the hallway.

"I haven't the time to argue, Gitty. My future is something I plan to mold myself, and I have an appointment with destiny."

Gitty blew out an exasperated breath and rolled her eyes. "Dragons and trolls, Morgan. I've barely had time to down my coffee and you're spouting rhetoric worthy of Shakespeare. You must've been drinking tainted mead, for it's surely gone to your head."

She looked around the room, noting she'd not seen Cary since storming from the meadow last evening. Had the tiff between the siblings frightened the little fae?

Gitty shrugged her shoulders. While the little fae was a welcome diversion and having her as a spy in the faerie camp would give Gitty a huge advantage, she'd done fine before the wee one appeared on the scene.

Morgan appeared and moved toward the back door. He was attired in the clan's red-brown colors; a dark brown cloak about his shoulders, black polished riding boots on his feet. His hair was tied back with a dark brown leather strip and he carried his fighting steel.

"I'm taking a horse from the stables. And Gitty," Morgan turned to face his sister, "I wouldn't go out after dark."

He departed before she could reply. Moving back to the window, she watched him gallop down the driveway on his brown steed. Out of the corner of her eye, she spied the tiniest distortion in the air. Peering to the valley, she scrutinized each inch of the scene below her. As she was about to give up and get more coffee, the air directly in front of her wavered.

Gitty sucked air to her lungs. *There's old magic here. If the Ancient Ones have been brought in, Morgan and his friends could be in trouble. Heck, we'll all be in deep trouble.*

Aethel ambled through the living room and toward the kitchen, dark circles under his blue eyes. He grabbed a cup from the cupboard and poured coffee for himself. Sitting at the kitchen dinette, he spooned two teaspoons of sugar into the black concoction and stirred.

Gitty slipped in behind him and watched as he dropped his head to his hands.

"Are things alright, Father?"

Aethel groaned. "No. Did you know your brother was involved in a duel last night?"

His question echoed through the room. He lifted his head and looked into the guilty eyes of his daughter. "As I suspected...you knew and you were there. Before you try to deny it, there were witnesses."

"Who says I was going to deny it?"

"Your brother and his renegade friends will be the death of us all. I've spent the night tossing and turning with the knowledge we are one step from war with the humans. We can't afford war with the humans. And if that isn't enough, my senses tell me there is Old Magic being used close by.

"My skin is crawling from the spell casting."

Gitty went to the stove and pulled out a frying pan. She collected eggs from the icebox and sliced bread from the breadbox. Muttering under her breath, she proceeded to magic the eggs to cook and bread to toast. Fixing the food on the plate, she handed it to her father.

"Thank you. This should help."

"Why are you so determined *not* to war with the humans? We're superior to them in every way and should control this entire valley, not the other way around. They should be trying to get along with us." Gitty dropped her long frame into a chair opposite her father.

"The world doesn't always work the way you think it should, daughter. You must remember we're visitors here."

"Not if we own all the land."

Aethel looked up from his food. "If the humans don't wish to sell to us, how do you propose we get ownership of the land?"

She leaned back in the chair and looked at the ceiling, her mind churning, as she formulated a non-confrontational answer.

"Magic."

The clattering of the fork on the china plate rang through the kitchen.

"You would magic the inhabitants to turn over their land to you? What about when they awoke from the spell? What then?" Aethel's eyes had turned a steely gray as he fixed an angry glare on his daughter.

Gitty stared at her father. *What's happened to the fearless warrior of yesteryear who'd peered into the jaws of death and charged ahead anyway?*

"By the time these witless wonders came around, we'd own their property and they'd have to pay taxes to live on it. We'd be the rightful rulers of this land. What else matters?" She furrowed her brow in disbelief.

Aethel stood, set his plate in the kitchen sink and magicked it clean then turned to his offspring.

"Take yourself elsewhere for the day. I'm not sure I can control my anger enough *not* to destroy you. Don't show your face to me until the rise of the sun tomorrow." Fists clenched against his side, Aethel stomped from the kitchen.

Gitty smirked. *Just as well.* She retired to her room and rummaged in her clothing chest. Many months had passed since she'd ridden her horse. Today would be a perfect time to remedy the situation. She pulled the white chaps from the chest and lashed them on, grabbing her long duster and a white hat in case the skies opted to dump rain on her.

She tromped to the back porch and sat on a wooden chair, slipping into her riding boots. The night elf craftsman who'd created her gear had spent many months bleaching the leather to a sparkling white. Gitty had demanded the leathers be created the old way, by hand, not by magicking the material to the desired color.

She slammed the door and strode to the stables, covering the quarter acre quickly in her fury. Her father had grown weak in his time in this inconsequential valley, but she had not. She'd watched him succumb to the taming imposed by the council. No night raids for him, no. He'd sat by the fire reading the old texts, trying to apply their wisdom to the new situation.

She could have told him it wouldn't work but he didn't want to hear it.

Gitty swung up on the finely crafted saddle and yanked the reins to the bit of her mare, directing the animal to the driveway running by the castle. The sooner she was away from here the better. She touched her pouch to ensure there were coins for necessities. A quick kick to the mare's flanks and she galloped away from the mountain's top. By the time she returned, her plan would be set in motion, father or no father.

~ * ~

Conn rubbed his hands together and flew loop-de-loops in delight.

Cary pumped her wings, feeling the lack of use in her shoulder blades.

"Why are you so happy? I'm tired, hungry and I want to sleep in my own bed. I can sense we're close to the place we settled in but I'm not completely sure I can find it. Will you stop acting foolish and get us home?" She scowled Conn's direction.

"There's going to be a wa-a-a-r-r-r. There's going to be a wa-a-a-a-r-r-r."

Cary stopped mid-air, hovering. She grabbed Conn's arm and jerked him around to face her.

"You're an idiot. Don't you remember the last time these humans fought? There was bloodshed all around us. We nearly lost everyone we cared about!"

"Pshaw! This time the magical folks will win and these humans will be gone. We'll have control of the meadows and forests again." Conn danced a jig.

"CONN!!"

He stopped and turned to stare at Cary.

"What is your problem? This is good news for us all."

"You've been listening to that Morgan elf. *We* aren't from here. *We* know nothing about these humans, this land, the night elves...need I go on?"

Conn floated, winging lazy circles around Cary. "I have been listening to Morgan and I agree with him. The Others here are very backward. They're nearly the same as the Others we left back home. How could we not succeed here? Once the night elf clans conquer the valley, we'll have free reign to do what we want. Isn't it great?"

He zipped up and turned somersaults in the air.

Cary moved in the direction she thought the oak where they were staying grew. "All I want is to go home to Ireland. This place is different. They talk funny and no one really believes in us here. I'm homesick and I want to go home. I don't want to see these Others kill each other over pieces of land."

Conn shrugged his shoulders. He'd never really understood Cary's love of the land. Oh, sure, he loved his Ireland, but this land was green and there was much to be gained by starting new. Maybe he could conjure that big red travel thing which had brought them here. If he could just remember the conjuring spell...

~ * ~

Aethel sat on the ledge of his bedroom window peering in the direction of the meadow. He couldn't shake the image of Skye from his mind. She'd aged, but then so had he and she'd apparently married, as had he. The young warrior Terran, with firm jutting jaw, straight back and tenacity reminded Aethel so much of Skye, he'd bet his best stallion the young gnome was her son.

He found his heart aching with the need to touch her again and flinching a bit in jealousy. What would have happened had the two of them mated? Ah, but these were the meanderings of a life long past. It could never happen. Night elves married and mated with night elves and gnomes married and mated with gnomes. Some lines weren't crossed. It didn't matter if he'd loved Skye. There, the truth had been revealed.

Sure, his wife had been tall, lean and elegant, just like Gitty. Unlike Gitty, his Ella had possessed a kind heart and they'd grown to appreciate each other, but Aethel had not loved Ella. It saddened him to lose her when Morgan was born.

Seeing Skye again brought a rush of feelings he'd thought dead. Oh well, not much he could do now. Because of his two renegade children, the valley and its inhabitants, including Skye and her family, were in great danger.

Aethel stood and looked over the meadow. They might think him old...but it was up to him to prove them wrong and save the valley from their arrogance. He might have propagated them but he didn't have to like them.

It was a sad fact, but Aethel's children had become his enemy, and he was determined to win this war. More than the night elves and gnome lives depended on his success.

Chapter Ten

Everything about the scene before her was wrong. Scorched spots blackened the earth and marred nearby trees. Splintered branches littered the ground and the scuffmarks crisscrossing the forest floor hinted at recent activity. Reaching over her shoulder, she guided the tempered blade from its leather encasement and held the weapon in front of her.

The air wavered and Tiamoon froze in place, holding her breath. The flesh on her arms rose and hair on the back of her neck prickled. Magic had been used here recently. She moved leather-clad feet slowly, silently around the edge of the scuffed area. Her lungs ached for air and the side of her lip pulsed where she clamped down with her teeth.

Tia poked the shrubbery with her blade. Under a mulberry leaf, wings crumpled beneath a tiny body, lay an inert fae of the wood clan. Tia let go the breath she was holding. The sight was worse than she could possibly have imagined. Moving quickly, she reconnoitered the area and discovered eleven dead fae and one barely clinging to life.

She placed her blade on the ground and knelt at the male fae's side.

"Who did this to you?" She placed a leaf over the tiny one's body.

Very faintly, the male whispered. "Morgan."

She leaned her ear close to his mouth. "Who?"

"Morgan."

Buzzing about her head alerted her she was not alone. Again the annoying buzz sounds, and now, pinpricks of pain. Tiamoon tried tracking the sound with her eyes. Just when she thought she'd determined the source, a stab of pain would distract her.

"Stop! I'm not sure why you've targeted me but stop. I'm not the enemy."

She stood still as the oaks growing nearby, listening as the buzzing slowed to the swishing sounds of many tiny wings.

Two male fae flew to the front of her face and pointed lances her direction.

"Do not move, gnome. We've seen the damage you've inflicted here." The speaker swept an arm at the lifeless bodies scattered on the ground. "You may have had the upper hand with my kinfolk but I bring reinforcements and we won't be so blindly trusting."

Tia watched as a multitude of faeries appeared before her eyes. She sheathed her sword. Slow, measured steps took her to a stump where she opted to sit and allowed the emotion of the sight she'd stumbled upon to overtake her. A tear meandered down her cheek.

"Such waste; such destruction. Your poor kinfolk had no chance. This is the work of the night elves. I can only guess they stunned your warriors and dispatched them with no conscience."

The male faes darted looks at each other and continued to hold their lances on the seated gnome.

"You lie. You're trying to divert attention from yourself from the heinous act of murder!"

Multitudes of wings fluttered with the murmured agreement of the crowd.

Tia stood. "No. I was searching to find the elves before something like this occurred. I'm trying to stop them. Everyone in the valley will be in danger if they gain the upper hand and take over.

"I've no quarrel with you. I think we need to join forces against the night elves. If all the forest and meadow folk get together in a united front, we can make sure the valley stays ours. If we don't, we'll be subject to the whims of the night elves."

The two male fae lowered their lances and winged backward.

Tia watched as they drew several others from the throng and conferred among themselves. She could only hope her argument was strong. It was difficult to gauge the fae community. For the most part, they were very unreliable, concerned only with life's enjoyments. But many were deceived by this attitude and knew not what fearsome warriors they could be when their homes were endangered. Most magic had been gifted to others by the fae. The extent of their magical understanding had never been tested.

Tiamoon was not about to be the first to test the depths.

The two male fae winged to her, their lances, once again, pointed her direction.

"We can't trust your word. All we know is we came to help our kinsmen but found most of them dead and you hovering over the last one breathing. Your prowess with a sword is legend, gnome. It's not beyond reason to think you inflicted all this destruction.

"We will handle our own affairs and take care of our own families. It might be in your best interest to leave this valley. Word will spread and you won't be welcomed in any community."

Tia clenched her fists at her side. "Do you threaten me, fae?"

The throng of faeries buzzed forward pointing weapons her direction.

"Fine. I offered my sword to you and you refused. Don't call on me when you find yourselves under the grinding boots of the night elves. I take my leave."

She turned her back on the warriors, leaving and keeping to the edge of the woods. Her heart pounded and she ran a tongue over her dry lips. She was in a precarious position. The night elves would run roughshod over the inhabitants of the valley if something wasn't done, but her offer of services had met with rejection.

The fae community was suspicious of all outsiders, a fact Tiamoon knew. But she'd relied on her being part of the magical folk of the area to help her win their trust, an obvious mistake. This valley was in for a war like no other and everyone, except the night elves, stood to lose.

I'm not sure I can stand by and watch my people get slaughtered.

A solution was needed and soon. At the moment, Tiamoon wanted to get home without becoming the next victim in the fray.

~ * ~

Gitty galloped her stallion across the meadow to the edge of the verdant forest opposite her home. An old ally had been rumored to be in the area. Slowing her steed to a walk, she kept herself vigilant. The old growth woods could shield many an opponent. Her horse tugged at the reins and snorted impatiently. Halfway up the first hill, the stallion stopped and could not be coaxed to move one step further.

Gitty kicked his flanks but the beast would not budge. In an angry huff, she flung her right leg over the saddle and dismounted, turning to stare down the shaft of a highly sharpened sword. Startled ice-blue eyes rose to gaze into deep green orbs.

"Glade." The whispered name floated through the air.

"You'd best be careful, Gitty. Next time, your opponent might not be as taken with a blonde, blue-eyed amazon." His lips curled into a smile that reached his eyes.

He lowered his weapon and stepped forward, gathering her in his arms and crushing her lips beneath his.

Gitty sucked in a deep draught of air when he released her.

"What makes you think I wanted that?" She furrowed her brows at him.

A deep bubbling sound echoed beneath the forest's green canopy.

"Because, my love, you didn't fight me in the least and I still hold you in my arms."

She tried to wiggle free but the arms holding her gently tightened as her captor pulled her close.

"I won't lose this opportunity to make up for lost time, love."

Glade lowered his lips and stopped just above hers.

Gitty waited but he moved no further. When she could stand it no longer she reached up and closed the space between them, slipping her arms around his neck.

He groaned deep in his throat as she pulled from him.

"It has been too long Gitty Saun, too long. I've missed your sharp tongue and quick wit. But most of all I've missed holding you in my arms. How have you been?"

"After all these years you ask now, Glade? Where did you go? Why didn't you contact me? You could have magicked a message to me. What happened?"

The dark-haired night elf pulled back, grabbed the reins of the horse and slipped his arm around the blonde amazon's waist.

"This is not a safe haven. I'll explain once we've arrived at camp."

He led her through a maze of trees and bushes, paths twisting, turning and doubling back on themselves. Just about the time Gitty felt truly lost, the thick forest opened to reveal a camp with many traveling caravans.

Curious eyes watched the striking couple enter the campsite.

Glade led the stallion and Gitty to a wooden caravan. Brightly painted designs covered the outside. Stairs descended from the door to the forest's floor and Gitty noted the wooden wheels were covered in rubber. Glade tied the steed to the side of the vehicle near a filled water bucket. He slid his hand beneath Gitty's arm and directed her to the caravan's door.

"Go inside. I'll bring hay for your stallion and give him a quick brushing."

Gitty turned to protest but Glade had disappeared.

She climbed the steps and entered the box on wheels. Surprised at the space within, she sat at a table and looked out a portal to the outside. The floor of the caravan was covered in hand woven rugs. Colorful pillows dotted the table benches and hurricane lamps hung from metal hooks protruding from the walls.

Glade came through the opening and slid next to her.

"What do you think of my home?"

"This is your home?"

"Has been for the last twenty years."

"I thought your family had a castle in the old country."

Glade heaved a sigh, his shoulders drooping. "We did. For millennia we had a castle with lands, rivers and towns. But the last one-hundred-fifty years have taken their toll on our land and clan. With more than a dozen wars happening, the last World War causing the most damage, my people have had to flee our homeland."

"Couldn't you just fight back?"

"We have magic like you but these humans, these Others, have weapons so destructive we were outmatched. Before we could organize and protect our lands, they had bombed the earth from beneath us. We fled over the North Pole and through Canada to come back here. Some of our southern cousins recalled these caravans from the early wandering night elves and created them for us here. They're mobile and contain all we need to survive. They'll do."

Gitty looked around. A shy smile touched her lips. "Yes, they will."

Glade gazed at her porcelain face. "Gitty, my love?"

"Hhmm?"

"What is it you want from me?"

She turned wide eyes on him. "What makes you think I want something?"

Glade burst into laughter. "Because I know you. We had a great love--once--but I've never known you to pine for a man, and *need* is not in your vocabulary."

Gitty felt heat rush to her cheeks. She hated it when Glade foresaw her every move. It was one of the reasons she'd walked away from him. He knew her too well.

"Okay, fine. My brother Morgan is gathering troops around him for a takeover of the valley."

"I was aware he was purchasing land from the Others at a rapid pace but I didn't know he was serious about a war."

Gitty nudged him to move and scooted from the table to pace the small room.

"I'm not really sure he wants to go to war but he wants to appear powerful so others will respect him."

"That's a dangerous undertaking, isn't it?" Glade frowned.

"Yes and he has no experience commanding anybody, let alone a bunch of young night elves out for blood."

Glade leaned back and crossed his arms. "So why are you so concerned? You have no love for the humans of your valley."

Gitty turned a lopsided grin his direction. "Because *I* want to control the valley and I *do* have experience commanding a group of blood-thirsty night elves."

He chuckled. "Aye, you do. Well, Gitty, my love, would it be worth my skin?"

She tilted her head and looked at him from beneath her eyelashes.

"Aye, Glade, aye."

Chapter Eleven

Smoke curled lazily from the chimney as Tiamoon padded toward home. She could only hope Thomas had decided to leave and quit living off the kindness of her mother.

The gate creaked as she opened it, reminding her yet again of the need to oil the hinges. She pushed open the cottage door and was met with the spicy aroma of mulled cider. Her stomach growled and Tia made for the stool by the fire.

She shed herself of the blade and scabbard, standing them next to the hearth before sitting to peel off her boots and stick her feet near the fire. *What am I to do?*

A hand reached around and placed a mug of the warmed cider in her grasp.

Tia turned and looked up at her mother. "Thanks."

"What troubles you, daughter?"

She sipped from the cup and contemplated.

"I came across a scene so horrific today, I can barely think on it."

Skye felt a shiver course down her back. "What would that be?"

"I set out to find the night elves. I'd heard from some of the river faeries Morgan and his cronies were traipsing through the woods destroying all in their path. I was wary, at first, but was forced to re-examine what I know about Morgan. He's no stomach for bloodshed, only for wooing the ladies.

"I started at the south woods and crept my way through the wood nymphs' glen. As I neared the woodland faeries home, I realized I couldn't hear any of the birds singing. No insects were buzzing and the air around me pressed heavy on my skin.

"I slowed my pace and silenced my footsteps. The ground in front of me was scorched and several trees had blackened spots on the bark. Branches lay broken on the ground. I let my eyes sweep the landscape and they fell on the most horrible of scenes. Scattered about the ground were dead faeries, their wings and clothes burnt, weapons scattered. I noted one male fae in front of me struggling to breath. I leaned down to see if I could help and he whispered one name...Morgan."

Tia looked up at her mother, eyes spilling tears. "Mum. They had no chance. Morgan killed them all! How could this happen in our valley?"

Skye dropped into the seat by the fire. *How, indeed.* She would have to find a way to contact Aethel and incorporate his help. The humans could be expected to fight and kill each other. It seemed to be what they did best, but the valley folk were better than that. They were supposed to get along and help each other. This... slaughter was unthinkable.

Skye placed her hand on her daughter's shoulder, feeling the young woman's body shake with emotion.

"Is there more to this, Labhoise?"

A deep sigh escaped the young gnome warrior. "Yes. They accused me of causing the deaths of the wee ones."

Blue eyes filled to the brim with tears looked pleadingly at Skye.

"How could they possibly think I would harm any of them? I offered to help them find Morgan, but they told me they didn't want my help and to stay away from them.

"Mum, what am I to do? I can't just stand by and let them be massacred."

Skye pulled Tia into her arms and held the young woman, stroking her red locks and allowing her to cry herself out.

"Whatever we attempt, child, we must do under cover of night. We'll protect our forest and meadow from those who would destroy the lands and us. This is not done. We won't lie down and let them annihilate us."

~ * ~

Dorinda gave the table one more swipe with the wet cloth and stepped around the back of the bar. Her keen eye noted the strange foreigners who'd started hanging out didn't come in as often as they once had.

The dandy Morgan was in almost every night, but all the others like him had quit appearing in her pub. She wasn't too disappointed. Oh, yeah, she liked the income, but the tall fair-haired men made the local boys nervous and caused more fights than she wanted to referee.

The women loved the attention but soon realized most of the foreigners had little or no money and were looking for a sugar mama.

It was while she'd been waiting to use the one restroom she'd heard the local females talking.

"Did you hear that braggart Morgan tonight?"

"No, what's he done now?"

"He was talking about buying the Thompson's farm. I didn't even know Bill and Joyce were selling. Did you?"

"No. Wait a minute. Didn't he say he'd bought the Williams' land last week?"

"Yeah. He did. What's he up to? He has enough money to buy a bunch of farms in the valley but can't buy his own drinks? I've had it with him. Beside, that new guy he brought in, the one called Glade? Well, he's really much cuter, anyway."

Dorinda stepped behind the door when the two women left the bathroom. She watched as they walked back to the restaurant. The news she'd just heard was very disturbing. She'd investigate first thing in the morning when the bank opened.

Morning arrived in a blaze of sunshine. Dorinda gazed out her kitchen window at glowing golden rays. She stood at the sink finishing the morning's dishes. With Mr. Florence gone, there were only two residents at her inn and they were leaving this morning for Eugene. When she'd made mention she needed to do some banking in town, Mr. Jones offered to give her a lift to the city. She'd take the afternoon bus home and arrive in time to get the bar ready for the evening crowd, if there was one.

She donned her going-to-town dress and grabbed her spring hat. You could never be sure in the early months of the season if it would rain or not so Dorinda brought an umbrella and a slicker. She stopped by her desk and opened the business drawer, retrieving a slip of paper which she stuffed in her bag. Quick stepping to the front door, she locked the handle and crawled in the passenger seat of Mr. Jones' business coupe.

Conversation was polite and brief on the way in, each rider enjoying the passing scenery.

Dorinda thanked the gentleman when he dropped her at the bank, wishing him luck on his business trip and inviting him to stay at the inn should he pass that way again.

She straightened up and marched boldly through the front door and up to the receptionist.

"I'd like to see the president of the bank, please."

The older woman peered over her glasses at Dorinda and raised an eyebrow.

"May I ask what this is about?"

"No. I wish to discuss personal business with the president."

The woman rose from her seat and pointed at a straight-backed wooden chair positioned at right angles to the desk.

"Take a seat. I'll see if he's available."

Dorinda fretted with her umbrella, turning the handle in her fingers and chewing her bottom lip as she listened to the clicking sounds of the receptionist's heels on the bank's marble flooring. She noted the smell of Murphy's oil and let a smile slip to her lips. She used the same oil on the pub's bar top. She started at the brusque voice interrupting her thoughts.

"Mr. Clive will see you now."

The receptionist frowned as she pointed to the partially opened door titled 'President'.

Dorinda nodded at the receptionist. "Thank you."

One hour later, Dorinda emerged from the President's office, agitated at the news she'd discovered. She felt pushed by the urgency of the situation to contact all the farmers and businessmen in her town. A meeting had to be held as soon as she could possibly get people together. The face of the valley was changing and not in a positive way.

~ * ~

Glade sat up and stretched his arms. He'd have to remember to purchase material for the women to create more rugs for his floor. There wasn't much difference from the earth's ground and his caravan's rug covered wooden floor; both were hard and cold.

Rising up and quietly slipping out the door, he made his way to the stream to splash cold water on his face. His heart pounded wildly as he thought of the silken haired she-elf sleeping in his bed. Were he to settle into monogamy, Gitty would be his first choice. She, on the other hand, was only interested in power and had made that abundantly clear when they spoke last evening.

He'd watched her eyes glitter with the thought of owning the valley below this mountain, controlling all the inhabitants. He sucked in a breath when the ice-cold snow runoff hit his face. His whole body shivered as he splashed more water against his skin. He needed his wits about him this morning as he gathered his clan to share the decision he'd come to last night.

What he had said in the council meeting was true; his clan was tired of moving from place to place and desired nothing more than twenty or so acres away from the humans to create their own town and settle. What he was about to do was throw them into the heat of battle; the reward was the entire mountain. Once Gitty conquered all the other clans with his help and bought all the property the humans had, she would sit on her hill and rule as the queen she fancied herself.

"Morning, love."

Glade twisted to face the silver-haired night elf. Sunlight backlit her hair, casting a glow about her face.

"Morning. Did you sleep well?"

"Yes, but as I told you last night, you could have lain with me."

Glade smiled as he ran his hand down her cheek. "No. I will only lay with you if we are mated."

Gitty humphed. "That's not going to happen."

Glade grabbed the bottom of his tunic and blotted the excess water from his face.

"You made that brutally apparent last night. Where are you headed today?"

The pair moved in the direction of the base camp.

"I think I'll head to the village and start asking around. I'm sure there are some of the Others who haven't been approached by Morgan yet. If I can buy their land before he makes an offer, I'll be on my way to owning all I see."

Gitty leaned over and placed a kiss on Glade's cheek. "Good luck with your meeting today. I'll send a messenger bird with our next move. Thanks for the great night's sleep."

With the flash of a smile and wave of a hand, she swung up in the saddle of her stallion and reined him to leave the camp. Glade had magicked the directions back to the valley into the steed's ear the night before.

Glade watched her leave, a strange sensation settling over him. The sight of her back felt very final. He shivered and moved to the caravan. A good breakfast then a gathering of his clansmen. Today, they would begin their future.

Chapter Twelve

Dorinda got off the bus and scurried home. She had just enough time to start her letters to the local farmers. She knew ten days was almost too short to ask folks to come to a meeting, but the information she'd received at the bank put an urgency to her task. She gathered her writing tools. If business were slow tonight, she'd be able to get all the letters done and posted by tomorrow's mail.

The quiet life everyone once knew was about to go up in flames.

~ * ~

Skye sat at the head of the table; Aethel faced her from the opposite end. The last two weeks in the valley folk lives had taken a decided turn for the worse. Reports were trickling in from survivors of raids on outlying communities. Forest gnome clans, wood nymph clans and even the laconic leprechauns were taking up arms. The survivors straggled in to the meadow and collapsed in the homes of cousins.

After Skye's third cousin, a forest gnome, had stumbled to her cottage with news of total annihilation of two communities by night elves in forest green leathers, she called this emergency meet.

Tension filled the room and weapons rattled in nervous apprehension.

Skye stood. "Thank you all for taking the time from the protection of your homes to be here. I know most of you are not in the mood to talk peace but how about we talk cooperation?"

Protests passed among the seated participants and glares were directed Aethel's direction.

Skye called for silence. "We, too, have heard the stories from survivors, my own cousin, Etain from the forest clan, watched the invaders tear down her village and burn the trees. She heard them laugh about leveling the northern clan's homes. Had she not been hunting mushrooms, she would have perished."

The company of magical creatures rose from their chairs and moved Aethel's direction.

"Stop!" Skye held her blade with both hands in front of her, chair on the ground where she'd jumped up. "The next soul who moves will be cut in two."

"Why shouldn't we slice him in pieces and hang the bits from all the trees? It's *his* people who are doing this."

Skye inched forward. "Do any of you doubt my word?"

The room was filled with mumbles and grumbling.

"Then set yourselves down and listen. If you can't or won't listen, I'll confiscate your weapons or, better yet, let you try to handle this alone. How long do you think you'll last against several clans of rogue night elves? A day? A week? How long?"

She slammed her sword on the table and planted her hands on her hips.

The clan members put away their weapons and scowling, sat in the assorted chairs, grudgingly giving Skye their attention.

"Thank you. I will vouch for Aethel."

He snapped his head up and stared at the warrior gnome.

"I have known this particular night elf longer than most of you have been on this planet. His heart is pure and his intentions honorable. He can no more choose his heritage than your or I but this man...this night elf guarded this valley from outside sources long before your families settled here.

"When my cousin described the invaders of her village, I knew immediately what we were facing. Glade has been true to his word. He and his clansmen are terrorizing the mountains and valley.

"Singularly, we stand no chance of saving our community. However if we unite, pool our resources and plan wisely, I believe we can defeat these marauders and run them out of our lives forever.

"Who's with me?"

Silence permeated the room. Each clan leader glanced at the other.

"Fine. Then you can kiss your loved ones and dig holes in the ground to be buried because alone we won't make it."

Skye grabbed her blade and headed to the door.

"What about him?"

She spun around to face the speaker. "Who?"

"The traitor night elf."

Skye walked to Aethel and placed her hand on his shoulder, ignoring the spark she felt flame in her heart.

"You call him a traitor; I call him a hero. He could have easily decided to throw his sword in with the mercenaries burning their way through our homes, but chose instead to stand up and be counted with us. His life is in danger every moment of the day because of his choice.

"Can you say the same?"

Low conversations buzzed in the air until Fergus of the river gnomes stood.

"I'll throw my sword in with you. But only if you lead, Skye."

Heads around the room nodded.

Skye stood straight and lifted her chin. "Fine. I'll take the lead on this but there is one hard and fast rule."

"What?"

"Do *not* question my orders or my authority. The first time either is put in doubt, I'll walk away and leave you to your own devices. Are we clear?"

"Aye."

"Form the circle."

The clan heads circled, facing the center, and placed their blade tip on top of the next.

Skye was the last to place her blade on the wheel of steel.

"These blades will fight for heart and home, until this land is again our own."

"To the death!"

Skye put up her free hand. "No. To life!"

"TO LIFE!"

The cry echoed through the building. When the swords had been sheathed and clan leaders filed out, Aethel stood from his seat.

"You took a huge chance today, Skye. Why?"

She gazed into the blue eyes which set her pulse racing. "Because I truly believe you are a man of honor, Aethel. You could have decided to throw your lot with the mercenaries. The one thing I didn't mention in the meeting was my cousin described a she elf with flowing silver hair in white leathers. You and I know there is only one person who fits that description."

"Gitty."

"Yes. But I didn't want these chieftains to have that bit of information. They wouldn't have united. They don't understand children who don't obey their parents. In our culture, it isn't tolerated or understood.

"Will you be able to help us even if it means working against your own kin?"

Aethel moved close to Skye. "Yes. I have love for my children but I don't have to like them. I do, however, wish to protect those I love and like. Will you allow me that honor?"

Skye felt the heat rush to her cheeks. It'd been a long time since any man had brought such personal feelings to the top of her heart. As much as she tried, denying her feelings for Aethel was going to be near impossible. She still loved him as much as ever.

She cleared her throat. "Thank you for helping our community."

Aethel leaned over and picked up her hand, placing a gentle kiss on the top.

"My pleasure."

Skye slipped her hand from his, knowing her cheeks were blazing red.

"Won't you be in danger if you go home?"

"Probably. I'll bunk at the inn until we've secured our valley. What about you? You surely can't go home with Glade and his clan roaming the woods."

"Hhmm. I hadn't thought of that. Well…"

"Allow me to pay for a room for you at the inn, too."

"Aethel…"

He smiled at her dangerous tone. She was always independent and determined to make her own way. It was a trait he admired.

"As you just pointed out to me, the danger out there is real."

Skye huffed out a deep breath. "Fine. But know I'll have the innkeeper marking down the costs so I can repay you."

Aethel smiled. "Of course."

Skye grabbed her sword and sheathed it. "Let's go. I find myself sporting a great hunger. You?"

"Aye. The innkeeper is quite a good cook. The food will fill the belly and please the soul."

Marching out the door and down the dusty road, the unlikely duo headed to the small community of humans. The war had begun.

Chapter Thirteen

Gitty sat in the caravan reveling in the tales Glade was spinning of his conquests of the small towns and villages.

"We galloped in and, blades whirling, took down all the menfolk. As you would expect, some of the women were in gear and fighting back so my kinsmen felt no remorse in taking them down too.

"Ahhh, Gitty, it was a sight. The first hut was set ablaze and the others went up in the blink of an eye. What a vision! I believe we'll be in control of this land in less than six moons. Taking their land is as easy as swirling a finger through water.

"Our deal is still in place, right?"

Gitty stretched her legs under the table and pushed her arms over her head.

"Of course. I just set the paperwork in motion to buy this mountain for you. When the bank manager approves the sale and issues the money to the human, we'll own everything you see.

"Will that keep your kinsmen happy?"

"Yes. Some of them are beginning to grumble a bit. They want a challenge in battle. So far none of these outposts have provided them a contest worthy of their talents."

"Tell them to have a little patience. By the fall of the first leaves, they can start wooing their sweethearts and planning little warriors."

Smiling, she rose from the table. "I've enjoyed the tales of valor, love, but I must go home. Can't have your kinfolk talking, can we?"

Glade blocked her path and snatched her into his arms. He leaned down and pulled her earlobe gently into his mouth. Releasing the soft tissue, he whispered.

"No, can't have the neighbors telling stories out of school."

Gitty moaned and turned her face to his accepting his lips. Fire raged through her body, tingling her skin and taking away her breath. She pushed him away.

"I-I have to go."

She rushed out the door and leapt on her stallion, galloping away from the camp to the sound of laughter chasing her out of the woods.

~ * ~

Dorinda stood in front of the assorted group, feeling her knees threatening to give way. She cleared her throat.

"Thank you all for showing up on such short notice. We don't often get together like this, but what I learned recently made me feel this was something of an emergency."

"What is it, Dorinda? You finally getting hitched?"

A ripple of laughter circled the room. Dorinda couldn't help but smile.

"No, Ollie. There's still no man in my life. You volunteering?"

More laughter.

"Okay, okay. I'm sure some of you have noticed we have had quite a few new folk in our community."

Heads bobbed up and down in agreement.

"Now, normally, as a business woman I wouldn't say that is bad, but what I've noticed is these folks seem to be flashing quite a bit of cash around."

"And that's bad?"

The group snickered.

"No, Dave, it's not unless you start thinking about how many of your neighbors are no longer in this room. Anybody seen the Thompsons lately? How about the Williams or the McCoys? Tell me, who else is missing?"

The gathered group started looking around and murmuring. Realization started to dawn on the members present.

"Dorinda, what's happening?"

"I made a trip to town to make my final payment on the inn and restaurant and got the bank president to talking. In the last three months, ten folk have sold their places to the family up on the hill--the Sauns. Most of the sales went to the young man, Morgan, but it seems the girl, Gitty, is now starting to purchase land.

"Have any of you been approached?"

Several hands rose in the air.

"Do you see what's happening here? If we don't watch out, they'll own every bit of land around here and all our hard work will be for nothing. To be honest with you, I don't think I want to live here if they become the main landowners.

"I've watched that young man when he comes in the pub. It makes my skin crawl just to think about it. If that doesn't scare you, think about this...Morgan Saun had no problem running a sword through a stranger who insulted his lady. What would he do to someone who hunted on his land or tried to plant wheat in his valley?

"We need to hang on to our property. If they're bound and determined to buy it, make them wait. What's the big hurry?

"Okay. I've said my piece. Who wants lunch?"

Dorinda watched as the members of her community bunched in small groups. She might not be able to completely stop the sale of her valley, but the Sauns weren't going to walk in and take over. Not if she had anything to say about it.

~ * ~

Tiamoon moved her feet slowly and watched every movement she made. Whispers had the night elves planning a raid on this settlement tonight. She, Terran and a dozen of her family clan had volunteered to patrol the perimeter of the village.

The shadows at the edge of the meadow stretched long into the forest backdrop. Every movement set Tia's teeth on edge. Her muscles ached from the intense control and her hands itched to be fighting.

"Tia." The whisper reverberated off the pines.

"What?" She couldn't stop the irritation in her voice. Of all people, Terran should know better than to try and communicate when they were on silent watch.

"I need to answer the call of nature."

"Now?"

"Yes."

"Then be as quiet as you can."

Muffled steps crushed against the needle strewn forest floor. Tia's ears keened to hear any unusual movements.

"AAAAHHHHH!!!!"

"TERRAN!"

The sound of her brother's cry set Tia racing in the direction she recalled him going.

"TERRAN!"

Thundering hoof beats came toward her. In her quick estimate, she guessed a dozen horses were heading her direction.

"INTRUDERS! INTRUDERS!"

She clutched her sword to her chest and nitched against a large pine. As the hoof beats rumbled closer, she muttered. "Please forgive me."

Turning the blade side away from the animal's shin, she grabbed the blade and swung the handle side at the animal with all her might.

The horse stumbled, sending the rider to the ground. Behind him two others went down. Tia rushed out and finished the night elf with a swift blow. She quickly glanced at the figure on the ground and caught her breath. She'd just put a sword through Glade. The ashen color of his skin indicated her prowess had not lessened since the last war.

Not having the time to think further on the situation, Tiamoon soon dispatched two other elven warriors. She ran between the trees to the village. Slowing her pace to a trot, she noted smoke rising from the chimneys and lights in the windows. She spun to face the remaining warriors headed this direction but heard no hoof beats echoing through the pines.

Tiamoon slowed her breathing and narrowed her eyes. A movement in the trees set her teeth to grinding as she tensed to fight. Three forms headed her direction. Two upright figures dragged a limp form between them. Tia's muscles went into overdrive.

She moved silently toward the trio.

"Tia?" A whisper pierced her concentration.

"Frey?"

"Yes. We've Terran and he's hurt bad. We need to get him to the healer."

She ran to the cottage known to house the healer and knocked on the door.

A sliver of light cut the darkness of the night as the gnome witch peeked out the door.

"What is it you need?"

"My brother is badly wounded. We need your healing powers."

"Bring him to me."

Tia ran to relieve one of the warriors. Moving with urgency, the gnomes made their way to the healer's cottage. Directed to a cot by the fire, Terran was laid on the straw mattress.

The healer turned to the warriors, centering her gaze on Tiamoon.

"Go. I will send for you when I have ministered to him."

"But..."

"Go. Your bond to him is too strong. It will interfere with my healing efforts."

Tia glared at the healer but left the cottage. She was a warrior, not a healer, and could respect the witch's need to perform her magic in private.

When the sun rose above the eastern mountains, a small child came and tugged on the tail of Tia's cloak.

"You must come to the healer's."

She hurried to follow the child and knocked before entering the cottage of the witch.

The woman looked up. "I'm truly sorry but they damaged his life source. I could do nothing to save him."

Tia looked at the broken form of her brother. She clenched her jaw, spun on her heel and left the healer's cottage. Barging past the gathered warriors, she barked orders.

"Give Terran a warrior's burial then head to your homes. The night has been long and we need rest before the next attack."

The men glanced warily at each other. Many had fought with her in the last war and knew this look did not bode well for the enemy. Many night elves would lose their lives to pay for the death of Tiamoon's brother.

Chapter Fourteen

Morgan paced the living room end to end. His deal on the Huff land had fallen through and for no reason he could fathom. He'd offered them more money than they could hope to get in a lifetime, yet just as they were about to agree to his terms, they changed their mind. The same situation occurred with the Millers down by the stream. If he didn't know better, he'd swear someone was undermining him. *Gitty?*

Scuffing across the floor in house boots on her feet, she meandered through to the kitchen, an enigmatic smile on her face. She hummed a Celtic tune she recalled her mother singing years earlier.

"What are you so happy about?" Morgan scowled at her.

"Why not? From what I hear, the forest elves are ridding the surrounding mountains of all the worthless creatures usurping our land."

Morgan stared at his sister. "What did you just say?"

Gitty rolled her eyes. "The forest elves are ridding the mountains of all the scum. Dragons, Morgan, don't you ever read?"

"Why? Won't make me rich."

"Seems you're not getting that way by your own means. Maybe reading will help you become the noble landowner you think you should be." She smirked his direction.

"I knew it! *You're* the one who's undermining my deals." He shot toward her, fury overcoming common sense.

Before Morgan could reach Gitty, she'd pulled a knife and held it at his throat, the blade inches from his Adam's apple.

"Don't tempt me, little brother. I've always wanted to be an only child. If your deals aren't working out, it's not because I'm undermining them. It's because you're a poor negotiator. I'm not experiencing problems."

He backed away and shot her a dirty look.

"If father were here, he'd tell you to back off. As the heir apparent, it's your duty to support me and my efforts."

Gitty's brows furrowed as she stared at her brother. She broke into laughter and walked away. "But he isn't here, is he? In fact, I haven't seen him in several weeks, Morgan. Have you?"

Morgan gazed out the window and mulled over Gitty's statement. She was right. He hadn't seen his father in several weeks. He walked back to the master bedroom and entered. The bed was properly made and a light layer of dust covered the furniture tops. Opening the wardrobe,

Morgan noted Aethel's riding boots were missing and his leathers appeared to be gone. He quick-stepped his way to the stables. Several fighting blades used by Aethel were missing, as was the thoroughbred mare he always rode.

If Aethel was gone then...he liked the idea of being the head of the house.

Gitty passed him on her way to the barns.

"Don't get any wild ideas about being the boss."

He whipped around. "What?"

"You had that dreamy look on your face like when you think you're going to get your way. Father is still in the area, just not here right now. I've seen him come in, change his clothing and leave. He usually checks to see if either of us is here.

"I believe, little brother, he fears us. If your buying deals are falling apart, our own father maybe responsible. What will you do if he's the one spoiling your plans? Kill him?"

Morgan growled. "I wouldn't be the first or the last to commit patricide, I suspect. I need to regroup. Where are you going?"

Gitty flipped her hair over her shoulder. "None of your business. Don't wait up. I'll be home late." She trotted through the stable opening, reappearing on her steed, and galloped down the driveway.

Morgan fumed as he stomped into the house, slamming the door in his wake.

He could sense Gitty was scheming against him and now he had to contend with his father conspiring against him, too? *What to do? What to do?*

"Well, pacing the floor here won't get things done. Maybe there's a young maiden new to the valley who'll appreciate my attentions. A bit of mead will help clear the brain and set the mind to working. That's what I'll do...go to the pub."

Grasping his night cloak, Morgan swung the cape about his shoulders and headed to the barn. He'd find a solution to his situation at the pub and things would go his way in the morning...just like always.

~ * ~

Gnomes, leprechauns and clans of fair night elves tromped in and out of the inn. Dorinda hadn't seen this much business in her family's restaurant, well, ever. During the evening hours, magical folk she'd grown up hearing the tales of came in for food and meetings. Her back rooms were beginning to resemble war rooms. Maps were constantly being unfolded and lines followed by fingers. Murmured conversations soon overtook the music from the radio. When she entered the room with beverages, the dialogues would cease until she left. No matter. Dorinda was thrilled to know the valley where she resided was guarded by the magic folk.

She started leaving plates out on the hearth at night and at the back door. Let the people talk. She knew she was ensuring her safety.

During the day, the farmers and villagers began to stop by and keep her posted on the offers being made by the tall blonde female and male newcomers. Offers met with negative answers.

But of all the wonders in her world, Dorinda was most fascinated by the unusual couple residing in her inn. She tried not to stare, but they brought looks to themselves from everyone.

It had been a month since she'd held the meeting with the village folk and the tall gent and tiny lady in leather clothing sat at a table in her restaurant speaking in low tones. Dorinda watched them, a spike of envy touching her heart. The pair were obviously in love, but something about their conversation suggested they held the worries of the world on their shoulders.

She came over to fill their water glasses.

"Excuse me, miss?" The gentleman's blue eyes held her attention.

"Dorinda, sir. How can I help you?"

He glanced at his companion and she nodded her head.

"You believe in the wee folk, don't you?"

"Yes. My mum was from the old country."

His smile sparkled lighting up his face. "Good. Could you spare my companion and me some time after you close tonight?"

"Sure. I can meet you in the sitting room around 10:00 pm if you wish."

"Perfect."

Dorinda watched as the two held hands. Her curiosity was wildly peaked. If she could only make it until ten without exploding...

~ * ~

Gitty tore through the forest. She hadn't heard from Glade in several days. He always sent a messenger bird after a successful battle and she hadn't heard a thing. Her stomach ached with worry. Slowing her steed, she pulled him to a stop and dismounted. She tied him to the nearest tree opting to walk the rest of the way to the caravan camp.

She followed the trail she'd memorized, breathing easier as the forest opened to the clearing. But the scene unfolding before her struck fear in her heart. The fire pit was black and dark. There were no caravans to be seen anywhere and by the disturbed dirt on the forest floor; the inhabitants had left in a hurry. Gitty ran to the spot where Glade's caravan had stood. Jammed into the ground through his green jerkin was his bloodied sword. Next to the sword stood his riding boots covered in blood.

Gitty sucked air into her lungs. Dropping to her knees, her fingers trembled as she reached out to the boots.

"No." The word whooshed from her mouth.

Snapping twigs alerted her to the presence of another. She looked up to see a haggard-faced, young forest night elf.

"Twelve went out, one came back. Keep your mountain and your wretched valley. It's not worth the price. He loved you more than any other woman and would have presented you many healthy sons. You wasted his life."

The young warrior spit on the ground next to her, turned on his heel and disappeared into the towering pines.

Gitty sat on her heels, determined to be strong, but the moment her hand touched the soft, green leather jerkin, she broke down and wept, the sighing wind through the pine boughs harmonizing with her keening wails.

It was at that moment any compassion felt by the she night elf disappeared.

Chapter Fifteen

Cary and Conn hid beneath the oak their wings shaking in fear.

"So you want to stay? For what? To spend the rest of your life hiding in a tree?"

Dozens of footfalls trampled past the oak and down the road.

Conn buzzed to the center of the room. "I'm not afraid. I just didn't want them to find you."

Cary narrowed her eyes at him. "You're a fool and a liar. What I wouldn't give to find that big red thing that dropped us here and fly away home."

Conn crossed his arms and lifted his head. "I'm not a liar. I'm not afraid."

The ground next to their tree rumbled and rocked the roots of the tree.

Cary screamed and flew to Conn's arms. "What is it? Are we going to die?"

Conn shook her from him and winged his way to the tree's opening. He peeked out the door. Turning, he flashed Cary a huge smile.

"Your magic seems to work just as well here as it did back home."

She furrowed her brows. "What are you talking about? I haven't cast a spell in many moons."

He wiggled his brows. "That big red thing is outside the door and the mangy mutt is running around sniffing. You ready to leave?"

Before he could blink his eyes, Cary had zipped past him and found the opening in the red thing. Recalling the thunderous, rowdy crowd of warriors who'd just passed by, Conn was a wing beat behind her.

He'd had enough adventure for one lifetime.

~ * ~

Morgan swaggered into the pub and reconnoitered the room. There were no night elves, no gnomes, no magic folk at all in the inn. The only woman at the bar was a grandmotherly type drinking cola.

He sauntered to the bar, removed his cloak and sat on a stool. Dorinda appeared and walked toward him.

"He's not welcome here, innkeeper."

The deep voice boomed through the empty room.

Morgan swiveled his chair to look upon a familiar face.

"Father. Since when do you give orders in this place?" A sneer marred the young night elf's chiseled features.

"Since the council gave me the power over all things in the valley and mountains. We've watched you try and steal what these humans have worked so hard to earn by playing to their sense of security. No longer, Morgan. You are not welcome on these premises. Your presence is offensive to all creatures magical and nonmagical.

"When you took the life of an Other without regard..."

"But *he* offended my companion and *he* is the one who issued the challenge." Morgan smirked, his knowledge of the rules of dueling well honed.

"Truth that may well be, but you could also tell from his ways and clothing he was not of this time."

Morgan shrugged. "I can't help it if he didn't know where he was."

"And that attitude is what has gotten you banned. Until this generation has grandchildren or has passed on, you will confine yourself to the castle grounds starting now."

Standing with his hand on his blade, the young night elf glared at his father.

"Are you going to enforce this decision?"

Aethel stood tall. "If you force me, I'll do whatever it takes to obey the council's decree. Don't push me, Morgan. I *will* cross swords with you and I'll win."

The air crackled with electricity and the two night elves faced each other. Morgan dropped his hand from his sword.

"This is a poor excuse for a proper pub anyway. I'll find my entertainment elsewhere." He snatched his cloak and stormed from the room.

Dorinda watched the older night elf melt away from the room. She looked up to see if Betty needed another cola only to find the seat empty. As the time was nearing ten, she locked the front door and started to clean up.

At the appointed time, Dorinda joined Skye and Aethel in the dining room. The three sat at a table staring at each other.

"What is it you wish to talk to me about?" Dorinda's voice wavered.

Skye smiled and gently touched her hand. "Don't be afraid. We're not here to harm anyone. We've watched you with the Others. You sense things they don't and I suspect you have the magic about you."

Dorinda felt the heat rush to her cheeks. How could this small woman see so well?

"Uhm, yes. It's strong in my family. My grandmother was a healer back in Ireland before we came here. I've been taught the old ways since I was a child."

"Aha! I knew I'd been feeling old magic in the air." Aethel rose from the chair and began to pace. "Are there many other humans with this power?"

Dorinda shook her head. "No. I'm afraid once I'm gone the old magic will die. No one in this country believes as I do and I don't believe they want to. They're too busy trying to survive in the here and now."

Aethel stopped pacing and stood behind Skye. "We asked you here to be an ambassador for the Others until the uprising has been quelled."

Dorinda sat back in her chair. *Me? An ambassador?*

Skye reached a hand out and touched the innkeeper's lightly. "You know that Aethel and his kin are night elves, right?"

"I guessed."

"I'm a gnome. While originally of the forest clan, I moved to the meadow and joined them when I wed. There are also wood nymphs, leprechauns and wee folk in the surrounding areas. We need an advocate who can make the Others, the humans, understand our plight. I know most humans in this country don't believe in us but they seem to listen to you.

"Will you speak for us?"

Sucking air into her lungs, Dorinda's only answer was a large smile.

Aethel patted Skye gently on the back. "I told you she would."

Skye rolled her eyes and huffed. "Men."

Aethel turned his attention to Dorinda. "The worst of the uprising has passed but there might be pockets of resistance to the peace plan we've set in place. We need you and your kind to be wary and let us know when unusual happenings occur. We'll send out our warriors to keep control of the few. I promise no human will be harmed."

Dorinda looked to the earnest faces of her guests. "How can I say no?"

"Then it is done." Aethel patted Skye's shoulder.

"It's done." Skye nodded her agreement.

"It's done." Dorinda agreed.

~ * ~

Tiamoon stood at the cottage's door gazing on the carefully manicured yard. When Skye had learned of Terran's death, she'd come back and worked furiously in the yard for three days, digging until her fingers bled. Tia knew her mother had watered the plants with her tears.

But Tia had been surprised when Skye had gone back to the inn, especially when Skye sent word via the mouse network she'd be staying with Aethel, the night elf.

Skye had instructed Tiamoon to retrieve a diary she kept in her wardrobe. The contents would explain her actions.

As instructed by her mother, Tia had read the early pages and received the shock of her life. She was half night elf. She wasn't sure whether to scorn herself or deny the connection. What she did was send a message to her mother to find her happiness.

Maybe among all the death there would be a spark of love and a promise of life. Only time would tell.

St. Batzy and the Time Machine
Genene Valleau

Chapter One

Horace Ainsworth patted the side of the giant red fire hydrant towering two stories above him then addressed the terrier mix dog staring at him curiously. "It's finished. Now don't you dig in my Maddie's roses any more or potty on the pansies."

Batzy stared at Horace's retreating back for a moment before he hiked his leg on the nearest flowering plant.

Then he turned his attention to the odd-looking structure the Big Human had erected. Not like any fire hydrant he'd ever sniffed. A canine would have to be the size of King Kong to give this thing a proper marking.

Though it did smell like the water that sprayed out of the hose when the human across the street yelled at him. Batzy grinned and lifted his leg, imagining he was returning the spray of the yelling human.

As he circled this mysterious structure, the smell of fresh paint and overturned earth drifted into his nostrils. It was bigger than the merry-go-round at the park where his human, Chloe, sometimes took him.

Wonder what's inside?

Batzy scratched at the side of the structure then trotted another few steps and scratched again. About halfway around he found an opening. Not tall enough for the Big Human, but just about perfect for his little girl, Chloe. Batzy darted inside and lifted his face to sample the aromas.

No scents of danger but much to explore. Like this box of dirt. Odd. Big humans usually didn't appreciate the joys of digging. Hadn't he just been told not to dig in the rose bushes? A sniff and a poke with his paw uncovered a bone. Fresh out of the package. Batzy looked around. What game was the Big Human playing?

"Batzy!" his little girl was calling him.

Batzy stepped out of the digging pit. *Hmm. I smell peanut butter.*

He put a front paw on a cabinet for balance and nosed a button. A bone-shaped treat fell into a bowl below. Also fresh out of a package. The Big Human was definitely up to something. Batzy gobbled it down quickly before looking around again.

"Batzy!"

Drat! He had to go. On his way out, Batzy stepped back into the digging box and snatched up the bone. Outside once again, he pushed the bone through the gap under the fence, and squeezed through after it.

He popped up on the other side with only a few more streaks of mud on the white of his belly and wagged his tail at Chloe. He'd go back to explore the Big Human's structure later.

~ * ~

Satisfied he had neutralized the threat to Maddie's rose bushes, Horace returned to the workshop in the basement of their castle-shaped home. In King Arthur's time, the sorcerer Merlin might have worked his magic in similar surroundings. Had Merlin simply been a scientist with an observing eye and a searching mind?

That's how Horace saw himself: open to possibilities and what others might consider impossibilities. He loved to explore "what if" and took delight in disproving "facts." Edison did it with the light bulb. The Wright brothers did it with airplanes. Horace continued that tradition with a flying car and a robot that served dinner, as well as a play structure made out of a water tower and painted like a giant fire hydrant for the dog next door. After all, who said inventions had to be serious?

Horace scanned the stone walls lined with tables and shelves stacked with high-tech inventions and mechanical gadgets in various stages of development. What should he work on next?

He nearly set aside the recipe card propped on the computer keyboard, except he hadn't seen the word "urgent" on a recipe before. Horace realized it was a phone message from his cousin, Clement. "Will arrive tomorrow with submarine."

Horace scratched his chin. What would his space engineer relative be doing with a submarine?

Suddenly, the alarm for the garages began wailing. A glance at the security monitor showed a truck pulling a trailer painted in vivid red and orange careening around the castle had clipped the gutter downspout and set off the alarm.

A net dropped over the trailer, tangling in a wheel and jerking it sideways. Unfortunately, the truck continued its forward momentum until it also lurched to a stop, now sitting almost side by side with the trailer.

If Horace didn't know his wife was safely painting in her studio, he would have sworn she was driving the truck.

He hurried out of his workshop to be sure both truck and driver were okay.

A tall, lanky man wearing a white shirt and black slacks jumped down from the driver's seat as the truck shuddered to a stop, grinning at Horace. "Hi, Cuz."

A frown creased Horace's forehead as he stared at the argyle suspenders that kept Clement Ainsworth's slacks pulled up into a permanent wedgie. The same suspenders Clement bragged had garnered him a date with the prettiest sorority girl at college some thirty-odd years ago. "But your message said you'd be here tomorrow."

Clement waved away Horace's confusion. "I called yesterday. You need a new secretary."

"My nephew took the message--"

"Like I said, you need a new secretary."

Horace made a mental note to come up with a more

efficient way to deliver messages. "Why are you here? This doesn't look like a submarine."

Clement frowned. "Paperwork hold-up. But we can start work without it."

"Work on what?"

After a suspicious look around, Clement dropped his voice to a whisper. "A probe to explore black holes."

Horace also looked around, seeing nothing of danger except his cousin's lack of driving skills. "You mean black holes in space caused by stars burning out?"

"Well, that's the generally accepted theory."

"And do you have a probe in the trailer?"

"Nah. This is a mobile fabrication laboratory." Clement walked to the back of the trailer, stepping over the tangled netting that had captured one of the wheels. "This will make us a working prototype of the probe."

Horace stepped inside the trailer behind his cousin. "What is all this?"

"Laser cutter, CNC machine tools, robotic water jet, a rapid prototyping device--just to name a few. All run by cutting edge computer software."

Horace's hands tingled with the desire to pry open the metal casings on the equipment and see how the machines really worked. "Don't you make anything by hand?"

"You're still living in the dark ages, Horace." Clement laughed again. "No one makes things manually anymore."

Horace squared his shoulders, determined not to let his older, city slicker cousin make him feel inferior the way he had in college. "I do."

Clement's expression turned immediately apologetic, something Horace had rarely seen. "That's why I need you."

With a deep breath and a frown, Clement looked Horace squarely in the eye. "You're the detail man. You make visions a reality. Others know the theories, but you know how to make them work."

"Um...right." Horace was still a bit off balance and definitely wary of his cousin's change in attitude. For the first time Horace could recall, Clement seemed to appreciate his skills rather than denigrating them. Surely Horace could give the man a chance to explain--and examine these intriguing machines--before Maddie threw Clement off their property. "Tell me what you have in mind."

"Saving the world."

Chapter Two

"By the way, I'm famished. What do you have to eat?" Clement patted his scrawny belly as he stepped out of the trailer and walked toward the house.

With a reluctant look toward the machines he wanted to explore, Horace followed his cousin. From past experience, Horace knew he would learn no more about Clement's project until his cousin had food--lots of it.

In the kitchen, Horace's nephew-in-law, Ryan, focused on a cooking show featuring a battle between chefs.

"Ryan, this is my cousin, Clement," Horace said. "Would you be so kind as to fix him a snack?"

Ryan muted the sound on the television and brushed his hand over his apron before extending it to Clement. "Sorry, flour on my hands. What would you like?"

Clement shook Ryan's hand. "A few sandwiches would be good."

"Just saw a recipe I want to try that will fit the bill. Should only take a few minutes."

While Ryan fixed the sandwiches, Horace rummaged through the pantry for a bag of potato chips and pulled a pitcher of lemonade out of the refrigerator.

As Ryan predicted, the sandwiches didn't take long. "Toasted peanut butter and banana sandwiches topped with sugar and cinnamon."

Clement took a couple bites and nodded. "Not bad. How about some pickles on the side?"

Clement was finishing up a third sandwich when Maddie walked into the room.

Horace smiled broadly as his heart rate accelerated. After all the years they had been married, his wife's presence still had the ability to discombobulate him. She was as tall as Horace's own six feet--the reason they saw eye-to-eye on most things, they joked. Her cherry wine eyes seemed almost black and shone with her emotions. To Horace, she was more beautiful than when they met thirty-some years ago.

Maddie greeted Horace with a kiss on the cheek and frowned at Clement. "Heard you came for lunch. Just passing through?"

"Good to see you again too, Madelaine." Clement started to wipe his mouth with his sleeve, stopped himself and reached for a napkin instead. "I came to ask Horace's help on a project."

"What kind of a project?" Maddie placed a chair between Horace and Clement and sat down.

"Classified." Clement scowled.

"Even though you're not working for NASA anymore?" Maddie poured a glass of lemonade for herself.

"You didn't mention that," Horace said. "What happened?"

"Politics. And we didn't have a chance to finish our discussion about the project." The scowl deepened between Clement's brows as he crammed potato chips into his mouth.

"How's Victoria?" Maddie sipped her lemonade.

Clement choked on a chip, coughing so hard Horace pounded him on the back. Clement coughed one more time then took a huge swallow of lemonade and aimed an angry gaze at Maddie. "My wife left me, which I'm sure you already know."

"But you've been married nearly as long as..." Horace's face scrunched up in bafflement.

"As you and Maddie. I know." Clement shook his head with a sigh. "She said I was an arrogant geek."

Silence settled over the group in the kitchen.

"Well, I hope things work out for the best." Though Maddie's softly spoken words responded to Clement's comment, her gaze rested on Horace. "I know I'd be lost without my Horace."

She rose and squeezed Horace's shoulders in a hug. "I have a painting to finish. Whatever your project is, keep both feet on the ground. No space flights or underwater exploring, please."

Horace clung to Maddie's hand an extra moment as the news sank into his mind that his cousin's marriage of twenty-five years had crumbled. Horace worried every moment Maddie was away on one of her misadventures. He couldn't imagine the devastation if she didn't come back.

As Maddie left the room after a lingering backward glance at Horace, he resisted the urge to run after her.

Maddie always came back, he reassured himself. He forced his mind to return to the trailer full of tempting machines his cousin had brought. "Tell me more about your project."

Clement eyed a triple-layer chocolate cake as they rose from the table. "How about a piece of that delicious looking dessert to fuel our discussion?"

Armed with a large wedge of the cake Ryan had topped with curls of dark chocolate earlier in the day, Horace and Clement returned to the fabrication lab.

Surrounded by humming machinery, Horace set aside his worry about Maddie not coming back from one of her journeys. "Tell me more about your plan to save the world."

"Right." Clement took a huge bite of cake, chewed and swallowed. "Perhaps you've heard rumors the world will end in 2012."

Horace shrugged. "Someone always thinks the world is ending."

"This time actually has its basis in astronomy. We're nearing the end of both Earth's 5,000-year cycle around the galaxy and 26,000-year cycle through the twelve Zodiac constellations. The incidence of earthquakes and hurricanes and other natural disasters is at an all-time high."

"How can black holes save the world?"

Clement finished off the cake and wiped his mouth with the sleeve of his white shirt, leaving a chocolate streak on the white linen fabric. "Space is more curved at the edge of a black hole and time behaves differently. I want to gather information from the year 2012 that the world isn't really ending, but simply entering another world age: the

Age of Aquarius."

"So you want a time machine?"

"No. A simple robotic probe we can manipulate from here to get pictures and data immediately. That's where your expertise at building gadgets comes in. I want you to build that probe."

"How far would it have to travel to the nearest black hole?"

"It wouldn't. We're going to generate our own black hole."

At Horace's puzzled look, Clement continued. "Most scientists have accepted two theories about black holes: what goes in can't get back out, and black holes are 'out there' somewhere. I challenge both of those assumptions, and we're going to prove it while the probe is gathering information the world is not going to end in 2012."

"Sending the probe into a black hole and having it return would certainly prove there is a way out," Horace said. "But how do you plan to generate a black hole?"

"Newer thinking expands on the theory that black holes are caused only by collapsing stars and proposes smaller black holes can merge into larger ones. Taking another jump, I think certain types of high energy collisions--such as those used in nuclear reactors--could cause black holes."

"And that's what the nuclear submarine was for."

"Exactly. I think those types of black holes can be recreated here on Earth, which will give us a prototype to explore without traveling into space."

Excitement buzzed through Horace. He could keep

his promise to Maddie not to travel in space or explore underwater and still make a huge contribution to science and technology. By the time Maddie returned from her latest adventure, time travel should be a reality!

~ * ~

Maddie eyed the painting critically as the peace sign that had become her signature statement blended into the tree trunk. *There--finished!*

And still a day to go until the plane left for her volunteer work for women's empowerment in Guatemala City. One day to get rid of Clement or at least threaten him with vile repercussions if he left Horace holding the bag for one of his madcap schemes as he had in college. If she hadn't signed on a year ago for this trip, Maddie would be tempted to stay home and protect Horace from his advantage-taking relative.

However, Horace's loyalty ran deep. It was one of the things Maddie loved about him. But Clement took advantage of Horace's naiveté. If Victoria was still in the picture, Maddie could simply ask her to keep Clement in check. But his estranged wife had made it very clear she was tired of her husband's arrogant, know-it-all attitude and had found herself a younger man with more looks than brains.

With twenty-four hours to come up with a plan to temper Clement's influence over Horace, Maddie called on her family to help.

Her sister, Daphne, was the first recruit. After her husband had died twenty-odd years ago, Daphne had retreated into an imaginary world based in the 1950s. She had recently recovered and was looking for a part-time career to help fill her time. "How would you like to explore being a private investigator as a new career option?"

"Cool. What did you have in mind?"

"Come with me." Maddie and Daphne crept quietly through the castle hallways and down the stairs into Horace's workshop. One of the many cabinets contained a myriad of gadgets designed for keeping tabs on suspicious characters. And Maddie definitely considered Clement a suspicious character.

"This pen should do the trick," Maddie whispered. "It records video and audio from across the room. Just click like a regular pen to start recording."

"And?" Daphne looked at Maddie expectantly.

"It's that simple."

"Oh." Disappointment colored Daphne's voice. "I thought there would be more."

Understanding dawned on Maddie. Her sister wanted the drama of being a private investigator. "Well, there can be more."

Over the next half hour, Maddie pulled items out of the cabinet for Daphne's consideration--a video recorder to be hidden in a faux house plant, a pair of earphones for a mini-stereo system that could also be used to amplify other sounds up to a hundred yards away, night vision goggles, a telephone recorder, and Daphne's favorite: an ornate cigarette lighter that doubled as a camera and recorder, even though she didn't smoke. Daphne also insisted on taking an evidence kit that included fingerprint powder, an ultra-violet light, tweezers to collect specimens and evidence storage bags.

As Daphne hurried back to her rooms to change into her spy clothes, Maddie wondered if she had overplayed the importance of watching Horace's cousin. She shrugged away the thought as she walked toward the kitchen to talk to her nephew. Daphne had been bored lately. Spying on Clement would give her something creative to do.

In the kitchen, Maddie's nephew was tuned into another cooking show on television. Ryan had been obsessed with these shows since his ex-fiancé had decided to become a star in a reality show rather than get married. He was as casual about watching Clement as Daphne was fixated with the task. Maddie hoped the two of them would at least remind Clement someone was watching out for Horace's good.

The next morning, Daphne appeared in a short leather skirt, trench coat, a fedora pulled low over one eye and stiletto heels. She put a finger to her lips and whispered, "Discretion is the word."

Maddie pushed away severe doubts about leaving and closed her suitcase with a determined zzzzip! "You'll call Ian and Rissa if you need them?"

"I've memorized my daughter's cell phone number and destroyed the evidence." Daphne giggled as if she didn't already know Rissa's phone number by memory. She clicked the heel of one of her shoes on the floor and a series of beeps signaled a telephone making a call.

"Hello, Mother," a voice answered. "Is this another

test?"

"Yes, darling," Daphne whispered into her hat. "All is working perfectly."

Daphne's eyes glowed with excitement as she ended the call with her daughter. "I've recorded video of all Clement's activities this morning. Did you know he sleeps in his suspenders?"

"Ah, no, I didn't." With less than two hours until she had to be at the airport, Maddie refused to question the wisdom of abandoning Horace to his smooth-talking cousin with only Daphne and Ryan to chaperone. She firmly settled her Victorian beefeater hat on her head and decided one more chat with Clement before she left would be beneficial. She hefted her suitcase off the bed and started down the hallway.

Maddie found Clement in the kitchen with Horace, sampling Ryan's latest cooking experiment. The clunk of her suitcase settling on the tile floor caught the attention of all in the kitchen. "I have some things to say, Clement, about what I expect while I'm gone."

Clement's Adam's apple bobbled hard as he swallowed the bite of food he had been chewing.

"Now, Maddie, don't be so hard--"

Maddie quieted her husband's protest with a kiss. A real one this time--full on the mouth. "I love you, Horace. More than anything or anyone in my life."

Maddie turned the full intensity of her attention to Clement who gulped. She removed the fork from his hand and used it to emphasize her words. "And that is why I expect you to behave with the utmost respect to my husband and the rest of my family. Just as if I was in the very next room, watching you. Because I will be. Daphne will be giving me daily updates on what's happening here."

Out of the corner of her eye, Maddie saw the flash of a camera as Daphne recorded another family moment. "My ultra-responsible niece, Rissa, has married an inspector from Scotland Yard, and they are only a phone call away. I'm sure Ryan could be persuaded to add a little something to your food if you misbehave. Nothing lethal, mind you, but you might develop more than a passing acquaintance with the downstairs bathroom."

Clement looked at the uneaten portion of food on his plate with suspicion.

"Oh, not to worry, as long as you are the perfect guest."

"Bravo, my dear, bravo!" Horace clapped his hands, his face beaming at Maddie with pride. "You haven't lost your flair for debate. But unnecessary, you see, as Clement and I have already resolved past issues, and he has assured me he has changed."

"Well, I'm not as kind and trusting as my husband." Maddie speared Clement with a pointed look as she placed his fork beside his plate. "I want proof an arrogant nerd has turned in his pocket protector."

"I understand perfectly, Madelaine." Clement pushed away his half-eaten plate of food. "And I appreciate you want to protect your family. However, as Horace stated, that's no longer necessary. I'm here to work on a project with Horace that will benefit all of mankind."

Maddie's smile clearly conveyed her wait-and-see

attitude as she readjusted her hat. "Ryan, I'd appreciate a ride to the airport now."

~ * ~

All the way to the airport, to the boarding gate, and into her seat on the airplane, Maddie thought about her family. Horace was her rock and her sanity. Without him...well, Maddie didn't even want to think about that.

Her sister, Daphne, seemed to have regained her zest for life after existing in a 1950's time-warp for twenty-some years since her husband's unexpected death. Maddie had mostly raised her twin niece and nephew, Rissa and Ryan. However, Rissa had recently married and Ryan had immersed himself in becoming a world famous chef via the wonders of cooking shows on television. Her entire family seemed to be realizing their dreams.

Am I? Maddie wondered. *Now that I can do anything I want to, what do I really want?*

An image of Horace came strongly to mind. *I want to renew my relationship with my husband. He's more intelligent than two or three "normal" people, yet he's humble. He never wants to hurt anyone or anything. He doesn't know the meaning of macho posturing. His goodness truly runs through his entire being.*

Maddie smiled as she thought of the evening she met Horace. He was standing alone at a college fraternity party, shifting from foot to foot and glancing around the room. The song, "Age of Aquarius," blasted from the stereo. Some of those who were only mildly stoned or moderately drunk gyrated in dance in the middle of the room. Maddie's attention was instantly captured by the only man in the room who was sober and clean-shaven. "Can I help you find someone?"

Horace's startled gaze zeroed in on her face. "A friend--I'm looking for a friend."

"One you know or someone you want to get to know?"

His puzzled frown kick-started her jaded heart. The man was a true innocent. Maddie had given up hope such an anomaly existed. She tucked her hand under his elbow and steered him toward the relative quiet of the kitchen. The swinging door muffled the sounds in the adjacent room as it drifted closed.

"What's your name?" Maddie offered the man a pickle she had speared out of a jar on the counter.

"Horace Ainsworth." He shook his head at her offer of a snack. "I was supposed to meet my cousin, Clement, here."

"He connected with Victoria from the sorority down the street. I doubt they'll be back tonight."

"Oh." A baffled look settled once more over Horace's face.

"Do you need a ride home?" Maddie was totally intrigued by this man, dropped like a choir boy amid the raucous atmosphere of a Saturday night fraternity party.

"No, thank you. It's only a few blocks."

"I'll walk with you."

They walked without talking through the crisp fall air, Horace automatically taking the position closest to the street. Maddie didn't feel the need to fill the silence.

A few blocks away, Horace stopped in front of an immense, two-story house. The baffled expression that already seemed dear to Maddie settled over his face again. "I can't let you walk back alone."

Maddie laughed. "I walk all over town by myself."

Horace shook his head firmly. "It wouldn't be right."

"Then I'll come in."

His frown deepened. "That wouldn't be right either."

Maddie was enchanted with this good-hearted, proper man. "Have you eaten dinner?"

"I don't believe so. I was working on a project and lost track of time..."

If the light had been better, Maddie would have sworn the man blushed.

"Come on. There's a diner nearby where some of my friends hang out. I'll stay with them." Once again, Maddie took Horace's arm and steered him down the sidewalk.

Their connection developed companionably from there. The delighted smile on Horace's face every time he saw her both humbled and amazed Maddie. She had never met a person so guileless and open.

The day Horace invited Maddie to see his workshop was the day she knew she had fallen in love with him. Gone was any shyness or uncertainty. Horace explained the machine he was building in words Maddie could understand, but without being condescending. His eyes sparkled with enthusiasm as he answered all of her questions, and later declared his appreciation for her interest in his work.

Their relationship shifted to a deeper level that day, and Horace even started taking the lead in asking her to lunch or to attend rallies he thought she might be interested in--if he didn't get involved in a project and forget what day it was.

Without any formal announcement, they had become a couple. Maddie's heart nearly stopped when Horace quietly told her he had finished all the requirements for his Ph.D. and would be moving. They stared at each other for a moment with tear-filled eyes then blurted out in unison, "Will you marry me?"

While Maddie finished her degree in Political Science, Horace worked on his inventions. They both believed they could change the world.

Had they remained true to the ideals they expressed all those years ago? Were they making the world better?

Sure, Maddie made weekly trips to the homeless shelter and blended hidden messages in each of her paintings. And this trip to Guatemala to lend her voice to women's empowerment would move the men and women in that small Central American country forward a few steps.

However, now the actual Age of Aquarius--filled with peace and harmony and understanding--was dawning, Horace was working on a project that could change the entire world. Maddie wanted to be part of that change. Wanted to work with the man who restored her passion so many years ago with his guileless sincerity.

After this trip, she promised herself. No more

commitments that would take her away from the man she loved.

~ * ~

"We need to set up a command center," Clement said. "We can use the computer in the fabrication lab--just find extra monitors as well as cameras for the probe..."

Horace nodded as his cousin listed the items they needed to set up the control center. He had a number of surveillance monitors that could be relocated and wired to the computer in the fabrication lab. There were also several cameras from a recent project he had done for a private investigator.

At least there were a couple months ago. Horace stared at the empty shelves in the cabinet where he was sure he had stored the pieces left from working with the PI.

From the corner of his eye, Horace thought he saw his sister-in-law peeking around the corner. Interesting that she seemed to have traded her 1950s poodle skirt for a trench coat. "Daphne, have you seen--"

But she wasn't there. Had Horace imagined her? Or was someone playing with the holographic projector?

With a shake of his head, Horace decided they could use the cameras from the surveillance van for the probe. They were much larger than the ones he had used for the private investigator's test equipment, but sturdier.

Within an hour, Horace had gathered all the items on his cousin's list to put together a control center, and Clement had output a shell for the probe from one of the rapid prototyping machines in the fabrication lab.

While Clement experimented with generating a black hole with the nuclear reactor in the submarine that had finally arrived, Horace assembled the internal workings of the probe.

As always when he worked on a project, time ceased to exist while Horace worked on the probe. He noticed at one point Clement had curled his lanky frame onto an old car seat in the workshop and had fallen asleep. Later, Clement got up and went back to experimenting with the nuclear reactor, muttering and making notes. Horace also vaguely remembered Ryan bringing in food and, on occasion, he thought he saw Daphne in her trench coat peeking around corners. However, these events simply happened in the background of Horace's mind while his attention focused on the probe.

He finished soldering the final piece of the probe into place as his cousin shouted, "Eureka! We have a black hole."

"And the probe is ready to explore," Horace said with a boyish grin.

Horace and Clement slapped hands in a high-five then sat down to compare notes.

"How long does the black hole stay open?" Horace asked.

"I can keep it pretty stable with the reactor, opening it and closing it as needed."

"Let's test the probe."

Once the probe was settled near the reactor, Clement started a countdown. Silently, Horace ticked off the seconds along with the computerized voice, "...three, two, one. Engage. Destination: the year 2012."

The probe disappeared from the workshop and materialized on one of the monitors via a camera mounted on the probe in such a way it showed the probe and what was happening around it.

"I didn't account for that much spin." Clement made a note on the pad by his left hand.

"Is that how fast it's traveling through time?" Horace asked.

"Perhaps. That could be a way to tell the year--by how fast the probe spins. Or link it to a clock or calendar in the computer." Clement made more notes on his pad.

"Look!" Horace pointed to one of the monitors. "It's spinning out of control."

Clement muttered under his breath as his fingers raced over the keyboard.

"Can you bring it back?" Horace asked.

The probe re-materialized in the fabrication lab, missing one antennae and the other one twisted into a coil. A series of scratches formed circles around the metal body.

"Definitely a lot of spin." Clement frowned in concentration as he typed some calculations into the computer. "Like cutting cookies on the ice in my old sedan."

"Didn't you crash that car?" Horace asked.

"I've learned a few things since then." Clement keyed another number sequence into the computer and sat back in his chair. "Let's try it again."

They activated the countdown again then the probe disappeared from the fabrication lab and appeared on the monitors.

"Ah, much better."

"We're getting video footage from a parade," Horace said. "I see a banner that says 2015. We overshot by a few years, but at least we can prove the world won't end in 2012."

"One more minor adjustment to the spin should improve the accuracy in getting the targeted year."

Horace and Clement exchanged satisfied smiles.

Within seconds, the probe materialized in the fabrication lab once again.

Clement stood and stretched his lanky frame. "This calls for a celebration. Wonder what Ryan has fixed for lunch--or dinner. What time is it anyway?"

Horace laughed. "Doesn't it seem ironic that we can send a probe to the future, but we don't know what time we're actually living in?"

"If we can travel through time, we can live in any time we'd like. Let's go eat."

Soon Horace would have cause for another celebration: his Maddie would be home from her week in Central America. She would be delighted to hear about this latest invention--no space travel or undersea exploration needed.

~ * ~

Maddie settled into her seat on the airplane, satisfied with their week's work in Guatemala City, grateful for no misadventures, and ready to be home with Horace.

The other passengers stowed their carryon luggage, sat down and pulled out magazines or plugged into videos.

The airplane's engines rumbled, building in a steady crescendo as they moved down the runway. Maddie clutched the armrests as the metal beast roared and separated itself from the Earth. No matter how many times Horace explained why airplanes could fly, the thought always flickered through Maddie's mind at take-off that this much metal shouldn't be able to stay in the air.

Then they leveled out of the climb, the "fasten seatbelts" light dimmed, and it didn't seem like they were moving at all. Maddie pulled a book from her carryon bag and began to read. Barely into the second Chapter, she fell asleep, making up for late nights on her trip.

An announcement from the flight attendant roused Maddie sometime later. "Please return to your seats and fasten your seatbelts."

Maddie stretched, anticipating a warm welcome home greeting from her family.

However, Fate had another twist in store as the flight attendant continued speaking. "We have been asked to make an unexpected flight correction--"

"You been hijacked, folks." A rough male voice interrupted the flight attendant's soothing tones. "And we're going to Ireland."

Absolute silence greeted the announcement then whispered conversations buzzed throughout the plane's cabin.

"Just sit down, shut up, and do what you're told."

So close to being home without incident. After the kidnapping she had experienced last year, Horace would be panicked about this hijacking. She hunched down in the seat and settled her hat so it hid more of her face, trying to be as inconspicuous as possible..

"You there! In the funny hat."

Please don't let him be talking to me. Maddie remained still--until her hat was snatched off her head.

"I'm talkin' to **you**."

Maddie turned a steely gaze toward the source of the rude voice. A man with his face painted green snarled at her, making the fake shamrock sitting atop a leprechaun's hat bounce at the end of its spring.

And the man had the audacity to call her hat "funny"?

"Stand up."

Drawing a deep breath, Maddie stood up. To her full six-foot height. At least a head taller than the man who disturbed her intention to stay quietly compliant.

"No! Sit down." The man stepped backward and bumped against the seats across the aisle.

Instead, Maddie took a step forward and snatched her hat back from the odious little man. As she did so, a man seated behind the hijacker clunked him up-side the head with a three-inch thick book.

"I say, Tolstoy would be proud." The British gentleman's silver moustache curved upward in a smile as he patted the book in his hand.

"Let's get him tied up while he's still unconscious." A businessman removed his tie and quickly wrapped and bound the hijacker's hands behind his back.

"Are there more of them?" Maddie asked the flight attendant.

"At least one more. In the cockpit with the pilot."

The airplane tilted abruptly to the right, tumbling

the passengers who had gathered around the hijacker like a line of dominoes. As they scrambled for something to hold onto, a voice once more brayed over the PA system, "Does anyone know how to fly this plane?"

The passengers looked at each other, shrugging one after another. The businessman who had removed his tie blew out a breath. "I'll give it a try."

While he followed the flight attendant toward the cockpit, Maddie and the British gentleman dragged the hijacker into the bathroom and locked him in, with his hands still bound behind his back.

The plane tilted again, this time in the opposite direction, once more tumbling passengers into each other.

"Sorry, folks, just a course correction." The businessman's voice crackled over the PA system.

A collective sigh of relief rippled through the passengers, cut short by a curse and a terse command from the cockpit. "Heads on your knees, folks! We're going down."

Maddie crawled toward a seat and held on as the plane's nose tilted downward. The plane jerked as they hit the highest treetops and Maddie flopped like a rag doll as she clung to the seat. The image of Horace settled in her mind. Sweet, brilliant, absent-minded Horace. Would she ever see him again?

*I love you...*was her last thought as the plane slammed into the ground, and a child's ant farm crashed into the side of her head.

Chapter Three

Though Horace's belly was filled after pasta and garlic bread, Clement heaped his plate three times before declaring it was time for dessert.

As he worked his way through a lemon bar nearly as large as the cook stove in the kitchen, the telephone rang. Ryan listened for a moment then handed the receiver to Horace. "You'll want to take this call."

Horace did not like the look of careful blankness on Ryan's face, nor the measured calm of Rissa's voice on the other end of the phone call. In fact, he didn't like anything about this call, especially the fact Maddie's plane had gone down shortly after take-off.

"What's wrong, Cuz?" Clement cleared the last of the crumbs off his plate.

"My Maddie's plane was hijacked and now leprechauns have her."

Clement blinked. Twice. On this rare occasion, his cousin, the NASA engineer, seemed speechless.

"If I could go back in time, I wouldn't let Maddie go by herself--" Horace stopped abruptly. He and Clement had sent a probe forward in time; why not send a human back in time? "We need to build a time machine to rescue Maddie before the hijacking actually happens."

Clement slipped his thumbs under his suspenders and rocked from the balls of his feet to his heels. "Interesting concept. Though some of my colleagues say there's a failsafe mechanism to prevent time travelers from changing what's already happened."

"I'm going to prove your colleagues wrong." Horace pushed past his cousin toward the fabrication lab. "We need to make some modifications to the probe to turn it into a time machine."

"You'll need an entire redesign if you want enough room for humans."

"Or something that's big enough to be retrofitted with a nuclear reactor." Mentally, Horace went through the structures on their property that could be quickly modified to carry a human time traveler. "The giant fire hydrant!"

Horace changed direction and dashed across the back yard. By the time Clement caught up with him, Horace had crawled inside the two-story red structure and was scrutinizing every square inch. Clement slowly stood up inside the water tower painted like a fire hydrant and looked around. "What is this for?"

"So the neighbor girl's dog doesn't potty on Maddie's flowers or dig up her rose bushes." Horace looked upward, mentally calculating what space would be needed for a human to travel through time to carry out a rescue mission. "How much room would the nuclear reactor take up?"

"You're serious?" Clement asked.

"I'll do anything to save my Maddie." Horace met Clement's doubting gaze with determination.

"I believe you would. Let's get busy." Clement crawled out of the structure, with Horace literally on his heels.

Soon they hovered over the computer in the fabrication lab designing a time machine centered around a refrigerator-sized nuclear reactor that could create its own black holes to travel through time.

"Since we know the probe will travel through time and back, let's incorporate it into the time machine," Clement said. "That will also give us many of the components we need."

On a pad of paper Horace sketched in the probe above the reactor. "I can move the monitors so they are mounted on the tower instead of inside the probe."

"It would be wise to place the monitors to see all around the structure to be sure it's safe to exit."

"Good idea." Horace made more notes on the paper.

"What do you have that will work for an instrument panel?" Clement asked. "Many of the gauges from the submarine are damaged. Do you have anything from an automobile?"

"My Maddie is a bit hard on cars." Wistfulness caused an ache in Horace's heart, but he pushed it aside. He needed to focus on saving Maddie. "I have a lot of spare auto parts."

"Great." Clement made a list of what they would

need: gauges, clock, bucket seats. "I think it would also be wise to include necessities such as a repair kit, first aid supplies, toilet, sink, and a place for food supplies and sleeping--"

"But I won't be gone that long--"

Clement held up his hand. "If all goes off without a hitch, you can tell me I worried for nothing. But if things don't go as planned--and they rarely do--you'll be prepared."

"Well, okay. As long as it doesn't slow down the project."

"By the time you gather all the components, the computer will have generated a design that will fit comfortably inside this tower."

True to his word, Clement was poring over a time machine design by the time Horace returned with faux leopard print bucket seats for a pilot and co-pilot, gauges from one of the classic automobiles Maddie had wrecked, a digital clock from a microwave, a camping port-a-potty for a bathroom, a mini-refrigerator from Ryan's college fraternity days, a drink and snack dispenser, and a sleeping bag and hammock for a bed.

"I think we should also have a second reactor here as a backup that can remotely control the time machine," Clement stated.

The full import of what they were doing finally struck Horace. Time travel was the stuff of wondrous fiction novels, not scientific journals. Did that mean it hadn't been done? Or couldn't be proven? Or that time travelers had failed and were stuck in the past or in the future with no way back?

What if he went back in time to rescue Maddie and miscalculated? What if going back in time wasn't the same as going forward, and he had to live out the rest of his life without his beloved Maddie?

Horace swallowed. "A backup reactor would be a good thing."

"You don't have to do this, Horace. Maddie has been on misadventures before and come back safely. She'll probably be back before we complete the unmanned test flight."

"Test flight." Horace didn't like the feeling of cowardice that tempted him to call off this project. All his life, he had proceeded with caution. That's what a good scientist did, he told himself. Checked and double-checked facts. Had he hidden behind that method? He wanted to be brave--not just for Maddie, but for himself. "But just one test flight. Then I need to rescue my Maddie."

~ * ~

"Get out! Quickly! Everyone down the escape slides!"

The shouts of the other airline passengers slowly became clearer as Maddie returned to consciousness.

"Save the Queen! Can you walk?" The British gentleman crouched in front of Maddie.

Maddie started to nod, but stopped as pain shot through her head and ants dropped into her lap. "My head hurts, but I'll be fine as soon as I clear the ants out of my hat."

Maddie set the ant farm that had clonked her on the head into an upright position. Then shook the ants out of her hat and back into their home.

The British gentleman helped her to a wobbly stand and outside where the other passengers gathered under the sheltering branches of a tall fir tree a short distance from the crumpled airplane. Maddie set the ant farm beside a tree, thinking the little creatures might enjoy being forest ants now.

"Where are we?" One of the hijackers demanded, waving his gun and squinting through the wreckage of his glasses. One lens was missing and the other was scratched and discolored. "This doesn't look like Ireland."

The passengers looked at each other and at the landscape. Hills covered with trees ringed the emerald green valley where they huddled together.

He can't be serious, Maddie thought. *Unless he hit his head harder than I did when we crashed.*

"We should salvage what we can from the plane before it gets dark," the businessman said.

The hijacker swung his gun and attention toward the businessman. "We're going to get as far away from this plane as possible. Where's my buddy, Jarvis? Jarvis!"

"Hurt in the crash, like some of the others," the businessman stated.

"Guess they'll just have to make it on their own."

"Ommmmmmmmmmmmmmm."

"What is that noise?" The hijacker spun around, the barrel of his gun wavering toward a small figure in purple twisted into a pretzel-like pose.

"Just one of the fae folk." Maddie watched for the hijacker's reaction, hoping if he wanted to go to Ireland, he might also have some superstitions they could use to unnerve him. "I'll chase it away."

Maddie hurried toward Greta, an older woman with blue-tinted hair who was part of Maddie's women's empowerment group. Greta had practiced yoga for many years and told Maddie that yoga and chanting helped her stay calm in stressful situations. This hijacking definitely qualified as stressful!

"Shoo!" Maddie said loudly as she approached the woman. Greta looked at her in surprise.

"The hijacker broke his glasses and thinks you're a faerie," Maddie whispered. "Hide quickly and see if you can signal for help after the rest of us have gone."

Greta blinked, unwound from her yoga pose, and slipped away into the forest.

"We don't want to see you again!" Maddie stated loudly.

She brushed her hands together in satisfaction as she returned to the rest of the group. "That should keep the wee folk from stealing our dreams tonight."

The hijacker stared at Maddie with one eye squinted closed. "What do you mean?"

"Oh, it's just an old wife's tale that if the wee folk steal your dreams, you won't ever wake up."

"Uh-huh." The hijacker glanced over his shoulder. "Let's get out of here. You with the funny hat--you go first."

Maddie shrugged and started down a path through the trees. The pain in her head didn't jolt too badly if she walked slowly and set her feet down carefully. If she could keep the hijacker distracted, she would just lead them in a big circle so they would be close to the airplane when help arrived. "Watch for fireflies. It means the wee folk are nearby."

From the corner of her eye, Maddie noted with satisfaction the hijacker glanced around nervously before prodding the other passengers into a single-file line behind her.

They walked in silence for a time until Maddie stopped abruptly and announced, "Time for a rest break."

"I didn't say you could stop." The hijacker pushed his way to the front of the line.

Maddie noticed a couple of the passengers slipped away from the group and back toward the airplane.

"I need to rest," Maddie stated.

"You don't need to rest. Keep moving."

"I need to go to the blimey loo," Maddie hissed loudly.

Titters rippled through the rest of the group then stopped abruptly as the hijacker turned to scowl at them. "Make it fast."

Maddie moved slowly off the main trail, pulling out her cell phone.

"That's far enough." The hijacker's voice carried loudly through the twilight.

Flipping open the cell phone, Maddie crossed her fingers she was far enough away so the hijacker couldn't hear any beeps the phone might make. Unfortunately, the phone wasn't picking up a signal.

With a sigh, Maddie slipped the phone back into her pocket then returned to the group.

"Gura míle." Maddie said thank you in Irish Gaelic and nodded regally toward the hijacker before resuming her place at the head of the line and moving slowly down the trail once more.

"By jove, I see fireflies ahead," the British gentleman commented as they reached a fork in the trail.

"Where?" The hijacker once more pushed his way toward the front of the line but stayed well back from the flickering points of light on the path ahead. "Take a different direction."

Obliging, Maddie took the fork in the trail that turned them back toward the downed airplane. This time the hijacker didn't move all the way to the back of the line but stayed beside the businessman and glanced repeatedly over his shoulder until the lights faded away.

After they had walked for a distance, Maddie judged they were once more fairly close to the airplane. She stopped again and announced they were going to make camp for the rest of the night.

"I didn't say you could take a break." The hijacker blustered his way toward Maddie.

"We've covered a good distance, and the wee people should be in bed for the night. If we sleep now we can move out again before they gather the dew at daybreak."

"What?" The hijacker glared at Maddie.

"Just another old wives' tale."

"Tell me," the hijacker demanded.

"Well, the faeries gather dew from the flowers just

before the sun rises to use in their magic potions. Anyone who sees them during this time will go blind."

"OK, we'll stop here--but not for long." The hijacker pushed aside his mangled glasses and rubbed his eyes before pointing his gun at the businessman. "You stand watch. Let me know if you see any fireflies--I mean anything suspicious."

Maddie sank gratefully down onto a mat of soft needles beneath a fir tree. The pain in her head was throbbing now.

"Here, take these." One of the other passengers pressed two tablets into her hand and handed her a bottle of water. "A couple of the others got some blankets from the airplane."

"How far are we from the plane?"

"About a hundred yards. You did a good job of keeping us close, but we'll need to be on the move again before it gets completely light so he doesn't suspect we're moving in a circle."

"Thank you." Maddie closed her eyes and slept for far too short a time.

Just before dawn, the businessman woke her with a gentle nudge on her shoulder. "Are you doing OK? You might have a concussion from hitting your head when we crashed."

"I'll be fine. Any sign of a rescue party?"

The businessman shook his head. "Not yet."

Their conversation was cut short by a panicked shout from the hijacker. "Argh! They got me! The wee folk got me!"

Chapter Four

As soon as she pulled to a stop, Horace grabbed Rissa's hands and helped her out of her car. "I'm so glad you're back! What did Ian find out?"

"Aunt Madelaine's airplane went down in a wilderness area of the national forest in Southern Oregon. So the good news is they aren't far away. The not-so-good news is there appears to be a couple hijackers on board."

Horace's heart slid to his belly. His Maddie was at the mercy of terrorists.

"One of the passengers managed to send a message that said the hijacker's face was painted green and he was wearing a leprechaun suit and hat. Aunt Madelaine can handle kooky people--and she has help this time from the other passengers."

The words meant to allay Horace's fears. Instead made him more determined to finish the time machine. He would not leave Maddie in the clutches of crazy green leprechaun hijackers!

"Ian is on his way to join the search and rescue teams," Rissa said. "He'll let us know when they find the airplane."

Horace wasn't going to just wait. The time machine was ready for a test flight. If everything worked as he planned, the rescue team wouldn't be necessary.

Leaving Rissa in the kitchen with Ryan and his cooking show, Horace rejoined his cousin, Clement, in the fabrication lab. "Is everything ready?"

"Countdown has started."

On the monitors Horace watched the giant fire hydrant. On the outside it looked much the same as it had when Horace set it up for the dog next door. However, the monitors showing the inside of the hydrant revealed major changes. Living quarters for human time travelers were contained on the second floor of the hydrant. On the ground floor a mini-nuclear reactor had been installed. A semi-circle around it contained a bank of monitors and control panels linked to the computer that controlled the time machine and contained a calendar program to calculate the day, month and year where the time machine had traveled.

"T minus thirty seconds and counting," Clement intoned.

Horace drew a deep breath to calm the buzzing of adrenaline through his veins. If this worked--no, when they proved the time machine worked, Horace would rescue Maddie and never let her travel without him again.

"Ten, nine, eight..."

A movement on one of the inside monitors caught Horace's eye. "What's that?"

"...two, one. Activate."

"I think we have an unexpected passenger." Horace

dashed outside to where the fire hydrant used to sit. Now only a flattened patch of lawn separated his back yard from the neighbor's fence.

A freckle-faced girl with bright red hair leaned against the fence. "Have you seen my dog, Batzy?"

~ * ~

Batzy felt dizzy. Disoriented. Like the time he ate a shoe and the metal fasteners didn't want to digest. *Some grass would be good right now.*

He hopped off the chair, wobbled a bit, and scratched at the door. *Funny, it didn't open like it usually did.*

He dug a little harder. Still nothing. Okay. Well, he wasn't in trouble until his little girl, Chloe, called him for dinner. In the meantime, he'd have a snack and a nap.

Batzy put his front paws up on the control panel and pushed the button that dispensed treats.

Instead of a treat, a voice spoke to him. "Manual override engaged. What year do you wish to travel to?"

"Woof!"

"Unknown command," the voice intoned. "Please state the day, month and year where you wish to travel."

"Woof, woof!" Batzy was not pleased with this change the Big Human had made. He was getting hungry and this strange voice was playing games. "Grrr."

The hydrant began spinning slowly then faster and faster until it stopped abruptly with a thump. The door bounced open and fresh air filled with many tantalizing smells filled the inside.

Well, that was better. Chloe should have his dinner waiting.

With his tail curled over his back, Batzy trotted outside.

~ * ~

"We've got to bring it back," Horace declared. "The neighbor girl's dog is inside the time machine."

"Okay, okay." Clement keyed a sequence of commands into the computer.

"Is it working?" Horace peered anxiously at the monitors.

"Our time machine should be back in 2011 about-- now."

Horace didn't wait to watch the touchdown of the machine on the monitors. He dashed into the backyard and watched the giant fire hydrant materialize on its original site near the neighbor's fence.

Crossing his fingers, Horace pushed open the door. "Batzy?"

However, instead of a small white dog inside, Horace came face to face with--Horace blinked. Well, he wasn't sure what they were. Would the little dog have metamorphosed while traveling through time?

Then the door of the time machine slid shut and it disappeared again.

"There were aliens inside!" Clement rushed across the lawn.

"They didn't look like aliens. They looked like faeries. Mad faeries."

"I told Maddie I'd keep you out of trouble. She'll do worse than kill me if something goes wrong with this project."

"Where did you send them?"

"To the nuclear testing grounds."

"Isn't that a bit extreme?"

"Let the military deal with them."

Horace frowned. "Well, I suppose. But we need the time machine back. We still have to save Maddie and go back in time to rescue the neighbor girl's dog."

Horace and Clement hurried back inside the fabrication lab. On the monitors that showed the interior of the time machine, the two faeries were frantically pushing buttons.

"They've hit the emergency eject button!" Horace watched in horrified fascination as the bodies of the two faeries wavered like bad reception on a very old television set then disappeared. "What happened?"

Clement remained silent.

"Clement?"

"They may have been sucked into the black hole."

"We can get them out, right? The probe came back."

"Well..." Clement stared at the monitor showing an empty time machine. "Maybe we should leave them in the black hole until we rescue your wife and the dog. That might be safer than having them causing mayhem throughout history."

Horace frowned. Perhaps time travel wasn't such a good idea after all. Yet he couldn't in good conscience leave Batzy in the past. Maybe by the time he saved the dog, his

Maddie would be home. "OK, I'll go get the dog. Can you send the time machine back to that landing place and year?"

"The command sequence is programmed into the computer. But I promised Maddie you'd keep your feet on the ground."

"My feet will be on the ground," Horace stated. "Just in a different century."

"I don't know about this, Horace."

"The neighbor girl is heart-broken. I have to bring her dog back."

"Then I'll go."

Horace shook his head. "Batzy doesn't know you. He'd just run farther away. And I don't know all the computer sequence commands. You have to stay here to bring us back in case the time machine malfunctions."

"I still don't like this."

"Maddie won't hurt you badly until I'm safely back in 2011."

"Forget humor and stick to inventions, Cuz. Let's get this done before your wife finds out where you've gone."

Squaring his shoulders, Horace grabbed a bag of dog treats and marched toward the time machine. His heart thumped loudly in his ears as his palms grew damp with nervousness. *This is no different than testing my other inventions,* Horace swallowed hard, *which always seem to need some fine-tuning before they work as expected.*

Horace forced himself to take deep breaths and keep walking. How could he face the little neighbor girl if he didn't rescue her dog? He had to do this.

Once inside, Horace buckled himself into the faux leopard skin seat and stared at his cousin on the monitor.

"You'll be back before Maddie knows you're gone." Clement's voice rolled out of the speakers as if he was standing over Horace's shoulder. "Start the reactor sequence. The year and place are already programmed into the computer."

Horace crossed the fingers on one hand as he pushed the "start" button with the index finger of his other hand.

The time machine hummed to life with a computerized voice sounding suspiciously like Clement's estranged wife relaying the countdown.

Horace closed his eyes and drew a deep breath. Adventures were Maddie's bailiwick. He much preferred to stay in his workshop. But he had to do this. He had to set things right.

The time machine vibrated slightly then spun slowly as the calendar on one of the monitors sped back through the years. Past 2000, then 1975, 1950, 1936. The spinning stopped.

Get the dog and go home, Horace reminded himself. Drawing a determined breath, Horace clutched the bag of dog treats in one hand and slid open the door of the time machine.

Batzy trotted inside and howled a greeting then plopped himself on a cushion and looked at Horace expectantly.

Horace blinked in surprise. That was too easy.

As the door closed behind him, Batzy barked a

reminder for his treat.

"Here, have two." He tossed a couple treats to the dog then settled at the console of the time machine once again. With the year 2011 entered into the computer, Horace activated the nuclear reactor to create a black hole so they could return to their own time.

"Woof!" Batzy demanded.

"Wait just a few minutes and you'll have all the treats you want," Horace stated as the monitor ticked the years forward again. From 1936, 1940, 1950, 1960...

"Woo-woo-woof!" Batzy launched himself toward Horace's lap, but missed and landed on the control panel.

"No!" Horace grabbed at the little dog as the years on the monitor started rolling backward: 1959, 1929, 1889, 1849...

As Batzy stepped on a red button, the time machine abruptly stopped spinning.

"Emergency stop executed," the computer voice intoned. "You have arrived in Ireland in the year 1849."

~ * ~

"What's taking so long?" The hijacker squinted through crooked frames--all that remained of his glasses. "We should have found a city by now."

Maddie plopped down on a log. Her head still hurt and she was getting mighty tired of leading this hijacker in circles while waiting for a rescue team to arrive.

"I didn't say you could stop!" the hijacker's shrill whine added fresh pain to Maddie's headache.

She cuffed him alongside the head and wrenched the gun out of his hand. "You are a rude little man and I'm tired of your behavior."

"I do not like guns." With a shudder, she handed the pistol to the businessman. "And I do not like being herded around the forest. We are going to tie you up and stash you in the bathroom with your partner."

The British gentleman tied the hijacker's hands behind his back with a double knot and prodded the man toward the airplane wreckage.

"Let's light a signal fire," Maddie stated. "I'm ready to go home."

The rescue teams arrived within an hour. However, much to Maddie's disappointment, Horace wasn't with them. When she asked her niece's husband about Horace, Ian's non-answer was everyone would be glad to see her when she got home.

Unfortunately, going home was delayed by interrogation from FBI agents then by the flash and shouted questions of the media. Maddie's irritation grew with each interruption, as did her suspicion Horace's cousin had talked him into some cockamamie scheme.

Her niece, Rissa, met Maddie at the door of the castle with determined cheerfulness and no eye contact. "Ryan fixed something special for lunch I'm sure you'll like."

Rissa relieved Maddie of her bag, stashed it in the closet, and walked toward the kitchen.

"What I'd like is to know is where Horace is. What has Clement done?"

"Now, Maddie, this was Horace's way to rescue you. It wasn't my idea..." Clement made sure the table was between himself and Maddie.

"So where is my husband?"

"Um, we're not exactly sure." Rissa still wouldn't meet her aunt's gaze.

Maddie frowned. Horace rarely left his workshop then only with another family member to keep track of him lest his incredible brain come up with another project that led him far astray. "What do you mean, you're not sure?"

Rissa scooped a generous serving of chili over a bun and placed it in front of her aunt. "In the 1800s somewhere."

"Eighteen hundreds?" Maddie's voice came out as a squeak as she pushed the plate away.

"Come and see for yourself," Clement said. He led the way to the fabrication lab and the monitors that tracked the time machine's travels.

The full story left Maddie dazed, but wishing she had gone with Horace on this grand adventure.

The monitor showed the time machine sitting slightly atilt in a shadowed forest. With flashlight in hand, Horace walked slowly around the metal structure then knelt beside it.

"What's wrong?" Maddie asked.

"The computer indicates something punctured the hull," Clement said.

"So my Horace is stranded?" Maddie stared at the monitor then noticed movement behind Horace. "Oh, dear, watch out behind you!"

~ * ~

Since Batzy hit the emergency stop button, the time machine was not responding to manual commands. Horace had checked possible causes inside, now he would have to go outside to check what was wrong. He gathered a flashlight and toolbox then told the dog to stay inside. The door slid open and, with a quick glance around, Horace stepped into the black of the night.

He knelt beside the time machine to examine a tear in the metal where a boulder pushed its way into the side of the machine. He and Clement had outfitted a sparse repair kit, but nothing to deal with this. With a sigh, Horace braced his hand against the metal and glanced up into the glowing eyes of a...

Well, he wasn't quite sure what it was. Another faerie? Or perhaps a leprechaun or an elf. Maybe a mutation of them all.

The creature chattered at him in what seemed like a video on fast forward. Horace closed his eyes and shook his head. Perhaps traveling through time scrambled the senses.

However, when he opened his eyes, the creature still stood before him--three feet tall from its tiny feet to the tips of its iridescent wings.

"I'm sorry. I don't understand what you're saying."

A frown crossed the creature's heart-shaped face then understanding dawned in her eyes. "Ahhh. Is this better?"

Horace nodded. "Who are you?"

"I am Dorinda. It's rare for a human to be able to see an elfenchaun."

"I've been told I'm not like most humans."

"Your craft has been disabled."

With a shrug, Horace slowly rose to his feet. The elfenchaun fluttered upward to stay at eye level with him, her wings stirring the chilled night air. "I need to make some repairs."

"How will you do that?" Dorinda cocked her head to one side and examined the hole in the metal.

"Ideally, I'll find a piece of metal to replace the damaged section."

"I know of a shipbuilder who might help. Follow me." Dorinda flew off into the night, leaving only a trail of iridescent dust in her wake.

"Wait!" Horace hurried after her, stumbling over tree roots and getting slapped in the face with branches.

A short distance away, a young woman in a pale green dress stood waiting for him. "I forgot humans can't fly."

"Dorinda?" Horace rubbed his eyes.

The young woman smiled and nodded.

Heavens! What other surprises would this time travel bring? "Thank you for considering the needs of an old man."

Dorinda's laughter drifted like a gentle breeze through the trees as she stepped onto a trail and glided through the night. Horace followed as quickly and silently as possible.

The eastern sky was beginning to show streaks of light when Dorinda slowed her pace and turned to Horace with a finger against her lips. "We must take care not to be seen by the guard."

Horace nodded, simply wanting to get the time machine repaired and return to 2011 to rescue his Maddie. He knew the Ireland of 1849 was in the midst of the Potato Famine and great political unrest.

Maddie would have a heyday here organizing protests. However, Maddie wasn't here. Her plane had crash-landed in the wilderness, and his grandiose plans to build a time machine to prevent her from getting on that plane had gone far astray.

As Dorinda led him through the narrow passages between buildings, the scent of the sea became stronger. At last she stopped beside a weathered building where the water slapped against a wharf on one side. Once again, she held a finger to her lips as a caution to remain silent then slipped through the doorway.

Inside, the sound of raised voices filled the building. With a frown, Dorinda motioned for Horace to stay hidden then glided toward the voices. "Good morning, Grandfather. Aidan, I didn't expect to see you here."

From his hiding place, Horace heard only muffled replies to Dorinda's greeting before and older man said, "Aidan has come to ask for your decision to his proposal, lass."

"Oh, Grandfather, I'm not ready to marry."

"You should already be havin' a babe or two." The younger man's strident comment startled Horace. He would never think of addressing Maddie or Rissa or any woman with such disrespect. Ah, he would do well to remember this was another time and country.

"My granddaughter will have an answer for you by tomorrow." The older man's stern voice effectively stopped any further discussion as the younger man huffed a response.

On his way out, the young man passed within a few yards of where Horace crouched in the shadows. Large, muscular, and definitely with a temper to match the mahogany red of his hair.

"The O'Briens are a fine family," the older man said. "If you tarry too long, Aidan will find another lass to bear his sons."

"And that's the problem, Grandfather. He doesn't really love me. He simply thinks it's time to marry and have children."

"There's nothing wrong with marriage based on respect and mutual need."

"I want love, Grandfather. Like Mama and Da."

"And an early grave like them too?"

Dorinda's indrawn breath squeezed Horace's heart. Just the thought of losing his Maddie sent chills down his spine, which reminded him of the mission that had landed him here. He needed to repair the time machine and rescue his wife.

He stepped from the shadows and walked toward the man who stood facing Dorinda--a man near in age to Horace's own fifty-four years and bearing an eerie resemblance to his cousin, Clement. Horace rubbed his eyes. Perhaps it was only lack of sleep that made it seem so. "My apologies for the interruption, sir, but I understand you might have what I need to repair my conveyance."

The older man's gaze narrowed as it turned toward Horace. "And who might you be?"

"Simply a traveler in need of assistance."

"What could you offer in return?"

"I have some expertise in building."

Dorinda's grandfather studied Horace for a few moments. Horace reminded himself not to shuffle from foot to foot, as any sign of nervousness might lessen his chances of repairing the time machine and saving his Maddie.

"What is it you desire for these repairs?"

"A curved piece of metal such as you use for your ships--but only a small piece." With his hands, Horace measured out the size he would need.

"Three days of skilled labor in exchange."

"Grandfather, that's too much--"

The older man frowned at Dorinda's interruption. "What do you say, sir?"

"Two days and I'll find my own meals."

"I am Hurley." The older man offered one hand to Horace and clapped him on the back with the other. "What should I call you, my building friend?"

"Horace." Though he chafed at the delay in getting to Maddie, Horace clasped the other man's hand. He had a time machine, he reminded himself. A day or two wouldn't matter once he got the time machine repaired. He could travel to any time he liked.

All that day, Horace labored over curving the hull of a boat just so. Many times he wished for the tools in his work shop or, better still, the computer-run machines in the fabrication lab.

As twilight fell, Horace rubbed his sore and blistered hands as he limped in the direction of the forest and the disabled time machine. He hoped the dog, Batzy, wasn't as hungry as he was, and he hoped he could find his way back without using the flashlight tucked inside his jacket and rousing suspicion.

Horace needn't have worried. Less than a block from her grandfather's warehouse, Dorinda appeared to guide Horace back through the forest.

"Who are you?" she asked as the trees shrouded them in silence.

"A traveler from the future who simply wants to get home and rescue my wife." Horace yawned; too tired to make up a story to satisfy this young woman's curiosity.

Dorinda's laughter faded as she studied Horace's face. "I believe you're serious."

Horace didn't respond, but simply continued to shuffle down the winding trail.

Dorinda hurried to catch up with him. "How far in the future?"

"The year 2011--one hundred and sixty-two years from now."

"But that's past the turn of the century--the turn of two centuries."

"Yes." Horace stopped at the entrance of the time machine and frowned. "Young ladies shouldn't be in the forest alone."

"The rules are different for elfenchauns."

Before his awestruck gaze, Dorinda the young lady faded into the diminutive winged creature who had surprised Horace before dawn that morning.

"I won't be allowed to metamorph after I'm married." Dorinda sighed.

"Must you marry if you don't love the man?"

"Grandfather says Aidan is a good provider." Dorinda cocked her head. "Do you love your wife?"

"More than anything."

"I want a love such as yours." Drawing a deep breath, Dorinda looked at the time machine. "Is this how you came from the future?"

"Yes. And I must repair the time machine to rescue my wife."

"May I see inside?"

Horace frowned. He doubted that protocol in 1849 would allow young ladies to be alone with any man, even one old enough to be her grandfather. However, they had already tramped through the forest together, and she had provided him a way to repair the time machine.

"I suppose that would be alright. But be careful--"

Chapter Five

Too late, Dorinda whisked open the door of the time machine and Batzy charged out in a frenzy of barking.

"--not to let the dog escape." Exhausted, Horace dreaded the idea of chasing the neighbor girl's dog through the forest in the dark.

"I'm so sorry." With a quick flutter of her wings, Dorinda zoomed after Batzy, her swoops and loops leaving an iridescent glow against the night sky.

When Batzy spotted her, his ears stood at attention. Totally focused on the creature, he followed her back through the forest and inside the time machine. Horace slipped quickly inside and slid the door closed.

"Is this what the future looks like?" Dorinda hovered in the middle of the time machine, turning slowly as her awed gaze traveled from the carpeted main level to the pointed dome two stories above.

Horace forgot his tiredness in the curiosity of Dorinda's eyes. For a young lady in the 1800s, the time machine must indeed seem magical.

"Sit down." Horace indicated one of the faux leopard print seats.

Dorinda ran her fingers over the soft, fuzzy texture before cautiously settling herself in the seat.

"Do you wish to activate time travel?" asked the female voice of the computer.

Startled, Dorinda flew from the chair and looked around. "Who is that? Is it your wife?"

"No." Horace chuckled. "It's the computer, who sounds very much like my cousin's wife."

"What's a computer?"

How do I explain technology to someone who has never seen a car or an airplane or even a radio? "It's one of the marvelous inventions of the future. It performs many of the tasks it would take a human days or even months to perform, like calculate how far back in time to travel to rescue this very curious dog."

"And this computer is a woman?" Dorinda asked.

"A computer's voice can be programmed to be a woman's or a man's or a cartoon character's."

Confusion wrinkled Dorinda's brow, but her curious gaze continued to examine every inch of the time machine.

Still in elfenchaun mode, she zoomed up to the second floor to examine the living quarters. "What is up here?"

Batzy the dog zipped up the metal circular staircase after Dorinda and Horace followed more slowly. "Space for sleeping or fixing meals."

Batzy sat in front of the refrigerator and barked.

"Our canine friend is hungry," Horace said. "Would

you like something to eat too?"

Her eyes still round with curiosity and amazement, Dorinda nodded.

"Ah, let's see." Horace examined the containers his nephew-in-law, Ryan, had labeled and placed in the mini-refrigerator. "Eggplant parmesan: Heat one minute or until it burns your fingers. My nephew was trying to be funny."

With a slight frown, Horace stared at the microwave controls for a moment, wishing it was voice activated like the time machine's computer. He'd have to add that adjustment to his project list. He slid the container inside and pushed several buttons, hoping they were the right ones.

"May I help?" Dorinda asked.

"I think I have it figured out," Horace shrugged in apology. "My nephew does most of the cooking at home."

"A man who cooks and a female computer who thinks faster than any human?" If possible, Dorinda's eyes grew even rounder. "I want to go to this future of yours."

"I think there are rules about not changing history," Horace said.

"Oh." Dorinda's mouth turned down in disappointment. "Not even just to visit?"

Horace was saved the need to come up with an explanation by a loud popping from the microwave. Dorinda ducked under the table as Horace pushed the off button and opened the door. "Oh, dear."

"What is it?" Dorinda hovered behind Horace and peeked cautiously over his shoulder.

"I believe I've ruined that dinner." With a sigh,

Horace dragged the container out of the microwave. "I forgot to take the top off and the food exploded all over."

Dorinda patted Horace's hand. "I wasn't really that hungry."

She fetched a damp cloth and began wiping at the spattered casserole inside the microwave.

"We can eat something else." Horace pulled another container from the refrigerator.

"Is there a lot of food in the future?"

The rumble of Dorinda's stomach reminded Horace the Irish of the mid-1800s had worries Horace never had to consider, such as where their next meal would come from--or if they would have a next meal. "Yes, there is plenty of food in the United States of the future, though people in some countries are still starving."

"Just as in our time. The English aristocracy feasts while Irish peasants starve."

"As my Maddie would say, humans are slow to learn some basic lessons."

"Tell me about your wife."

A smile spread across Horace's face as he scooped potato salad--no heating needed--onto three plates for himself, Dorinda and the dog.

When they were seated, he told Dorinda the story of how he and Maddie had met. How he loved her from the first moment, and never thought a woman as bold and brave would ever love him in return. "My Maddie still goes on grand adventures to change the world. I worry about her, but I'm so proud of her."

Dorinda remained quiet for a few moments after

Horace stopped talking, then said softly. "I would like to live in a world where there is plenty of food and women are allowed to follow their passions."

In the next breath, she pushed out a sigh and stood. "'It is not productive to grumble about what cannot be. I will leave you to rest, and I have much to think about. Thank you for a look into the future. You have given me hope."

"Let me accompany you back to the village." Horace also rose.

However, Dorinda shook her head. "As an elfenchaun, I'll be quite safe with the creatures of the forest."

Still, Horace watched Dorinda from the entryway of the time machine until the trail of shimmering green faded into the night. Elfenchaun or not, he worried about the delicate creature who had shown him such kindness. Would she truly be forced to give up the life of relative freedom she had known and marry a man who would control her every move? He would not want to smother his Maddie's bold spirit, even if it cost him days of worry when she was gone.

All the next day, Horace toiled under the watchful eye of Dorinda's grandfather. As the light of day faded into twilight, the man shook Horace's hand and presented him with a curved piece of metal to repair the time machine.

Though exhaustion threatened, the desire to return to the year 2011 and rescue his Maddie gave Horace the energy to drag the metal back through the forest and replace the damaged panel of the time machine.

As Horace gathered his tools and placed them back inside the time machine, he looked forward to seeing Maddie again. He walked the short distance to a small stream and splashed cool water over his face, any tiredness dripping away with the water that ran down his skin. Soon he would see his Maddie!

The short distance back to the time machine took only a few moments, yet Horace knew something was not as he left it. His steps slowed and he looked cautiously around, listening carefully for any clue to what might have happened in the moments he had been gone.

A moan near his feet was all that prevented him from stepping on a tiny crumpled body on the ground. "Dorinda?"

He bent over the little elfenchaun, stunned by the pallor of her face and the broken remnants of her iridescent wings. "What happened?"

"Over here! I saw her fly this way." Strident shouts tore the peace of the night to tatters as lanterns bobbed closer and closer.

Adrenaline surged through Horace. As carefully as possible, he lifted Dorinda and carried her into the time machine. Laying her on a pad next to Batzy, Horace locked the door panel and started the sequence for the reactor. "Clement, can you give us a boost to get us out of here?"

"Thank the heavens!" Maddie appeared on the monitor beside Horace's cousin.

Clement's fingers flew over the computer keyboard. "What took you so long to make repairs?"

"I'll tell you when we get back." Thuds and

pounding rattled the time machine. "And hurry--it seems I have offended the natives."

Horace welcomed the whoosh of the reactor opening a black hole and the spin of the time machine as it hit the edge of the time warp. On the external monitor, Horace saw the surprised faces of several of the local townspeople, including Aidan O'Brien, who had issued a marriage proposal to Dorinda. Had he also had a hand in injuring her in elfenchaun form?

Rare anger flared in Horace's belly as he turned to his unexpected passenger. She seemed as small as the little girl next door who loved Batzy so much. Why would anyone hurt such a delicate creature?

The calendar pages turned rapidly on the computer monitor as the time machine raced forward. In only a few seconds, they passed 1900 then the year 2000--the turn of two centuries Dorinda had seemed so fascinated by.

Was he wrong to bring her with him? Perhaps. But Horace couldn't have left her broken body on the forest floor. His Maddie would know what to do.

~ * ~

Horace's family crowded around the time machine as it materialized gently in the back yard behind the castle. Maddie was the first to step through the doorway as Batzy darted outside. "Horace, thank heavens you're back."

Beyond grateful she was safe, Horace clung to his wife as he hadn't since the early years of their courtship. Her presence reassured him. Comforted him. Completed him.

"How did you escape from the leprechauns? Never mind. Time for that after we help Dorinda."

Holding Maddie's hand, Horace led her to the pad where the little elfenchaun lay in pale silence.

"Who--what is she?"

"A young woman who helped me find a metal piece to repair the time machine. But she's also an elfenchaun and she was chased by a mob and they hurt her badly..."

Maddie knelt beside the small creature and lifted her delicate wrist. "Her heartbeat seems strong."

"Look! She's changing..." The startled gazes of his family reflected what Horace had felt the first time he saw Dorinda change shapes.

Soon it was Dorinda the young lady who lay moaning on the pad, her pale green dress torn and stained.

"We need to get her to the hospital." Ryan swept Dorinda into his arms. He strode across the lawn toward the garages, Maddie and Horace close behind him.

Chapter Six

"We'll take the Woody."

After Horace punched in the code to open one of the garage doors, Maddie hurried inside. The classic Woody station wagon started with a rumble. Ryan climbed into the back and settled Dorinda on his lap. Horace scrambled into the front and closed the doors as Maddie revved the engine then squealed around the garages and out onto the road leading to the hospital.

Focusing on staying to the right of the dotted line in the middle of the road, Maddie pushed the wagon as fast as the road would allow. No one complained she was driving too fast. No one closed their eyes in a prayer for safety. All were concentrating on making the trip as quickly as possible.

Three miles in three minutes, Maddie thought as she cranked the steering wheel in a tight turn into the emergency entrance of the hospital.

The doors burst open and three attendants with a gurney raced toward them, one almost tripping in his haste. "Your niece called ahead and said you'd found a young lady in bad shape."

"Her wings were broken and she was unconscious," Horace said.

"What was broken?" The attendant asked as they rushed inside.

"Um, we're not sure if anything was broken, but we couldn't just leave her lying there." Maddie exchanged a glance with Horace.

"We'll check her over thoroughly."

The double doors into the exam rooms whooshed shut, leaving Maddie, Horace and Ryan staring at laminated panels.

"What if she changes back into an elfenchaun while they're examining her?" Ryan whispered.

"Let's hope that doesn't happen." Maddie settled into a seat in the waiting room beside Horace and watched her nephew pace. Ryan seemed especially concerned with the young woman. She knew he had deeper emotions than the easy-going, playboy image he tried to project. Since his twin sister had married and his mother no longer lived in a 1950s time warp, Maddie had seen more frequent signs Ryan was finally becoming a mature adult; this concern over a stranger being one of them.

After what seemed like hours, a doctor came out to talk to them. "Madelaine, Horace, it's been awhile since I've seen you. No explosions lately?"

"My inventions have taken a different direction," Horace said.

"Glad to hear it." The doctor smiled briefly then turned business-like once more. "Now, this young woman-- what do you know about her?"

"Well, her name is Dorinda..." Horace said.

"And that's about all we know," Maddie interrupted with another quick glance at her husband.

"She has numerous contusions on her torso and cried out when we examined her back. The x-rays show fractures in several ribs and there may be some internal damage. Do you know how she was injured?"

Maddie squeezed Horace's hand. "We didn't see what happened."

"Well, Dorinda is an unusual name," the doctor said. "Our staff will do a search for relatives and we'll notify the police to check their missing persons file."

"I want to see her," Ryan said. At the doctor's frown, he softened his demand. "If she's feeling up to it."

"She asked to see Horace. Once she's set up in a room, she can decide who she wants to visit her."

"How long will she be here?"

"At least overnight. We're waiting for some test results. Horace, come on back."

Maddie touched Ryan's arm as Horace followed the doctor toward the exam rooms. "Let her get settled."

"I keep seeing her before she changed." Ryan's voice rumbled low. "Like a broken child."

"The doctor will do all he can."

"But what if elfenchauns are different?" Ryan glanced around and kept his voice low. "I mean, do they have all the same organs and body parts as humans?"

"Well, she seems human now. We'll just have to wait and see."

"I don't want them using her as some experiment."

Ryan's statement ended on a heartfelt hiss.

"We'll just have to make sure that doesn't happen." Maddie winked at her nephew. Perhaps the boy--er, young man, had picked up some of her penchant for causes after all.

While Dorinda slept, Ryan sat close to her bed, and Maddie and Horace huddled in a corner of her hospital room, talking quietly.

"Her grandfather will be worried." Horace tossed a glance at the young woman in the bed. "She'll be alright, won't she?"

"Of course." Maddie patted Horace's hand. How lucky she was to have such a caring husband! Then an arrow of guilt touched her heart. Did he worry about her each time she went on an adventure? The thought strengthened her decision not to travel without him again. "We'll make sure of that."

Horace turned his hand over and squeezed Maddie's. His eyes said "I love you" as clearly as if he had said the words out loud.

She was indeed a lucky woman.

~ * ~

A week had passed since Dorinda's emergency visit to the hospital. After one night in the hospital, she had begged Horace and Maddie to free her from the prison of tubes and wires and nurses who monitored her every breath and heartbeat.

So she had settled into a room at Horace and

Maddie's castle--much to Ryan's delight--and grew stronger every day.

And each day Horace thought about her grandfather and how worried he must be about her. Finally, he approached Maddie with his decision. "I think we should let her grandfather know Dorinda is alright."

Maddie was in her studio, working on a portrait of Dorinda that combined her images as a young woman and a delicate elfenchaun. Without a pause in her painting, Maddie replied, "That would be a very long distance letter."

"Wouldn't you worry about your sister or your niece or nephew if they disappeared with no word?"

"Of course I would." Maddie paused and looked at Horace. "And her grandfather probably assumes the worst."

"I think we should go back and tell him."

"We agreed not to use the time machine unless Dorinda wanted to go home."

"I've made some adjustments so the controls can't be accidentally activated. And Batzy has a different fire hydrant to explore."

"Are you sure she won't change her mind?"

"When she learned Aidan was leading the mob that attacked her, she absolutely refused to return. She fears her grandfather would still try to force her to marry the man."

"Barbaric." Maddie shook her head in disgust. "I won't let you go on this grand adventure without me."

Horace smiled. "I hoped you'd say that."

When Horace and Maddie presented their plan to Dorinda, she seemed troubled instead of happy.

"What if Grandfather insists I go home?"

Maddie smiled. "You're more than a century and a half away from him. How could he force you to do anything?"

With a shrug, Dorinda responded. "He couldn't, I guess. Sometimes I just feel so overwhelmed with all the choices."

"Take your time, dear." Maddie patted the younger woman's hand. "You're welcome to stay here for as long as you want."

"But I have no way to repay your kindness--"

Maddie waved away Dorinda's protest. "There's always plenty to do around this big house. When you're strong enough, we'll talk about that."

"I am not used to sitting about. I want to do more than watch reality on that television thing."

"We'll talk about it when Horace and I get back from visiting with your grandfather."

Dorinda nodded in a jerky motion. "Please tell Grandfather...be sure he knows I am happy and safe."

"Of course, dear." Maddie watched Dorinda walk slowly down the hallway, her shoulders sagging.

That afternoon, excitement coursed through Maddie's veins as she thought about their upcoming trip to see Dorinda's grandfather. She never imagined actually traveling through time and, as she had hoped for years, Horace would be a partner in one of her grand adventures.

In preparation for their journey, her husband had dressed in trousers, a white shirt and vest, with an Irish flat cap hiding his normally chaotic hair. "How is your disguise coming?"

Maddie applied glue to a moustache and pressed it in place. "I'll be done as soon as the glue dries." She wiggled her upper lip. "It's rather ticklish. Ah-ah-ah-choo!"

One side of the moustache slipped over her mouth. "Are you certain this has to be part of my disguise?"

"Unless you want to face the restrictions of a beautiful woman in the middle 1800s."

Maddie's heartbeat raced. How she loved this man! "Do you think I'm still beautiful?"

"The most beautiful woman I know." Horace kissed Maddie and ended up wearing the moustache.

"We'll have to save the displays of affection for private places." Maddie laughed as she retrieved her moustache. "I doubt two men kissing would meet with approval in 1849."

"I'm sure you're right, Madison, my brother." Horace chuckled. "Clement has fired up the reactor so we can leave any time."

"Are you sure he's reliable? If we need to make a quick escape, I don't want to wait until your cousin comes back from a food binge."

"Clement promised someone would be at the monitors at all times."

"The neighbor girl's dog doesn't count, I hope."

"Being the worry-wart is my job." Horace patted Maddie's hand.

"My last two adventures have included a kidnapping and a hijacking. I'm starting to see the value in a back-up plan."

"Come on. Let's go see Dorinda's grandfather. We

should be back before Clement eats all the lasagna your nephew is fixing for dinner."

~ * ~

The time machine performed flawlessly on the trip back to 1849, materializing at the edge of a small clearing near the woods where Horace met Dorinda. Though Horace loved the landscape, he felt a tingle of fear the mob who had hurt the little elfenchaun might still be roaming nearby.

As the door of the time machine slid open, Horace cautiously stepped out. Maddie almost bumped into him as he stopped and listened. Where were the chattering birds? Where was the gentle rustle of the underbrush?

"What's wrong?" Maddie asked.

Horace looked at his wife, the adventuress, disguised as a man. Was he putting her in danger? "The woods are too quiet. I always heard birds singing and small creatures moving about when Dorinda was here."

"Maybe they are mourning her absence. All will be well after we talk to Dorinda's grandfather."

Hoping Maddie was right, Horace led the way along the trail. They were nearly to the small village when a group of men slipped out of the shadows and surrounded them.

"Where did you journey from?" one of the men demanded.

"My brother and I heard the local shipbuilder, Hurley, might have need for a skilled craftsman or two," Horace said.

"Did you see a young lady in the woods--blonde and wearing a pale green dress?"

"Wouldn't it be unusual for a young lady to be alone in the forest?" Horace responded.

"I have seen you before," one of the men said. "You disappeared about the same time as Dorinda."

"Now I remember you," another man said. "Her grandfather will want to talk to you more closely."

The group closed ranks around Horace and Maddie, escorting them toward the docks where Dorinda's grandfather operated his shipbuilding business. Horace wanted to take Maddie's hand to reassure her, but knew he dared not lest he give away her true identity as a woman.

When they reached the shipyard, they were taken to a small room and left with the terse message the grandfather would talk to them soon.

"I didn't think we would be suspected in Dorinda's disappearance." Horace spoke in a low voice.

"We'll be fine." Maddie patted Horace's hand. "We'll simply tell her grandfather the truth then go home."

However, the truth didn't seem like such a good idea when confronted with a distraught grandfather surrounded by a hostile group of men, including Aidan.

"What do you know of my granddaughter's disappearance?" Hurley crossed his arms over his chest.

"Your granddaughter was badly hurt," Horace began.

"How did she get hurt?" Aidan demanded.

"By the mob hunting the fae people."

"Pah. Any fool can tell the difference between a

woman and a leprechaun." Aidan crossed his arms and glared at Horace.

"She was being chased by a mob, including yourself," Horace responded.

"We only hunt the fae people. They cursed our potato crop, and now our families are starving."

"Your potato crop has a fungus, not a curse."

"What my brother means is we might be able to help your crop." Maddie spoke for the first time since the men had herded them through the village.

A muttering of disbelief rumbled through the men.

"The only way to save the potatoes is to kill all the evil fae people," Aidan insisted.

Maddie shrugged. "Well, if you want your wives and children to starve..."

"Maybe we should listen to them," one of the men said.

"Listen to a man who kidnapped one of our own?" Aidan pointed a finger at Horace. "Perhaps a dousing in the sea will loosen his tongue."

Maddie's protest died in the face of the rising mutter of agreement from the mob and the shake of Horace's head as his frightened eyes met her gaze.

"Time machine," he mouthed.

Maddie forced down her natural inclination to wade into the mob to snatch Horace to safety and instead faded into the gathering twilight behind the boat house. She clenched her fists as they tossed Horace off the dock and into the cold sea. She would be no good to him if the crowd overpowered them both. He came up spluttering, heaved himself onto the dock, and they tossed him into the water once again.

"Enough!" Dorinda's grandfather shouted. "I will deal with the man myself. Go on home now."

The crowd grumbled, but slowly dispersed. Then the grandfather tossed Horace a blanket and locked him in a storage room. As soon as all was quiet, Maddie sought out Dorinda's grandfather.

She found the man sitting by a meager fire, his shoulders hunched and sadness carving deep lines in his face.

"Your granddaughter will be fine."

The man spun around quickly at the sound of Maddie's voice, grabbing for a nearby walking stick to use as a weapon.

"There's no need for more violence." Maddie handed the man a piece of cloth from Dorinda's dress.

"What have you done with her?"

"She is safe. But the mob who hunted the fae people hurt her badly."

"No." The grandfather shook his head. "Aidan wouldn't hurt my Dorinda."

"He wanted her gifts. Wanted her to remove the curse from the potato crop."

"You're talking crazy. Only the fae people can do that."

He doesn't know, Maddie realized. In all her years, Dorinda had somehow kept her secret of being an elfenchaun from her grandfather. "If you want to see your granddaughter, free Horace and come with us."

The man's eyes narrowed. "You be tryin' to trick me."

"I want my hus--my brother. You want your granddaughter. Why can we not work together so both of us get what we want?"

Maddie met the grandfather's suspicious gaze without looking away.

"Perhaps," he said, eyes still wary. "You stay here."

A few moments later the grandfather returned with Horace, his hands bound behind his back and shivering with cold. "Any tricks and your brother will be payin' the price. Now go."

Slowly, Maddie picked her way through the forest toward the time machine, stumbling occasionally along the unfamiliar trail. Once or twice, she thought she heard the crack of heavy footsteps behind them. However, when she paused to listen, she only heard the sounds of the night creatures singing to each other through the darkness.

When they reached the site where the time machine had landed, Maddie froze.

It wasn't there!

She turned toward Horace with a question in her eyes and saw a flash of white between the nearby trees. "We're being followed."

"Who is there?" the grandfather called loudly.

Aidan stepped closer, his white shirt glowing in the pale light of the moon. "Will you be fallin' for their tricks, old man?"

"I only want to see my granddaughter safe."

"No one will be safe with the likes of these strangers

sneaking around near our village." Aidan raised a club as if to strike Horace.

"Stop!" The grandfather stepped between Aidan and Horace, his arm raised to ward off the blow. "There is no need for more bloodshed."

"They are in league with the fae people."

The grandfather sighed. "You be obsessed with faeries and leprechauns, Aidan. It would be more productive to find a way to feed our people."

Maddie nudged Horace and directed her gaze toward the edge of the clearing, where the time machine was materializing. "You can talk to your granddaughter now."

"What manner of ship is that?" The grandfather clenched the walking stick in his hands like a baseball bat, ready for an attack.

"It's our time ship. Come quickly before it fades away again."

"It is a trick of the fae people." Aidan trembled as he stared at the time machine, still painted fire hydrant red.

"And you will turn into a toad if you get too close," Maddie said. "Come on, Horace."

Horace and Maddie trotted toward the time machine. The grandfather followed them after only a moment's pause.

As Horace placed the palm of his hand against a panel on the ship, the door slid open. Suddenly, an ear-splitting yell erupted from Aidan as he charged across the clearing toward them, his club-like mace raised high above his head.

"Get inside quickly!"

Maddie pulled Dorinda's grandfather into the time machine and pushed a button to close the door. Outside, she heard a thunk against the time machine.

"Sorry, Hurley. You'll have to go with us. March 17, 2011." Horace spoke a command to the computer and the time machine started its slow spin through time.

Dorinda's grandfather sat dazed on the floor, leaning against the edge of the dog's digging pit. As he spotted a bone sticking out of the sand, he whispered, "What have you done with my granddaughter?"

"She's quite safe," Maddie said. "You'll see for yourself in a moment."

As the time machine's calendar rolled to 2011, the spinning gently settled to a stop. Once again, Maddie heard a thunk against the side of the time machine. "What is that?"

"Seems we brought another visitor from Ireland with us." Horace pointed to one of the monitors, showing Aidan clinging to the time machine, his mace bumping against the side.

The door slid open and Maddie stepped outside. Dorinda's grandfather cautiously followed, looking around. Horace exited last, sliding the door closed behind them.

"Ha-halt." Aidan staggered toward them, squinting his eyes and blinking. Then he sank into a heap at their feet.

"The spinning on the outside is definitely more intense." Horace stroked his chin. "Interesting."

"Aunt Maddie! Uncle Horace!" Rissa ran across the lawn toward them. "Thank goodness you're back."

"She's not my granddaughter." The grandfather watched Rissa's approach with disappointment.

"My niece," Maddie said, folding Rissa in a hug.

"Look out behind you!" Horace shouted.

Maddie turned as Aidan staggered to his feet, his eyes nearly crossing with the effort of doing that at the same time as lifting his weapon.

"Ah-ah-ah-choo!" As Maddie sneezed, her fake moustache blasted off her face and landed on Aidan's cheek.

"Vermin! Get it off of me!" Aidan spun around, whirling his arms wildly as he tried to dislodge the moustache. His gyrations stopped abruptly as he clonked himself in the head with his mace, and crumpled to the grass.

"Well, that will save me the trouble of subduing him." Maddie's nephew-in-law, Ian, bound Aidan's hands behind him as he lay unconscious on the lawn. "Can we hear this long story over dinner?"

By this time, Ryan and Dorinda had joined the rest of the family. Dorinda and her grandfather engaged in a cautiously joyful reunion while Ryan fetched a pan of cold water to revive Aidan. As the big man sputtered awake, Ian and Ryan helped him to his feet.

"If you're calmed down, you can eat with the rest of us," Ian informed Aidan.

Aidan scowled but accompanied them silently to the house. When he stepped through the door, his nostrils expanded with the aromas that filled the dining room. Then he firmed his jaw. "I simply came to retrieve my property: Dorinda."

"Not bloody likely." Ryan set the bowl of mashed potatoes on the table with a resounding thud.

"Gentlemen." Maddie rejoined the group, dressed in one of her satin gowns.

Aidan gaped at her. "You're not a man."

"Welcome to the twenty-first century." With a regal nod, Maddie sat in the chair Horace held for her at the head of the table. "While you are in my house, I expect you to behave like a well-mannered guest. If you choose not to do that, I'm sure my nephew Ian has a few defense skills to remove you. Do I make myself clear?"

"Twenty-first..." Aidan blinked in confusion and shook his head as if to clear his addled brain. He glanced around the gathered family, his gaze at last resting on Dorinda who nodded slowly. Aidan drew a deep breath. "Yes, ma'am."

"Thank you. Ian will show you where to clean up then please join us."

When they returned, Ian nudged Aidan to the chair between himself and Ryan who glowered at Aidan as he passed the okra and tomatoes.

Over the next half hour, both Aidan and Dorinda's grandfather ate more food than they had seen for many months.

With one final belch and a muttered apology, Aidan rose from the table. "Thank you for your hospitality. And now Dorinda and I will be going."

"Please sit down," Maddie said.

With a scowl, Aidan sank back into the chair.

"I haven't heard Dorinda say what she wants to do:

return to old Ireland or stay here."

As everyone looked at Dorinda, she flushed and twisted her hands. "I-I..."

She looked from Ryan to Aidan to her grandfather.

"She is promised to me." Aidan rose and braced his fists on the table.

"You almost killed her." Ryan shook a serving spoon at Aidan.

"I would never harm my beloved."

"I sat at her bedside for days until the danger of death was gone--from injuries you inflicted."

"I hunt only those who would harm our families and curse our potato crop." Aidan stood erect in self-righteous anger.

"He doesn't know," Maddie stated. "Neither does Dorinda's grandfather."

"How can they not know someone they claim to love is an elfenchaun?" Ryan waved the serving spoon in a question mark.

Again, all attention to Dorinda. Quietly, she said, "It is true."

"Pah! Cannot be. I have known Dorinda since she was a wee one." Aidan crossed his arms over his massive chest.

"Ignorance," Ryan muttered.

"Not every family is as open to uniqueness as we are," Maddie gently chided.

"I didn't tell them because I feared their reaction," Dorinda said.

"It is simply another trick to try to keep me from

claiming what is rightfully mine." Aidan moved toward Dorinda and Ryan smacked his arm with the serving spoon.

Aidan bellowed and turned his anger toward Ryan. However, Ian stopped any further aggression by applying a nerve hold at the base of Aidan's neck. The brawny Irishman crumpled into the mashed potatoes.

"Probably not a good choice to anger a man so much larger than yourself." Ian hefted Aidan out of the potatoes and let him slide to the floor, his back braced against the wall.

Ryan snorted. "Aunt Mads could take down that wimp."

"That doesn't mean you could."

"Well...true." Ryan scowled at the bulky Irishman now shaking his head as he roused once again.

Aidan wiped at the potatoes smeared on his face and looked suspiciously at the group assembled around him.

"One of those defense maneuvers I spoke of," Maddie stated. "Now, I would suggest we all behave like civilized..."

Aidan roared to his feet. "I want what is mine..."

Ian moved toward him, and Aidan stopped then held up his hand in a placating gesture.

"Dorinda, the choice is yours whether you return to Ireland or stay here," Maddie said. "And please know you are welcome in my house for as long as you wish to stay."

"I-thank you. I'm a bit tired right now," Dorinda said. "If you don't mind, I'd like to rest for a while and think about this."

"Of course," Maddie said.

As Dorinda swayed, Ryan put an arm around her waist to steady her.

"You will not be touchin' my property!" Aidan charged forward and Ryan thumped him on the forehead with the serving spoon.

Aidan blinked and bellowed. "If it is a duel you be wantin', a duel you shall get. Choose your weapons."

Chapter Seven

Ryan grinned. "Serving dishes at five o'clock."

"You mock me," Aidan stated.

"All in good fun, my man. But if you want to duel, I choose something I'm very good at: cooking. We'll each prepare a dinner for tomorrow evening and the family chooses whose food is better."

Aidan's brows remained furrowed on his brow like a thundercloud on the horizon. "Cooking is woman's work."

With an exaggerated shrug, Ryan said, "Well, if you can't manage a simple meal, you can concede now..."

"An O'Brien does not concede."

"Great. Dinner to be served at five o'clock tomorrow. I'll even let you have the kitchen first." Ryan held out his arm to Dorinda and they left the room.

As the rest of the family fell silent, Aidan said stoutly. "This cooking can't be very difficult if one such as that can do it."

"In all fairness, I believe someone should help you with the basics," Maddie said. "Rissa? Ian?"

"We have commitments all day tomorrow." Rissa

shrugged as she and Ian placed leftovers on the conveyor belt to the kitchen. "Sorry."

Maddie glanced at Clement, knowing his specialty was eating, not cooking. Horace was more likely to blow up the kitchen with a new invention than produce something edible from the oven. And her sister, Daphne, was out searching for a job as a private investigator So that left her to coach their unexpected guest in the fine art of preparing tomorrow's evening meal.

However, Ryan hadn't specified the food had to be prepared from scratch, so she had a loophole. A trip to the supermarket to pick up some almost-prepared foods would at least teach her nephew not to be quite so cocky.

"I'll be happy to show you how I prepare meals," Maddie smiled at Aidan.

With one more glance around the room that was deserted except for him and Maddie, Aidan suddenly looked overwhelmed. "Thank you, ma'am. And if I could use a corner to rest my weary bones, I would appreciate it."

Maddie showed Aidan to one of the guest bedrooms, his eyes growing wide when he tested the mattress on the sturdy king-sized bed. She didn't have the heart to ask him to change his clothes for something more appropriate when he lay down and shuddered a sigh as if he had found a cloud in heaven. Almost immediately his snoring filled the room, and Maddie thought beneath his bluster he was a fine fellow.

She eased the door closed and mentally prepared a shopping list. With her guidance, Aidan would at least give Ryan a gourmet run for his pasta.

Ryan got up early to prepare a strawberry-sugar biscuit trifle from fresh, natural ingredients. He was just swirling the whipped cream on top of his creation when Aidan entered the kitchen.

"Hey, big guy, you can still concede and save the embarrassment of ruining dinner."

"An O'Brien..."

"I know, I know," Ryan said. "An O'Brien does not concede. Well, try to have any disasters cleared up in a couple hours. I'll need a corner of the kitchen to prepare my winning entree."

Maddie waited until Ryan swaggered out of the kitchen before joining Aidan as he stared at the array of kitchen appliances in bewilderment.

"Are you sure you can show me how to prepare an evening repast?" Aidan asked.

"Enough to bring my beloved nephew down a notch or two."

Over the next two hours, Maddie coached Aidan on how to work the appliances. She was impressed with how quickly he learned. Because of Ireland's dependence on potatoes, he knew a variety of ways to spice up this often ordinary vegetable. Today, he added chunks of tomatoes, squash, and mushrooms on skewers, which he cooked over the natural gas grill with chunks of steak.

Just before Ryan returned to the kitchen, Maddie slipped away.

"Hey, Bucko, there's still time to concede..." Ryan gazed around the kitchen and frowned.

Ah, my nephew realizes this won't be quite the cake walk he thought it was going to be. Maddie smiled from her vantage point in the hallway.

"I was just going to set my humble offerings on the conveyance, if you would be so kind as to show me how to turn it on."

Ryan nodded, the look on his face showing he clearly understood Aidan had received help.

As the family gathered around the dining room table, Ryan complimented Aidan on his culinary skills.

"I had help," Aidan stated.

"Which one of my devoted family decided I should be put in my place?"

"We all knew that, brother dear." Rissa grinned at her twin. "But Ian and I were gone all day."

"Horace isn't allowed in the kitchen without the fire department nearby, and Clement only eats. With Mother still searching for a job, that leaves my dearest aunt."

"I'm your only aunt." Maddie kissed Ryan on the cheek and slid into her chair at the head of the table.

"Touché. Both on the comment and putting me in my place." Ryan turned to Aidan and offered his hand. "Good job. Too bad we both want the same woman or we could be friends."

Aidan looked around the table at the family watching him expectantly then slowly reached out and shook Ryan's hand.

"Well, everyone here is a winner," Ryan said. "We get to eat all this delicious food."

As the others heaped their plates and started, Aidan sat silently with his plate empty.

"What's wrong, Aidan? Don't trust your own cooking?" Maddie teased.

"I eat like a king while my countrymen are starving." He pushed away from the table. "I wish to be excused, ma'am."

As Aidan disappeared down the hallway, the others stopped eating.

"He's right," Maddie said. "The Irish in 1849 look much like those starving in African famines today."

"We agreed not to do anything that might change history," Horace said.

"History says food came from other countries, including our own. What would it hurt to add a few bags of grain or vegetables to help one small village?"

"Ah, Maddie, you've always wanted to change the world."

"And you too, with your inventions that help us live better."

"We could add shelves to the time machine to hold packages of food," Clement said. "Perhaps even some plants so they could vary their crops."

"Excellent idea, cousin. I'll get to work on that while my beautiful wife strong-arms donations from the locals." Horace smiled affectionately at Maddie, kissed her on the cheek, and hurried out the door, his dinner forgotten.

"Looks like leftovers tomorrow," Ryan said as he placed still full serving dishes on the conveyor belt.

~ * ~

"I feel like I should do more to help the Irish." Dorinda helped Maddie sort through the donated food items to load into the time machine and send to the famine-stricken Ireland of 1849.

"What do you **want** to do?"

"Part of me wants to go back, but I also want to stay in this exciting new time and explore." Dorinda shrugged. "Is that selfish?"

"Yes and no. If we're not selfish in some ways and take care of ourselves, we aren't able to help others."

"I will miss my grandfather if I stay here, but I will have to give up my life as an elfenchaun if I go back."

Maddie patted Dorinda's hand. "With the time machine, you really don't have to make a decision right now."

"Aidan said if I do not go back with him, he will marry one of the other village girls."

"How do you feel about that?"

"In some ways, I would be glad. But then I would be a burden to grandfather. He wants me to be taken care of when he dies. With the famine, that might not be too long for any of us. I know grandfather gives up some of his food for me and to help out others in the village."

"Your grandfather seems like a fine and honorable man."

"Yes, he is. I am struck by how much like Clement he is."

Maddie snorted. "Clement and I have had our disagreements. We'll see if he's learned anything from being ditched by his wife."

"He wrote her a letter of apology."

"At your urging?"

Dorinda shrugged. "He looks so much like my grandfather I feel like I know him. And from living in another century, I perhaps understand male pride better than women in these times."

Maddie considered the younger woman. "I think perhaps you do. Let's tell all those prideful males the food is ready to load."

However, muscle wasn't needed to load the food. Horace had rigged up a conveyor belt from the food collection point to the time machine. Ryan and Ian loaded the donations onto the belt, while Aidan and Clement arranged the food inside the time machine on the other end. As Horace and Dorinda's grandfather looked on, the conveyor worked flawlessly.

Before long, all the food was loaded and Aidan was ready to return to 1849 with Horace as the time machine pilot.

In the shadow of the time machine, Aidan took Dorinda's hands. "I need to have your answer now, lass. My life is in the Ireland of the past where I can help my people."

Dorinda blinked away tears and nodded. "If I go back, it will be to certain death--not just because of the famine, but because I am an elfenchaun. You may understand me better now, but others will still think my kind caused the potato crops to fail. If you marry me, you too will be an outcast and not able to help the people you love so well."

Silence fell between them then Aidan's head jerked in a nod. He turned and strode into the time machine where Horace was waiting to spin them into the past.

"Are you sure?" Dorinda's grandfather cradled the portrait Maddie had painted of her as both a young lady and her elfenchaun self.

"It will be better if I stay here," Dorinda said.

Slowly, her grandfather nodded. "I will miss you, lass."

Dorinda clung to her grandfather for long moments then wiped the tears from her eyes, and watched him walk away. As the time machine disappeared, Ryan slung a comforting arm over her shoulders.

~ * ~

As the family ate the leftovers of the gourmet meal Ryan and Aidan prepared previously, a horn tooted in the circular drive of the castle. A lovely dark-haired woman wearing a hat that would do Maddie proud emerged from a red convertible.

"Victoria." Clement froze with his fork in mid-air. A moment later, the fork clattered onto his plate as Maddie ushered their visitor into the dining room.

Victoria rushed to Clement as he slowly stood up and threw her arms around him. "Oh, my darling, I've missed you so."

In slow motion, Clement's arms circled his wife, a stunned and disbelieving look still on his face.

"I've been such a silly old woman. Will you forgive

me?" Victoria leaned back and braced Clement's face between both of her hands.

"Um, sure."

Victoria planted a smacking kiss on Clement's mouth. "Please take me home."

"Of course, dear."

As Clement and Victoria drove away in the red convertible, Maddie looked at Dorinda. "That must have been quite a letter Clement wrote."

Dorinda just smiled.

~ * ~

As twilight settled in shades of purple and orange on the horizon, Maddie and Horace sat on the balustrade of one of the castle turrets overlooking the grounds and the time machine. A flash of pale green momentarily arced through the night, followed by the sound of male laughter entwined with the lighter tinkle of an elfenchaun's giggle.

"Should our next adventure be to retrieve the pagan faeries from the black hole?" Horace asked.

Maddie squeezed her husband's hand. "It sounds as if there was quite a furor at their last stop in history. Maybe they should stay where they are and out of trouble for a while."

Horace nodded. "Perhaps you're right, my dear. Perhaps you're right."

The End

ABOUT THE AUTHORS

Born in Medford, Oregon, novelist Christine Young has lived in Oregon all of her life. After graduating from Oregon State University with a BS in science, she spent another year at Southern Oregon State University working on her teaching certificate, and a few years later received her Master's degree in secondary education and counseling. Now the long, hot days of summer provide the perfect setting for creating romance. She sold her first book, *Dakota's Bride*, the summer of 1998 and her second book, *My Angel* to Kensington. Each fall, Christine returns to the classroom as a high school math teacher. Her teaching and writing careers have intertwined with raising three children. Christine's newest venture is the creation of Rogue Phoenix Press. Christine is the founder, editor and co-owner with her husband. They live in Salem, Oregon.

~ * ~

C. L. Kraemer has been a gypsy all her life. From her military child beginnings to her might-not-get-this-chance-again attitude after she left home, she's seen most of the continental United States as well as Hawaii and Alaska. She hopes to travel the world but is content to stay close to her family in the great Northwest.

She has written several romance novels under the pen name of Celia Cooper but continues to pursue fantasy, mystery and sci-fi novels as C.L. Kraemer. Currently, she is busy on a Dragon series having finished Dragons Among Us and Dragons Among the Eagles to date. At this point, another dozen dragon books are expected. For lighter fare, she writes the stories included in the anthology series by RoguePhoenixPress.com.

~ * ~

For years Genene Valleau has been fascinated by the puzzle of why some people collapse under life's traumas and others emerge triumphantly stronger. Her dramatic action stories explore the lives of heroes and heroines who overcome those traumas, often using touches of humor. However, sometimes humor demands its own vehicle, such as the wayward time machine in this ST. PATRICK'S DAY TALE. So settle into your faux leopard print chair and join us for a tumble through time!

OTHER BOOKS BY THE AUTHORS AT ROGUE PHOENIX PRESS
www.roguephoenixpress.com

Christine Young

Forever His

The Talisman

The Locket

Allura

Highland Song

My Angel

Dakota's Bride

A Valentine's Day Anthology

Writing as AnnChristine

Safari Moon

~ * ~

C.L. Kraemer

Healthy Homicide

Dragons Among Us

A Valentine's Day Anthology

A Different Kind of Valentine

~ * ~

Genene Valleau

Feathers on the Floor

Stars in Your Eyes

A Valentine's Day Anthology

VISIT OUR WEBSITE
FOR THE FULL INVENTORY
OF QUALITY BOOKS:

http://www.roguephoenixpress.com

Rogue Phoenix Press
Representing Excellence in Publishing

Quality trade paperbacks and downloads
in multiple formats,
in genres ranging from historical to contemporary romance, mystery and science fiction.
Visit the website then bookmark it.
We add new titles each month!